HELLENIC STUDIES 38

The New Sappho on Old Age

Textual and Philosophical Issues

Selected Titles in the Hellenic Studies Series

http://chs.harvard.edu/publications

The New Sappho on Old Age
Textual and Philosophical Issues

Edited by
Ellen Greene
and
Marilyn Skinner

CENTER FOR HELLENIC STUDIES
Trustees for Harvard University
Washington, DC
Distributed by Harvard University Press
Cambridge, Massachusetts and London, England
2009

The New Sappho on Old Age: Textual and Philosophical Issues
Edited by Ellen Greene and Marilyn Skinner

Published by Center for Hellenic Studies, Trustees for Harvard University,
    Washington, D.C.
Distributed by Harvard University Press, Cambridge, Massachusetts and London,
    England
Printed in Ann Arbor, MI by Edwards Brothers, Inc.

LIBRARY OF CONGRESS CATALOGING-IN-PUBLICATION DATA
The new Sappho on old age : textual and philosophical issues / edited by Ellen Greene
and Marilyn B. Skinner.
    p. cm. -- (Hellenic studies series ; 38)
    ISBN 978-0-674-03295-8
1. Sappho--Criticism and interpretation. 2. Sappho--Translations into English. 3.
Greek poetry--History and criticism. 4. Aging in literature. I. Greene, Ellen, 1950- II.
Skinner, Marilyn B. III. Sappho. Poems. English & Greek. Selections. IV. Title. V. Series.

PA4409.N49 2009
884'.01--dc22

2009013858

Contents

A Note On Classics@

THIS VOLUME, *The New Sappho on Old Age*, is Issue 4 of the Center for Hellenic Studies journal Classics@, available free online from the Center's website (http://chs.harvard.edu). The goal of Classics@ is to bring the best of contemporary classical scholarship to a wide audience. Each issue is dedicated to its own topic, often with guest editors, for an in-depth exploration of important current problems in the field of Classics. The journal stresses the importance of research-in-progress, encouraging collegial debate (while discouraging polemics for the sake of polemics) as well as the timely sharing of important new information. This issue is the first one also made available in a print volume, with the intention of reaching an even wider audience. Although the print volume is necessarily static, the digital issue can remain dynamic, responding to new developments and reconsiderations of the evidence.

1
Introduction

Marilyn B. Skinner

Papyrological finds, no matter how momentous for papyrologists and other specialists studying the ancient world, ordinarily do not make international headlines. Yet M. L. West's 2005 article in the *Times Literary Supplement* announcing the apparent recovery of a virtually intact poem by Sappho, only the fourth to have survived almost complete, was quickly picked up by newspapers on both sides of the Atlantic, with follow-up mentions on poetry websites and even personal blogs.[1] In literary circles, it was a happening of the first order. To Sappho scholars, at least those of my generation, it is the *trouvaille* of a lifetime.

The "New Sappho," as it immediately became known, is actually a collective designation for two of Sappho's poems contained in fragments of a Hellenistic-era florilegium, one previously unknown and very lacunose, the other already partially preserved. In the short time since their initial publication in the *Zeitschrift für Papyrologie und Epigraphik*, scholarly discussion of these texts has burgeoned. Articles addressing pertinent textual, philological, and metrical issues now appear on a regular basis and several elegant translations of the second poem, often labeled "the Tithonus poem," are available in print and on-line. Subsequent publication of a third set of verses found on the same papyri, clearly of Hellenistic date but thematically linked to the two preceding texts, has extended the debate as experts attempt to determine

---

[1] West, M. L. "A New Sappho Poem." *Times Literary Supplement*, June 25, 2005. Three major London newspapers carried the story: the *Times* (June 24, 2005:24), the *Guardian* (June 24, 2005:5), and the *Daily Telegraph* (June 25, 2005:3). In this country, the *New York Times*, the *Seattle Times*, and the *Washington Post* all announced the discovery. Poetry websites: http://poetry.about.com/b/a/181700.htm and http://international.poetryinternationalweb.org/piw_cms/cms/cms_module/index.php?obj_id=310&x=1. Blog discussion: see comments from posters at http://monkeyfilter.com/link.php/8947 and http://www.languagehat.com/archives/001966.php.

their content and explain why and how the overall sequence of poems might have been assembled.

In January 2007, at the 138th annual meeting of the American Philological Association in San Diego, two separate panel sessions featured specialists in papyrology and archaic Greek poetry speaking on the "New Sappho." The group of essays that follow are, with two exceptions, revised and expanded versions of papers originally presented at those sessions. While most of the contributors devote a large part of their attention to the particular challenges posed by the Tithonus poem, they range widely in their attempts to contextualize it and relate it to other poems in the Sappho corpus, and the diverse conclusions they reach are a reflex of the volley of questions the papyrus finds have provoked. Chief among such questions is the problem of the poem's alternative endings. Addressing a chorus of young people (*paîdes*), the speaker laments her debilities—white hair, depressed spirits, weakened knees—then rhetorically checks herself: "Yet what can I do?" (*allà tí ken poeíên?*). Aging is part of the human condition. Even a goddess' love could not preserve Tithonus from decay. The shorter version, which ends with that exemplum, seems to terminate in resigned acceptance of the human lot. If, on the other hand, the text went on for four more lines, as some suppose, it would conclude with a highly positive and affirmative statement: yearning after the beauty of the sun, the most luminous of objects, compensates for the losses of old age. Each ending provides a psychologically satisfying closure, but as philosophical responses to mortality the two differ profoundly. As some of our papers show, the position one takes on that specific question will have ramifications for interpreting several other Sappho texts as well.

Following this introduction, two essays deal with textual and paleographical features. Dirk Obbink, in "Sappho Fragments 58–59: Text, Apparatus Criticus, and Translation," supplies us with a newly edited text and apparatus criticus of the three poems, incorporating all supplements and emendations proposed before posting. Obbink also reproduces, *exempli gratia* and for the reader's convenience, West's restored text of frr. 58–59 with his translation of the Tithonus poem, since other contributors frequently refer to it. In "The Cologne Sappho: Its Discovery and Textual Constitution," Jürgen Hammerstaedt gives us a publication history and a summary of the papyrological issues, accompanied by photographs of the papyri. The fragments first edited and published by Gronewald and Daniel (2004a) are scraps from an early third-century BCE poetic anthology arranged by content, comprising passages dealing with old age and death, but also with music and poetic immortality. *P.Köln* 21351, a pair of fragments from adjacent columns, contains two poems of Sappho. Both are in the same aeolic metre, acephalous Hipponacteans with internal double-choriambic expansion:[2]

$$^\wedge\text{hipp}^{2c} = \quad \times \; - \; \cup \; \cup \; - \; - \; \cup \; \cup \; - \; - \; \cup \; \cup \; - \; \cup \; - \; -$$

The second of these poems coincides with twelve verse endings previously known from the second-century CE Oxyrhynchus papyrus no. 1787, frr. 1 and 2, printed in the editions of Lobel (1925) and Voigt (1971) as Sappho fr. 58. With the new papyrus readings, five lines of poem 58 could be restored almost entirely. Subsequently another small piece from the same anthology, *P.Köln* 21376, was seen (Gronewald and Daniel 2004b) to supply the beginnings of three more lines immediately following the restored passage, thereby providing a substantially complete text of what had been lines 11 through 22 of fr. 58. After that a new poem commences in a different hand. Its dialect is not Aeolic and the metrical features also exclude the possibility of Sappho's authorship. Published by Gronewald and Daniel (2005) as the "lyrischer Text" from the Sappho papyrus, it has already given rise to conflicting explanations of its genre and import.

    Three successive essays investigate the unusually complicated problems of textual transmission. André Lardinois takes up the matter of where the "Tithonus poem" is supposed to end. Scholars agree that a new poem begins at *P.Oxy.* 58.11. Before the Cologne papyrus was published, it was also agreed that fr. 58 continued on after the Tithonus *exemplum* and presumably ended at line 26, four verses below, where Lobel in his 1925 edition marked a coronis (perhaps mistakenly). The gist of lines 25 and 26 was already known from a quotation of Clearchus transmitted in Athenaeus' *Deipnosophistae* (15.687b), though the construction of the Greek in the final line, and therefore the meaning of the statement, was debated. In the Cologne papyrus, however, the second Sappho poem terminates with the Tithonus *exemplum*, at what is line 22 of fr. 58, and the "lyric text" follows. What we might seem to possess in the newly restored verses 58.11–22, then, is a whole twelve-line poem by Sappho, with only slight restoration needed at the beginning; West reckoned it complete, but others insist that the poem continued with the lines quoted by Clearchus. As yet there is no emerging consensus. Lardinois discusses the arguments for each ending and reviews external evidence from an epigram of Posidippus that may add weight to the claims for the longer version.

---

[2] See Lidov's two contributions to this volume. West terms the metre "hagesichorean" and abbreviates as "hag2c".

Lowell Edmunds posits the need to take formal conventions of Greek lyric into account when deliberating upon this question. Does the typical occurrence of the narrated mythical *exemplum* in comparable poetry show that the Tithonus *exemplum* can properly function as a closural device? The rhetorical structure in which such a paradigm is typically embedded requires that speakers return from the myth itself to point out its applicability to the immediate situation. The unusual use of imperfect *éphanto* at line 9 (frr. 58–59 Obbink) to introduce the Tithonus story, instead of the present tense of a verb of saying, suggests a contrast between what the speaker used to hear when young and what she now understands. That distinction might have been explicitly articulated in the closural "adversative statement" putatively represented by lines 23–26 of *P.Oxy.* 1787. However, Deborah Boedeker considers the likelihood of textual deviation arising from performance conditions, a possibility raised elsewhere. She notes that some medieval poetic traditions reflect the phenomenon of *mouvance*, whereby variations in oral performance create textual variations in manuscripts. Instead of postulating a single "original" text, we might adopt the premise that alternative forms of the same poem may have been circulating as early as the archaic period, each suited to particular performance contexts. Both versions, then, could be termed in some sense "authentic."

The following four papers are chiefly concerned with relations among the texts on the papyrus. After surveying other fragments known to have come from books 3 and 4 of the Alexandrian edition of Sappho, Joel Lidov suggests that both the first and the second Cologne poems were forthright assertions of rewards after death earned by dedication to music in life. On that basis, he challenges previous supplements to the Tithonus poem and offers alternatives. In a succeeding essay, Lidov reviews evidence for the Alexandrian arrangement of Sappho's poetry and makes observations on the unusual metrical features of the new Sappho poem. Connections between the first and second poems are also reinforced by Eva Stehle's demonstration that both use the temporal markers *nun* and *pota* in the same way to indicate the speaker's different relationships to present and past. The poems work together to create a chronological trajectory from mythic plenitude in the past, to the present in which song recreates the vanished past experience, and then, in future time, to the immortality conferred by song. Tithonus, on this reading, takes on a unique import as a foil for the singer whose art persists into old age. Dee Clayman concentrates upon determining the relationship of the third, unfortunately quite fragmentary, poem on the papyrus to the preceding Sappho selections. Earlier scholars (Gronewald and Daniel 2005; Rawles 2006b; Lundon 2007a) found no direct association with Sappho herself, but Clayman argues that, though really the work of a later Hellenistic author, it poses as Sappho's own composition in which she is portrayed as undergoing the descent to Hades anticipated in the authentic poems.

The last three papers are concerned with larger interpretive questions: the effect of these poems upon our understanding of the rest of the Sappho corpus and their arguable role as performance texts in the light of the Greek oral poetic tradition. Ellen Greene, who regards the Tithonus poem as a philosophical pronouncement upon the human condition, examines the occurrence of other didactic statements by Sappho in the light of similar metaphysical statements attributed to Pre-Socratic thinkers. Hence even in the face of human mutability and loss, Greene argues, the poet articulates her coherent sense of transcendent experience, and even immortality, achieved through song. Conversely, an intertextual reading of the Tithonus poem against corresponding fragments of Mimnermus leads Marguerite Johnson to postulate a new intratextual reading of fr. 31 Voigt, in which the bodily transformation of the speaker might be deemed a consequence of *geras* as well as *erôs*. Finally, Gregory Nagy discusses the respective performance traditions in archaic Greece and classical Athens and how each might have influenced the form of Sappho's texts. Existence of a long and a shortened version of the same song can be explained, he argues, by the differing conventions of the sympotic event and the citharodic competitions at the Panathenaia. These are just a few considerations that must be weighed as we debate the textual and literary problems surrounding these miraculously recovered lines.

As co-editors of this volume, Ellen Greene and I wish to express deep gratitude to the two anonymous referees for their many valuable suggestions. Thanks, too, to Mary Ebbott, Executive Editor of *Classics@*, for her patience and invaluable technical assistance, and to Gregory Nagy for his generous encouragement throughout. Jill Curry Robbins, the CHS Visual Resources Specialist, diligently tracked down and obtained permission for the requisite images. For photographs of *P.Köln* 21351 and 21376, we are grateful to the Institut für Altertumskunde, Universität zu Köln and the Curator of the Köln Papyrus-Sammlung, Dr. Robert Daniel. We are indebted to Dirk Obbink and the Imaging Papyri Project, Oxford, for images of the fragments comprising *P.Oxy.* 1787. Illustrations for Jürgen Hammerstaedt's essay were supplied by Dr. Fabian Reiter, curator of the papyrus collection for the Ägyptische Museum und Papyrussammlung, Staatliche Museen zu Berlin, and by Christopher Naunton, Deputy Director of the Egypt Exploration Society. Professor John Tait, University College, London, kindly responded to Mr. Naunton's inquiries on behalf of the project. For Gregory Nagy's essay, Dr. Robbins drew the two illustrations of the Bochum vase, and Valerie Woelfel those of the Munich vase. Ellen Greene is extremely grateful for Jim Hawthorne's support, and I am indebted to Ron Skinner, as always, for quick technological advice. Lastly, our deepest gratitude to our contributors: working with you all has been a pleasure and a privilege.

Bibliography

Gronewald, M., and Daniel, R. W. 2004a. "Ein neuer Sappho-Papyrus." *Zeitschrift für Papyrologie und Epigraphik* 147:1–8.

———. 2004b. "Nachtrag zum neuen Sappho-Papyrus." *Zeitschrift für Papyrologie und Epigraphik* 149:1–4.

———. 2005. "Lyrischer Text (Sappho-Papyrus)." *Zeitschrift für Papyrologie und Epigraphik* 154:7–12.

Lobel, E., ed. 1925. ΣΑΠΦΟΥΣ ΜΕΛΗ: *The Fragments of the Lyrical Poems of Sappho.* Oxford.

Lundon, J. 2007. "Il nuovo testo lirico nel nuovo papiro di Saffo." *I papiri di Saffo e di Alceo* (ed. G. Bastianini and A. Casanova) 149–166. Studi e Testi di Papirologia, N.S. 9. Florence.

Rawles, R. 2006. "Notes on the Interpretation of the 'New Sappho'." *Zeitschrift für Papyrologie und Epigraphik* 157:1–7.

Voigt, E.-M., ed. 1971. *Sappho et Alcaeus: Fragmenta.* Amsterdam.

2

Sappho Fragments 58–59
Text, Apparatus Criticus, and Translation

Dirk Obbink

“THE NEW SAPPHO” ACTUALLY COMPRISES A GROUP of papyrus fragments, quotations, and testimonia for Sappho's poetry dating back more than two millennia. Scholars who were amazed to learn that Sappho had "composed a new poem" when Edgar Lobel published it a half-century ago—she had, after all, been dead for over 2600 years—would have been even more surprised at finding the same fragmentary poem's missing line-ends, conjecturally and limpingly supplied by scholars since Lobel, now actually supplied by another papyrus manuscript of the same poem, overlapping but preserving the other ends of the lines, that appeared as late as 2004. The result, like so much else in the archaeology of our textual knowledge of the ancient past, has raised more questions than it has answered about the complex interrelations of language, performance, and context of poetry, as well as its transmission and reception. Not all of these are likely or even able to be solved by the simple constitution of texts, reporting of witnesses, and compilation of suggestions. What follows presents the textual basis for the discussions of the papers in this volume. It has the same basic form and function as David Sider's edition of Simonides' elegiac fragments 1–22 W^2 (Sider 2001). It critically collates the evidence of the manuscript witnesses, both for the ancient editions of Sappho's poems, and for the testimony, ancient and medieval, relating to these two fragments. As an appendix, the text as originally restored and translated by M. L. West is reproduced *exempli gratia*, and against which other translations, interpretations, and emendations are critically compared in the contributions to this volume.

Oxyrhynchus Papyrus 1787 was recovered from the ancient land-fill dump on the outskirts of the provincial capital city of Oxyrhynchus in central Egypt by B. P. Grenfell and A. S. Hunt during their excavations there in 1898–1907, and is now in the Papyrology Rooms of the Sackler Library, University of Oxford. As published by E. Lobel in *The Oxyrhynchus Papyri* vol. XXI, it contains numerous fragments of what was once a professionally produced, critical edition of book 4 of Sappho's poetry in one edition circulating in the Roman period, as can be seen from the colophon (in fr. 44) containing the fragmentary remains of Sappho's name and the title of the collection (*Mele*). The book-number itself is not preserved in the papyrus, but is recoverable by ancient references to the book containing poems solely in this meter. The handwriting enables us to date the copying of the manuscript to the later second century AD. Fr. 2 of this papyrus preserves the line-ends of the verses that came to be known as Sappho fr. 58, together with the line-beginnings of the meager fr. 59.

Cologne Papyrus inv. 21351 was acquired from an antiquities dealer in 2004 by the University of Cologne, and was published by R. W. Daniel and M. Gronewald in *Zeitschrift für Papyrologie und Epigraphik* in 2004; subsequently, in the same year, an additional fragment (inv. 21376) was identified and placed in the ensemble of fragments, the remains of a papyrus roll containing poems by Sappho and at least one other poet, copied by two different hands in the early part (first quarter or a little later) of the third century BC. The fragmentary papyrus manuscript had been dismantled from painted mummy-cartonnage, viz. covered with a thin layer of gesso plaster and painted, of which the fragments still bear traces. A site in the Fayum, the rich agricultural oasis southwest of Cairo, and the only area in Egypt known certainly to evidence the practice of using recycled papyrus for decorative funerary art, may be assigned as the provenance.

Sappho's authorship of verses in the Cologne fragments is secured by their overlap with the Oxford manuscript of Sappho in fr. 58: Cologne supplies the earlier portion of the lines (not preserved in the other papyrus), Oxford supplies the ends of the lines, while the two manuscripts overlap for a thin strip of several centimeters in the middle. A new set of verses, referred to below as the "New Fragment," however, appears before the verses about Tithonus in the Cologne manuscript, entirely different from those in the Oxford one (termed below "Success Poem") and that stand here in modern editions of Sappho. In both manuscripts there follow the verses held in common by the two manuscripts, called below (in the absence of ancient testimony for a title) the "Tithonus Poem." After these, in Cologne a series of verses follow that cannot be by any Lesbian/Aeolic poet (for they are in a meter that admits a series of more than two successive short syllables); in Oxford there follow verses which are certainly of Sapphic pedigree, since Athenaeus quotes them (in a defective form partially garbled in our medieval manuscripts) and attributes them to the poetess. In the text below, the former is called "Continuation 1" (its priority reflecting the fact that it is witnessed by the earlier manuscript), and the latter "Continuation 2."

The terms "New Fragment," "Success Poem," and the Continuations 1–2 will become better understood at a later stage of this book, as they are more fully explained by the contributions below. For convenience of reference here, I have numbered each of these sections independently; it should be noted, of course, that the verses of the "Tithonus Poem" continue on after the "New Fragment" and the "Success Poem," in Cologne and Oxford respectively: i.e. the first verse of the "Tithonus Poem" is actually line 9 of the Cologne papyrus, but is line 11 of the Oxyrhynchus papyrus (and similarly with Continuations 1 and 2).

In both the Cologne and Oxford papyrus manuscripts, the distichs (Asclepiadean verses grouped into pairs) are separated by a short horizontal line (*paragraphos*) penned in between two verse-beginnings, extending slightly into the blank intercolumnium before and slightly into the column of writing. Here and there, both manuscripts also bear final graphics or *coronides*, which are known to have marked the ends of poems in ancient manuscripts of Sappho. Where the left margin of a column of writing survives to such an extent as to preserve these, they provide an invaluable control of the point at which ancient editors and readers thought one of these poems ended and a new one began (as at the end of the "Tithonus Poem" in the Cologne manuscript). But where the left margin does not survive to determine the placement of a *coronis* (as at the end of the "Tithonus Poem" in the Oxford manuscript), we cannot be certain that in this case the ancient reader was warned of a division between poems here, especially when (as in the case of the Oxford and Cologne manuscripts at precisely this point) different sets of verses follow.

Much debate and discussion focuses on considerations of division, whether at the beginning and ending of poems, or on possibilities for the grouping of verses transmitted by both manuscripts into poems, and, of course, the "vexed problem of the ending" (as one of the anonymous press-readers for this volume put it, mildly). It therefore seemed useful, in the critical edition offered below, to represent graphically these lectional signs as they occur in one or both manuscripts at the left edge of the columns of writing. The sign ⊗, by contrast, placed in the right margin at line-end, denotes (as conventionally in modern editions since Voigt) that, in the judgment of the modern editor, a division between poems occurred (or should be posited) at this point, regardless of the corresponding presence, or preservation, of the final graphic (*coronis*).

The economy of the evidence suggests that, as in West's reconstruction, the verses transmitted in common by both manuscripts (i.e. the "Tithonus Poem") ought to constitute a complete poetic unit, in and of itself. And this seems to be borne out for the unusually abrupt conclusion of the "Tithonus Poem" by the presence of a *coronis* in the Cologne manuscript at this point. However, in the Oxford papyrus witness, the left margin at this point disconcertingly does not survive to confirm whether the verses that follow there (i.e. those quoted by Athenaeus) were signaled in this later manuscript as belonging to a separate poem, or to a continuation of the "Tithonus Poem" entirely unknown, as far as we can tell, to the editors and writers of the Cologne manuscript.

Finally, I have marked the point at which, in the Cologne manuscript, the handwriting changes. This change to a deceptively similar style of script is a subtle and easily overlooked one, but a change of which we can be certain. It is all the more notable, in that it accompanies the transition to a poem that neither Sappho nor any Lesbian poet from antiquity could have written. About this poem much remains to be said, and new readings continue to emerge from scrutiny of this part of the papyrus, which has received little attention thus far by comparison. It will suffice here merely to note that the change of handwriting, together with the change in authorship, marks out the Cologne manuscript as a book-roll produced more informally, at its relatively early date, than the Oxyrhynchus copy four centuries later, and places it in the context of an early anthology of poems constructed for private use or of a copy-book for practice, perhaps in a school-setting.

Text

Sigla: Π¹ = *P.Köln* inv. 21351+21376 (3ʳᵈ c. BC papyrus roll); Π² = *P.Oxy.* 1787 fr. 1 (2ⁿᵈ c. AD papyrus roll)

New Fragment

] ου[

] εὔχομ[

]. νῦν θαλία γε[

]. γέρθε δὲ γᾶc γε[νοίμα]ν·

5   ].. ν ἔχοιcαν γέραc ὠc [ἔ]οικεν

]ζοΐεν, ὠc νῦν ἐπὶ γᾶc ἔοιcαν

] λιγύραν [α]ἴ κεν ἔλοιcα πᾶκτιν

χε]λύγγαν. αλαμοιc ἀείδω.   ⊗

Source: Π¹ (verses lacking in Π², which has the beginning of fr. 58 in this place)
2 εὔχομ[Di Benedetto:].υχ...[Gronewald-Daniel   3 γε[Di Benedetto: πα[

Gronewald-Daniel, West   4 γε[νοίμα]ν Gronewald-Daniel, Di Benedetto: πε͙ [. . .] West   5 κῆ μοιcοπόλων ἔc]λο͙ν Di Benedetto   6 ψῦχαι (or cκίαι) κέ με θαυμά]ζοιεν Di Benedetto comparing Horace Odes 2.13.25–30: πάνται δέ με θαυμά]ζοιεν already suggested by West   7 φαίην δὸc ἀοίδαν] Di Benedetto (ἀοίδαν already suggested by Gronewald-Daniel) 8   ἔμαιcι φίλαιcι(ν) Di Benedetto comparing Sappho fr. 160

Fr. 58
"Success" Poem

```
 5                 ]ύγοιcα͙[
            ].[..]..[  ]ι δάχθην
          ]χυ θ[.]ο͙ι[.]αλλ[.......]ύταν
          ].χθο͙[.]ατί.[.....]ειcα
                  ]μένα ταν[....ώ]νυμόν cε
10                ]νι θῆται cτ[ύ]μα[τι] πρόκοψιν.  ⊗
```

Source: Π² (verses lacking in Π¹, which has the "New Fragment" in this place)

The "Tithonus poem"

ἰ]ο͙κ[ό]λπων κάλα δῶρα, παῖδεc,
τὰ]ν φιλάοιδον λιγύραν χελύνναν·

] ποτ᾽ [ἔ]ο͙ντα χρόα γῆραc ἤδη
ἐγ]ένοντο τρίχεc ἐκ μελαίναν·

5 βάρυc δέ μ᾽ ὀ [θ]ῦμο͙c πεπόηται, γόνα δ᾽ [ο]ὐ φέροιcι,
τὰ δή ποτα λαίψηρ᾽ ἔον ὄρχηcθ᾽ ἴcα νεβρίοιcι.

τὰ ⟨μὲν⟩ cτεναχίcδω θαμέωc· ἀλλὰ τί κεν ποείην;
ἀγήραον ἄνθρωπον ἔοντ᾽ οὐ δύνατον γένεcθαι.

καὶ γάρ π[ο]τα Τίθωνον ἔφαντο βροδόπαχυν Αὔων
10 ἔρωι φ͙.͙αθειcαν βάμεν᾽ εἰc ἔcχατα γᾶc φέροιcα[ν,

ἔοντα͙ [κ]ά͙λ͙ον καὶ νέον, ἀλλ᾽ αὖτον ὔμωc ἔμαρψε
χρόνωι πόλι͙ο͙ν γῆραc, ἔχ[ο]ν͙τ͙᾽ ἀθανάταν ἄκοιτιν. ⊗

Sources: Π¹ Π² (Π¹ preserves earlier portions of lines; Π² preserves ends of lines)
1 ὔμμες πεδὰ West: ὔμμες τάδε Janko: γεραίρετε Di Benedetto: φέρω τάδε Gronewald-Daniel   Μοίσαν ἰοκόλ]πων so already Stiebitz on Π²   2 σπουδάσδετε
West: σπουδάζετε would have been expected in Π¹, cf. 7: χορεύσατε Di Benedetto: λάβοισα πάλιν *vel* ἔλοισα πάλιν Gronewald-Daniel   καὶ West: κὰτ F. Ferrari   τὰ]ν West: τὰ]μ Π², Gronewald-Daniel   φιλάοιδον recognized by Maas
in Π²   3 ἔμοι δ' ἄπαλον πρίν] West   ἔμοι Snell: κέκαρφ' Gronewald-Daniel
δ' Di Benedetto: μὲν Snell   ἄπαλον Gronewald-Daniel   πρίν Di Benedetto: μοι
Gronewald-Daniel   ποτ' [ἔ]οντα Gronewald-Daniel   4 ἐπέλλαβε, (perhaps
too short) or κατέσκεθε, λεῦκαι δ' West: διώλεσε Di Benedetto: ὄγμοις(ιν) or
ὄγμοι δ' ἔνι Gronewald-Daniel   λεῦκαι Hunt   δ' Lobel: τ' Hunt   ἐγ]ένοντο
Hunt   ἐκ Π²: ἐγ Π¹   5 θ]ῦμος Gronewald-Daniel   6 νεβρίοισι West: -ciν
Π¹ Π²   7 τὰ ⟨μὲν⟩ West:⟨ταῦ⟩τα *vel* ⟨ὄν δὲ⟩ (i.e. ἀνὰ δὲ) Gronewald-Daniel: τὰ
⟨νῦν⟩ Janko   στεναχίζω Π¹: στεναχίcδω West: not preserved in Π²   κεν Π²: κεμ Π¹
9 π[ο]τα Gronewald-Daniel   10 δ.[.]α.εισαμ Π¹ (Π² not preserved here): φ..αθεισαν
West: δέπας εἰσάμ- Gronewald-Daniel: λα[λ]άγεισαμ Janko   βάμεν' articulation
West: εἰσαμβάμεν' Gronewald-Daniel, although εἰσομβάμεν' would be required
in the Aeolic dialect   φέροισα[ν Stiebitz on Π²   11 ἔοντα [κ]άλον or ἔοντ'
ἄ[π]αλον Gronewald-Daniel   12 πόλιον or πόλιον Gronewald-Daniel   ἔχ[ο]ντ'
Gronewald-Daniel

Translation

"(several words missing) the violet-rich Muses' fine gifts, children, (several
words missing) the clear-voiced song-loving lyre: (several words missing) skin
once was soft is withered now, (several words missing) hair has turned white
which once was black, my heart has been weighed down, my knees, which once
were swift to dance like young fawns, fail me. How often I lament these things.
But what can you do? No being that is human can escape old age. For people
used to think that Dawn with rosy arms (several words uncertain) Tithonus
fine and young to the edges of the earth; yet still grey old age in time did seize
him, though he has a deathless wife."

Continuation 1 (in non-Lesbian meter)

ψιθυροπλόκε δόλιε μύθων αὐτουργ[(έ)
ἐπίβουλε παῖ ⟦β`ι´οτον` ⟧. [.]γε´[...]ακ[..].[
ἑταῖρε ἀφέρπω : δ[.
[.] ⟦.... ⟧....:(?). [

5   [.]..ν :(?) ἄπγουϲ πρ.[
[φ]άοϲ ἀϲτέρων τε [καὶ ϲέλαϲ
[.]ϲ πυριφεγγὲϲ ἀελ[ίου ϲέλαϲ
[.]ϲ πᾶϲ᾽ ἀκούω : θρη[
[γ]ρου κόρον Ὀρφέα κ[

10 [ἑρ]πετὰ πάντα κ[
[..]. τὰν ἐρατὰν λα[
[εὔ]φθογγον λύραν..[
[ϲυ]νεργὸν ἔχοιϲα παγ[

.   .   .   .   .

Source: Π¹ (verses lacking in Π², which has "Continuation 2" in this place)
5 ὀμνύω τό] Puglia ([τό] already Gronewald-Daniel)   7–8 ψόγουϲ (e.g.) ἀναίτι|ο]ϲ
Puglia   8 θρή[νοιϲα μιμοῦμαι Puglia (μιμουμένα suggested by Gronewald-
Daniel)   9–10 τὸν | ἑρ]πετὰ πάντα κ[ηλοῦντα or κ[ηλήϲαντα (ἀοιδᾶι) Puglia
13 πάγ[των πόνων ἐμῶν Ferrari and Puglia: πᾶγ[or πάγ[τα Gronewald-Daniel

Continuation 2 (in Sapphic meter)
[Sappho fr. 58 (continued)]

            ]ιμέναν νομίϲδει
            ]αιϲ ὀπάϲδοι
ἔγω δὲ φίλημμ᾽ ἀβροϲύναν,   ]τοῦτο καί μοι
τὸ λά[μπρον ἔροϲ τὠελίω καὶ τὸ κά]λον λέ[λ]ογχε.

Sources: 1–4 Π² (verses lacking in Π¹, which has "Continuation 1" in this place)
3–4 line-beginnings restored from the quotation of these verses by Athenaeus
687b (Clearchus fr. 41 Wehrli)

Fr. 59

ἐπιν[   ].[...]νό.[
φίλει.[

καιν[

.   .   .   .

Source: Π² (verses lacking in Π¹, Athenaeus)

APPENDIX
The Text and Translation of Sappho frr. 58–59 as restored and translated by
M. L. West

Fr. 58
New Fragment

           ] νῦν θαλ[ί]ᾳ πα[ρέςτω
           ]. νέρθε δὲ γᾶς περ[ίςχ]οι
   5   κλέος μέγα Μοίςει]ον ἔχοιςαν γέρας ὡς [ἔ]οικεν,
       πάνται δέ με θαυμά]ζοῖεν, ὡς νῦν ἐπὶ γᾶς ἔοιςαν
       κάλειςι χελίδω] λιγύραν, [α]ἴ κεν ἔλοιςα πᾶκτιν
       ἢ βάρβιτον ἢ τάνδε χε]λύγγαν θαλάμοις' ἀείδω.   ⊗

The "Tithonus poem"

       ὔμμες πεδὰ Μοίςαν ἰ]οκ[ό]λπων κάλα δῶρα, παῖδες,
       ςπουδάςδετε καὶ τὰ]ν φιλάοιδον λιγύραν χελύνναν·

       ἔμοι δ' ἄπαλον πρίν] ποτ' [ἔ]οντα χρόα γῆρας ἤδη
       ἐπέλλαβε, λεῦκαι δ' ἐγ]ένοντο τρίχες ἐκ μελαίναν·

       βάρυς δέ μ' ὁ [θ]ῦμος πεπόηται, γόνα δ' [ο]ὐ φέροιςι,
       τὰ δή ποτα λαίψηρ' ἔον ὄρχηςθ' ἴςα νεβρίοιςι.

       τὰ ⟨μὲν⟩ ςτεναχίςδω θαμέως· ἀλλὰ τί κεν ποείην;
       ἀγήραον ἄνθρωπον ἔοντ' οὐ δύνατον γένεςθαι.

       καὶ γάρ π[ο]τα Τίθωνον ἔφαντο βροδόπαχυν Αὔων
       ἔρωι φ..αθειςαν βάμεν' εἰς ἔςχατα γᾶς φέροιςα[ν,

ἔοντα [κ]ά̣λο̣ν καὶ νέον, ἀλλ' αὖτον ὔμως ἔμαρψε
χρόνωι πό̣λ̣ι̣ο̣ν γῆρας, ἔχ̣[ο]ν̣τ̣' ἀθανάταν ἄκοιτιν. ⊗

Pursue the violet-laden Muses' handsome gifts,
my children, and the loud-voiced lyre so dear to song:
But me—my skin which once was soft is withered now
by age, my hair has turned to white which once was black,
my heart has been weighed down, my knees give no support
which once were nimble in the dance like little fawns.

How often I lament these things. But what to do?
No being that is human can escape old age.
For people used to think that Dawn with rosy arms
and loving murmurs took Tithonus fine and young
to reach the edges of the earth; yet still grey age
in time did seize him, though his consort cannot die.

Bibliography

Bernsdorff, H. 2005. "Offene Gedichtschlüsse." *Zeitschrift für Papyrologie und Epigraphik* 153:1–6.

Bettarini, L. 2005. "Note linguistiche alla nuova Saffo." *Zeitschrift für Papyrologie und Epigraphik* 154:33–39.

———. 2007. "Note esegetiche alla nuova Saffo: i versi di Titono (fr. 58,19–22 V.)." *Zeitschrift für Papyrologie und Epigraphik* 159:1–10.

———. 2008. "Saffo e l'aldilà in *P.Köln* 21351, 1–8." *Zeitschrift für Papyrologie und Epigraphik* 165:21–31.

Boedeker, D. Forthcoming. "Sappho Old and New (P.Köln 21351 and 21376, and P.Oxy. 1787): An Overview of Texts and Contexts." In Pierris, forthcoming.

Danielewicz, J. 2006. "Bacchylides fr. 20A, 12 S.-M. and Sappho, P.Köln fr. I–II, 12." *Zeitschrift für Papyrologie und Epigraphik* 155:19–21.

Di Benedetto, V. 2005. "La nuova Saffo e dintorni." *Zeitschrift für Papyrologie und Epigraphik* 153:7–20.

———. 2006. "Il tetrastico di Saffo e tre postille." *Zeitschrift für Papyrologie und Epigraphik* 155:5–18.

Edmunds, L. 2006. "The New Sappho: ἔφαντο (9)." *Zeitschrift für Papyrologie und Epigraphik* 156:23–26.

Führer, R. 2007. "Zum neuen Sappho-Papyrus." *Zeitschrift für Papyrologie und Epigraphik* 159:11.

Gronewald, M., and Daniel, R. W. 2004a. "Ein neuer Sappho-Papyrus." *Zeitschrift für Papyrologie und Epigraphik* 147:1–8.

———. 2004b. "Nachtrag zum neuen Sappho-Papyrus." *Zeitschrift für Papyrologie und Epigraphik* 149:1–4.

———. 2005. "Lyrischer Text (Sappho-Papyrus)." *Zeitschrift für Papyrologie und Epigraphik* 154:7–12.

Hardie, A. 2005. "Sappho, the Muses and Life after Death." *Zeitschrift für Papyrologie und Epigraphik* 154:13–32.

Janko, R. 2005. "Sappho Revisited." *Times Literary Supplement* December 23.

———. Forthcoming. "Tithonus and Eos in the New Sappho (fr. 58, 11–23), with a note on Horace *Odes* I 22." In Pierris, forthcoming. Expanded version of Janko 2005.

Magnani, M. 2005. "Note alla nuova Saffo." *Eikasmos* 16:41–49.

Pierris, A., ed. Forthcoming. *Symposium Lesbium: Poetry, Wisdom and Politics in Archaic Lesbos: Alcaeus, Sappho, Pittacus.* Oxford.

Puelma, M., and Angiò. F. 2005. "Sappho und Poseidippos: Nachtrag zum Sonnenuhr-Epigramm 52 A.-B. des Mailänder Papyrus." *Zeitschrift für Papyrologie und Epigraphik* 152:13–15.

Puglia, E. 2008. "Appunti sul nuovo testo lirico di Colonia." *Zeitschrift für Papyrologie und Epigraphik* 164:11–18.

Rawles, R. 2006a. "Musical Notes on the New Anonymous Lyric Poem from Köln." *Zeitschrift für Papyrologie und Epigraphik* 157:8–13.

———. 2006b. "Notes on the Interpretation of the 'New Sappho'." *Zeitschrift für Papyrologie und Epigraphik* 157:1–7.

West, M. L. 2005. "The New Sappho." *Zeitschrift für Papyrologie und Epigraphik* 151:1–9.

3

The Cologne Sappho
Its Discovery and Textual Constitution

Jürgen Hammerstaedt

Discovery and Acquisition

IN 2002 A GROUP OF MORE THAN 20 PAPYRI WAS ON THE MARKET. They belonged to a private collector outside Egypt. We do not know how and when the papyri became his property. But only after acquisition by the Cologne Papyrus Collection could these ancient documents of inestimable cultural value be finally restored, mounted and conserved properly. It is perhaps even more important that the acquisition of these papyri by a public institution led to their publication and made them accessible not only to the scientific community but also to a broader audience. In this way they at last received the attention they deserve.

First Edition, Partial Overlap with *P.Oxy.* 1787 fr. 1

Two fragments (inv. 21351) of the Cologne Sappho papyrus were published by Gronewald and Daniel in a first article (2004a). The two fragments do not join physically (Figure 1), but the first editors recognized that the text partially overlapped that of a fragment of Sappho (fr. 58.11–22 Voigt) on *P.Oxy.* 1787 fr. 1 of the second–third century AD (Figure 2).[1] It was thus clear that the verses contained in the upper part of the column of one of the pieces, which still preserves the top margin, were the immediate continuation of the verses written in the lower part of the columns of the other, which still preserves the bottom margin.

In the second fragment the lines which the Cologne papyrus has in common with *P.Oxy.* 1787 fr. 1 were followed by a slightly wider interlinear space and the remains of two lines of writing in a different script (Figure 3). These could not be identified with the lines which come after the same poem of Sappho in *P.Oxy.* 1787 fr. 1.[2]

---

[1] MP³ 1449 (together with *P.Hal.* 3 as fr. 44; and *P.Oxy.* XVIII 2166); LDAB 3899.

[2] The text which above (p. 13) is called "Continuation 2".

The new Cologne Sappho confirmed some of the previous restorations which had been proposed for the Oxyrhynchus fragment: [ἰ][ο̣κ][ό][λπ]ων by Stiebitz (fr. 58.11 Voigt); ⌊ὄρχ⌋ηϲθ' by Edmonds (fr. 58.16 Voigt); ⌊ἔϲ⌋χατα by Lobel (fr. 58.20 Voigt); ⌊ἀθαν⌋άταν by Stiebitz (fr. 58.22 Voigt). Five verses of Sappho's poem could now be reconstructed almost completely.[3] They confirmed that the metre of the poem is an acephalous Hipponactean expanded within by two choriambics. This was probably the principal metre of the fourth book of the Alexandrian edition of Sappho.[4]

The Third Cologne Fragment with More Sappho and an Anonymous Lyric Poem

At a later date, the editors recognized a third fragment (Cologne papyrus inv. 21376) and combined it with the second column (Figure 4). Its lower part continues the second text,[5] of which up to then only the remains of two lines written in a different script had survived. Its upper part also contains the missing beginnings of the last four lines of Sappho's "Tithonus poem". These were published by Gronewald and Daniel in a second article 2004b (P.Köln inv. no. 21351+21376). The rest of the third fragment was first edited in Gronewald and Daniel 2005 (Figure 5). The remainders of 13 lines run down to the end of the column. There is much uncertainty about the content, extension, metre and form of the poem. But the first editors pointed out one certainty: this text is definitely not by Sappho. None of the forms are specifically Aeolic, and not all of them can be explained as Aeolic.[6] Words like αὐτουργός, ἐπίβουλος, [ϲυ]νεργός and ἀφέρπω are not found in early poetry. Moreover, the mention of Orpheus, son of Oeagrus, all

---

[3] Lines 5–9 of the "Tithonus poem", see above (p. 11).

[4] For a brief review of the evidence for metrical arrangement, see Lidov, "Notes on the Meter," this volume. See already Hunt 1922:26 in the *editio princeps* of *P.Oxy.* 1787. Ancient references show that the first book of the edition of her poems was written in Sapphic stanzas, and that the second and third book each also consisted of one single metre (for book 2 cf. Hephaestion 7.7 p. 23 Consbruch, for book 3 Hephaestion 10.6 p. 34 C.). Page (1955:144f.), expanding Lobel's hints (cf. Liberman 2007:48) concluded from the fact that the numerous fragments of *P.Oxy.* 1787 are all of the same metre that the book which contained them consisted entirely of the same metre. Since the fifth book offered at least two different metres, as probably did the seventh, Page assigned *P.Oxy.* 1787 and its metre to Book Four, the only book besides the sixth about which nothing else is known. However, Acosta-Hughes (forthcoming:103) points out that Hephaestion does not attribute this metre to a certain book of Sappho's Alexandrian edition (Hephaestion 11.5, p. 36 C. Consbruch), as he does in yet a third case (regarding book seven: Hephaestion 10.5., p. 34 C.). Liberman (2007:50–52) develops some further ideas about the relationship between the Cologne Sappho and the Alexandrian edition.

[5] See above (p. 13), "Continuation 1".

[6] Line 8 πᾶϲ, or πᾶϲ(α) instead of παῖϲ(α). There is a strong Doric coloring, with the only exception of κόροϲ in line 9, which in Doric would be κῶροϲ (Ep.-Ion. κοῦροϲ). Cf. Lundon 2007a:155–157.

the beasts of the land (ἑρπετά) and the fine-voiced lyra imply a myth which is not attested earlier than Simonides PMG fr. 567 (Gronewald and Daniel 2007:8). The metrical features of these lines, however, are, in so far as they can be identified, even more cogent. These are written apparently without distinguishing the colometric units. The first line contains a sequence of at least five short syllables. Aeolic metre is therefore excluded. Gronewald and Daniel (2007) analyzed the beginning as lyric anapaests, followed after several gaps by an iambic penthemimeres and further sequences of double and single shorts between the long syllables. Lundon (2007a) points out that the first line could also be interpreted as two dochmiacs. Dochmiacs are the prevalent metre in the *Fragmentum Grenfellianum*.[7] This lyrical monologue, which contains the lament of a woman abandoned by her companion, had already been indicated by the first editors as a possible parallel for the lyric text in the Cologne Sappho papyrus also on account of other features, like the use of dicola (Figure 6).

In view of this parallel and the fact that the first word, the hapax ψιθυροπλόκε ("whisper-weaving"), recalls the epithet δολόπλοκε in Sappho's Hymn to Aphrodite (fr. 1 Voigt), Gronewald and Daniel (2007a and 2007b) supposed that the lyric text was erotic in content.

Rawles (2006) proposed a different interpretation, expanding an alternative explanation of Gronewald and Daniel. Taking the dicola in their well-attested function as marks for change of speaker, he suggested that the poem contained an antiphonal exchange between two musicians and focused not on love but on music, specifically the invention of the lyre and its early use by Orpheus. However, as Rawles himself admits, his interpretation does not account for the female character certainly alluded to at the end of the poem.

The most detailed examination of all the relevant evidence has been given by Lundon 2007a, who quotes, besides the *Fragmentum Grenfellianum*, the lament of Helen in the Hellenistic *P.Tebt.* I 1 as another parallel.[8] Puglia (2008) accepts and expands Lundon's conclusions, reconstructing the monologue of a woman who replies to the accusations of the man who had left her and accompanies her laments with the lyre, as Orpheus did.

In spite of differences in their interpretation, both Rawles and Lundon observed several features common to this text and the poems by Sappho that precede it. The most striking aspect is the mention of musical instruments in the three texts. The anonymous poem was apparently added with reference to

---

[7] Ed. Esposito 2005, who reveals further points of contact between the *Fragmentum Grenfellianum* and the anonymous lyric poem (Esposito 2005:62; cf. Lundon 2007a:162f.).

[8] MP[3] 1606; LDAB 6894.

the preceding poems.[9] But if we want to understand the relationship between Sappho's two poems and the lyric text properly, we also have to take the hands and other aspects of writing of the Cologne papyrus into consideration.

The Hands and Their Probable Date

Gronewald and Daniel 2005 observed that the letters ε, ζ and θ in the literary hand which wrote Sappho's two poems[10] in the Cologne papyrus are generally still written in the epigraphic form. There are also some fine examples of the archaic form of ω.[11] One ω (Figure 8, number 2) takes a further step in the direction of the shape in which it normally appears in the papyri, and in most cases in this papyrus too. Lundon (2007a) draws attention to α, whose middle stroke is horizontal, written as a separate stroke after the first diagonal. However, there is one exception (Figure 10), and there are also a few instances of round ε, written in two strokes (Figures 7 and 8).

Generally speaking, the epigraphic features, even if they are not applied throughout, lend a rectangular character to this hand. Nonetheless there are also more curved lines. These are especially noticeable in the right-hand vertical of η, and also in π (underlined in Figure 8), which is rather broad, like that appearing in the oldest dated papyrus document (*P. Saqqara* inv. 1972 GP 3; Turner/Parsons 1987 no. 79; between 331 and 323 BC; Figure 11). The same rounded features sometimes reappear in υ, which is occasionally written in two strokes (Figure 8). Compare the μ, in three strokes. c always has the lunate form.[12]

As for the other letters, ι extends above and below the line, as the vertical of κ frequently does too, while τ, υ, and ρ descend below the base-line. ω and c are smaller than the other letters.

Gronewald and Daniel (2004a) compared the hand of Sappho's two poems on the Cologne papyrus with Turner/Parsons 1987 no. 52, of the early third century BC (Figure 12). This manuscript containing anonymous fragments of tragedy (*TrGF* 625), seems even more archaic, because c is written in four strokes (Figures 13a and 13b), and ω always has the epigraphic form. However, there are also striking similarities between the two hands (Figures 13a and

---

[9] For further cases of imitation of Sappho's songs in this period, mainly by Theocritus and Apollonius Rhodius and in the Hellenistic epigram cf. Acosta-Hughes (forthcoming:ch.2).

[10] "New fragment" and "Tithonus poem", text see above (pp. 10-11).

[11] Comparable forms of ω are known, for example, from the Berlin Timotheus papyrus of the fourth century BC (Figure 9).

[12] As it already has in the early document *P.Elephantine* 1 (311/10 BC) and in *P.Vindob*. G 1 (UPZ I 1).

13b), in regard to not only the archaic letter forms, but also the long verticals of ι and κ and the descenders of τ, υ, and ρ.

I agree that Turner/Parsons 1987 no. 52 is the closest parallel to the first hand of the Cologne papyrus, which the editors dated on this basis to the early third century BC. So it is by far the earliest manuscript of Sappho which we now possess.

The anonymous lyric poem[13] is written in broader pen strokes. As a result the writing is less compact than that of the Sappho poems and the distance between the lines larger (Figure 5). No epigraphic letter-forms can be seen (ε is written in two strokes). For this reason the writing appears rounder than the hand of the Sappho poems (Figures 14a and 14b).

Shortly after the beginning of the anonymous lyrics there are in the second and third lines two major deletions and at least one interlinear correction (Figure 5, number 1). Lundon takes these as possible signs of an autograph, of a text composed and altered by the writer himself. Indeed, the ductus of the writing seems less regular and certainly less formal.

We should also note, with Lundon, that the middle strike of α tends to be inclined, and at least sometimes it seems to be drawn in the same movement as the preceding diagonal stroke (Figure 5, number 2) without the lifting of the pen. But sometimes α seems to be written in three strokes, as it was in the Sappho verses, and the inclination of the middle stroke is not always so accentuated (Figure 5, number 3).

In any case, I strongly believe that these are not just differences in the style of writing, but that the lines are in fact written by a hand altogether different from the one that wrote the Sappho poems. The observation that the τ of the lyric poem never descends below the line (cf. Figure 5, number 4), as it so often does in the hand of the Sappho poems (Figures 7 and 8, *passim*), seems to confirm this impression.

In view of the apparent similarities of the two hands and the fact that the archaic features of the first hand are not maintained throughout, Lundon concluded that the lyric text might have been added to the papyrus by a second hand in roughly the same period as the poems by Sappho.

I believe that the closest parallel for the hand of the anonymous lyrics is Turner/Parsons 1987 no. 30 (mid-third century BC; Figure 15), although there are of course some differences. The hand of the anthology of lyric passages from Euripides writes a very straight and severe ν and a rather broad δ. It is also more carefully executed. But all in all it looks quite similar (Figure 16). We find

---

[13] "Continuation 1" (text, see above, p. 13).

the same alternation between α in three movements with horizontal stroke and α in two movements with oblique middle stroke.

At any rate, I am still inclined to date the second hand of the Cologne papyrus some time later in the third century than the first hand. But what is more important: the noticeable difference in formality and execution between the two hands does not favor the idea that the lyric text was added to the papyrus at the same time or in the same situation as the poems by Sappho.

The Division of the Two Poems by Sappho in the First Column of the Cologne Papyrus

It is now generally believed that the verses which the Cologne and Oxyrhynchus papyri preserve before the twelve they share (see Figures 1 and 2) belong to different poems[14] and that the first of the common verses is the beginning of a new composition.[15] Gallavotti (1947) had already suspected the beginning of a new poem in this line of *P.Oxy.* 1787 fr. 1, while Lobel (1925) had conjectured one two lines later. Gronewald and Daniel recognized three further reasons for distinguishing two poems between lines 8 and 9 of the Cologne papyrus: (1) λιγύραν is repeated in lines 7 and 10; (2) if the constitution of lines 8 and 9 is right (cf. below), κάλα is repeated and line 8 contains an apostrophe to a single Muse,[16] while line 9 seems to mention the "fragrant-bosomed Muses" in the plural; (3) there is a thematic difference between lines 1–8, which compare Sappho's present existence with her life after death, and lines 9ff, which treat Sappho's old age.

There are accordingly good reasons for believing that the Cologne Sappho papyrus and *P.Oxy.* 1787 fr. 1 preserve the ends of two different poems by Sappho in their first lines, followed in both of them by the same poem dealing with old age. All the poems are written in the same metre.

P.Oxy. 1787 fr. 1 and 2: Papyrological and Textual Evidence Concerning Poem-Division

The evidence of the Cologne Sappho Papyrus proved the suspicion that two poems were to be distinguished in *P.Oxy.* 1787 fr. 1. The last four lines of the Oxyrhynchus papyrus (fr. 58.23–26 Voigt)[17] do not occur in the Cologne fragments either (cf. Figures 1 and 2). But no scholar had previously suspected that these lines might belong to a different poem. Those who assume that Sappho's

---

[14] "New Fragment" and "Success" poem (texts, see above, p. 10-11).
[15] "Tithonus poem" (texts, see above, p. 11).
[16] Reading with the first editors κάλα, Μοῖϲ'; for the reading cf. below, p. 26.
[17] "Continuation 2" (text, see above, p. 13).

poem on old age extended further than fr. 58.22 Voigt need to give convincing reasons to explain why the poem in the Cologne papyrus stops at this point and, of course, to interpret in this sense the remaining parts of lines 23–26.[18]

My contribution tries to set out some of the papyrological and textual evidence concerning Sappho fr. 58.23–26 and fr. 59 Voigt.

The Oxyrhynchus papyrus (text see above) has preserved only the very last words of these lines, but Athenaeus 15.687b gives a partial quotation of the last two lines.[19]

ὑμεῖς δὲ οἴεσθε τὴν ἁβρότητα χωρὶς ἀρετῆς ἔχειν τι τρυφερόν;
καίτοι Σαπφώ, γυνὴ μὲν πρὸς ἀλήθειαν οὖσα καὶ ποιήτρια,
ὅμως ᾐδέσθη τὸ καλὸν τῆς ἁβρότητος ἀφελεῖν λέγουσα ὧδε·

ἐγὼ δὲ φίλημμι ἀβροσύναν,   καί μοι
τὸ λαμπρὸν ἔρος ἀελίω καὶ τὸ καλὸν λέλογχε,

φανερὸν ποιοῦσα πᾶσιν ὡς ἡ τοῦ ζῆν ἐπιθυμία τὸ λαμπρὸν
καὶ τὸ καλὸν εἴ‹λη›χεν (Hunt) αὐτῇ· ταῦτα δ' ἐστὶν οἰκεῖα τῆς
ἀρετῆς.

But do you imagine that daintiness can comprehend anything luxurious when divorced from virtue? And yet Sappho, truly a woman, if there ever was one, and a poetess besides, nevertheless was ashamed to separate honor from daintiness when she said: "But I love daintiness ..., and for me brightness and honor belong to my yearning for the sun"; thus she makes it plain to all that the desire to live contained for her the idea of brightness with honor; for these are natural properties of virtue.[20]

For metrical reasons, Athenaeus's second verse needs emendation. The first verse cannot be completely reconstructed, but the Oxyrhynchus papyrus offers us one more word: τοῦτο.

---

[18] I still believe that in fr. 58.23 a new poem begins.

[19] The *scriptio plena* in the Sappho quotation follows the Athenaeus codex A. I plan to prove in a further article that the Sappho quotation does not derive from the third book of Clearchus *On Ways of life* (fr. 41 Wehrli²).

[20] Translation by Gulick (1941:VII 179); his translation of τοῦτο, which is inserted in the Sappho fragment from *P.Oxy.* 1787, is not reproduced. The interpretation and translation of the second part of the Sappho quotation is extremely doubtful.

The four letters τολα at the beginning of the last line in Athenaeus' Sappho quotation return in the first line of *P.Oxy.* 1787 fr. 2 (Figures 2 and 17). Hunt 1922 was the first to identify this line beginning with the first letters of the verse whose end is preserved in fr. 1.26. He may be right, but his identification is not altogether certain. In this case the other three lines of fr. 2 have to be combined with the remains of the letters at the bottom of fr. 1.[21]

Lobel and subsequent editors up to and including Voigt regarded the last three verses of fr. 2 as the beginning of a new poem (now Sappho fr. 59 Voigt). However, the horizontal stroke beneath the first line of fr. 2 is not necessarily part of a coronis, but can just as easily be interpreted as a mere paragraphos, like the one the editors recognized after the next two lines. The differences in position and appearance between the coronides, used to separate the poems, and the paragraphoi, used to distinguish the strophes of two lines each, can be illustrated very well at *P.Oxy.* 1787 fr. 3 (Figure 18). In the *intercolumnium*, before the lines, we see three coronides, which mark the ends, and the beginnings, of different poems (fr. 61 Voigt; fr. 62 Voigt, of 12 lines; fr. 63 Voigt, of 10 lines).

In the same fragment (Figure 18), several paragraphoi are beneath the first letters of the line. If we compare fr. 2 (Figure 17), the first horizontal stroke has a position, well inside the interlinear space, very similar to that of the paragraphoi in fr. 3.[22]

From this difference observed in *P.Oxy.* 1787 fr. 3 we might well conclude that the trace under fr. 2, line 1, must be a paragraphos and that a new poem did not begin here at all. Di Benedetto saw this in 1985; Luppe (2004) and West (2005) restated this fact.

However, as Lundon (2007a) observes, some coronides in other fragments of the same papyrus extend beneath the line in exactly the same way as the paragraphoi line (clearly in *P.Oxy* 1787 fr. 21.1–2 and fr. 24.3: figs. 20 and 21). The papyrological evidence does therefore not prove that a new poem begins in *P.Oxy.* 1787 fr. 2 (Voigt fr. 59), but it does not rule it out completely either.

Some Further Notes on the Text of the Cologne Papyrus

In the places where different readings were proposed I checked the Cologne papyrus on the original.[23]

---

[21] Cf. the text in Sappho fr. 59.1 Voigt.

[22] Half a millennium earlier, they had already served the same purpose in the Cologne Sappho papyrus (Figure 19).

[23] Regarding the anonymous lyric poem, the only readings that differ from Gronewald and Daniel's *editio princeps* are some corrections and suggestions which were offered by Lundon 2007a:154n23.

"New Fragment":[24]

Cologne papyrus line 3:] . νῦν θαλ[ί]ᾳ γε[νέcθω] or γέ[νοιτο] Gronewald and Daniel 2004a ([ἔμαιcιν ἑταίραιc' ἀμ' ἔμοι] νῦν θαλίᾳ γε[νέcθω] Bettarini 2008 *exempli gratia*): πα[ρέcτω] (or πά[ρεcτι] or πὰ[ρ ἄμμι]) West 2005. — The top of an upright before νῦν can be reconciled with Bettarini's proposal ἔμοι νῦν. On the other hand, there is no papyrological evidence to decide between γ and π, but Michael Gronewald excludes West's supposed ᾳ after π (cf. Figure 22).

Cologne papyrus line 4:] . νέρθε δὲ γᾶc γέγ[εcθ]αι ed. pr., γε[νοίμα]ν Di Benedetto 2005 (who defends Gronewald and Daniel 2004a), πε[ρίcχοι] West 2005, [ἐπεὶ δέ κε γήραιcα θάνω,] νέρθε δὲ γᾶc γέγ[ωμαι] Bettarini 2008 *exempli gratia*. — No clear papyrological evidence allows a decision between the readings at the line end (cf. Figure 23). The broad horizontal trace of ink at medium height before νέρθε does not contradict Bettarini's ([θάν]ω, νέρθε).

Cologne papyrus line 5:] . . ν ἔχοιcαν γέραc ὡc [ἔ]οικεν, West 2005: κλέοc μέγα Μοίcει]ον ἔχοιcαν γέραc; Hardie 2005: [μολπά μ' ἔτι Μοίcε]ιον ἔχοιcαν γέραc (Livrea 2007:76n23 would prefer κλέοc *vel* μνάμα instead of μολπά); Di Benedetto 2005: [κῆ μοιcοπόλων ἔc]λον ἔχοιcαν γέραc, ὡc [ἔ]οικεν (Bettarini 2008 supplies καί instead of κῆ). — Gronewald does not exclude]ον, but the supposed ο would be unusually large, as θ, and the space between ο and ν seems to be rather long and probably contains further traces of ink (cf. Figure 24).

Cologne papyrus line 6:] . οιεν, West 2005: πάνται δέ με θαυμά]ζοιεν, Di Benedetto 2005: ψῦχαι κέ με θαυμά]ζοιεν, Bettarini 2008: [οὔ κέν μ' ἔτι θαυμά] ζοιεν. — ζοιεν is quite possible: the surface was once torn upwards in such a way that the lower horizontal was obliquely disposed (cf. Figure 25).

Cologne papyrus beginning of line 8:] . . . . α . ; West 2005 (after Gronewald and Daniel 2004a app.): [ἢ βάρβιτον ἢ τάνδε χε]λύνναν, contested by Di Benedetto 2005. — χε]λύνναν is ruled out by the evidence. I myself checked α, then τ or π, the rest is not clear (cf. Figure 26).

Cologne papyrus, middle of line 8: κάλα, Μοῖc', ed. pr. (who rules out, for obvious reasons, καλάμοιc'), θαλάμοιc' West. The question cannot be decided (cf. Figure 26).

"Tithonus poem":[25]

Cologne papyrus line 15: †ται† cτεναχίζω θαμέωc Gronewald and Daniel 2004a (the metre requires a further syllable); <ταῦ>τα cτεναχίζω or <ὄν δὲ> cτεναχίζω Gronewald and Daniel 2004a comm., comparing Anacreon PMG 395, at the

---

[24] Cf. the text (above, p. 10), and the constitution of the text by West (p. 14).

[25] Text, see above p 11.

end of a description of the poet's ageing body: διὰ ταῦτ' ἀναστυλίζω / θάμα Τάρταρον δεδοικώς; West 2005: τὰ <μὲν> στεναχίζω; Janko forthcoming: τὰ <νῦν> στεναχίζω; Führer 2007: <ἦ> τὰ στεναχίζω Burzacchini 2007:100 (*defendit* Lundon 2007b; *reiecit* Bettarini 2008:30n53): <ζὰ> τὰ; στεναχίςδω θαμέως; Burzacchini 2007:100: τά<δε> στεναχίζω.

The most debated single place of the Cologne papyrus is line 18 (Figure 27): Gronewald and Daniel 2004a read ἔρωι δέπας εἰςανθάμεν' εἰς ἔςχατα γᾶς φέροιςα[ν (l. εἰςομβάμεν'), and translated: *"dass die rosenarmige Eos aus Liebesverlangen den Sonnenbecher bestiegen habe, (ihn = Tithonos) zum Ende der Erde tragend"* (the reading was supported with further arguments by Di Benedetto 2005:18–19).

West 2005 proposed: ἔρωι φ . . αθεισαν βάμεν'. — I am convinced that φ cannot be read.

Magnani 2005: ἔρωι δί[φρ]ον εἰςανθάμεν', comparing Nonnus *Dionysiaca* 15.280 (δίφρον ἐὸν στήσαςα φαεςφόρος ἥρπαςεν Ἠώς). — The ν at the end of δί[φρ]ον certainly does not fit the traces.

Austin 2007: Ἔρῳ ἄρμ' <ἀν>αθεῖςαν βάμεν', translating: *"confia son char à Eros et s'en alla aux extrémités de la terre en emmenant Tithonos"*; Bettarini 2007 Ἔρῳ ἄν[ι]' ἄφειςαν βάμεν', taking ἄνι(α) as Aeolic for ἡνία and proposing three different interpretations. — In spite of two examples of "broad" α pointed out by Bettarini the α of ἄρμ' or ἄν[ι]' seems highly improbable.

Janko forthcoming: ἔρωι λα[λ]άγειςαν βάμεν'. — The traces do not fit the first λ and the following α well; the γ seems to be ruled out by the traces.

In Figure 28, the two pieces of papyrus are combined more closely using an imaging program. The probability of this recomposition can easily be confirmed by the recomposed letters α and η at the beginning of line 16 in the Cologne papyrus and by the second α of line 17. In line 18, the short trace of a high horizontal line seems to form an ε together with the remaining traces after δ. Before ειςαν there is the upper left part of a round letter (θ, ς, ο), preceded by what seems to be the right end of an α (cf. the first α in line 14, or the second α in line 16).

The textual basis for possible restorations is either ερωιδε[.]αθεισαν or ερωιδε[.]αςεισαν. Besides the proposal of Gronewald and Daniel 2004 in the *editio princeps*, only three of the restorations proposed up to now fit the traces: δέμα θεῖςαν Danielewicz 2006; δέμας εἶςαν Austin 2007; δέμας εἰςαμβάμεν' Livrea 2007.

Bibliography

Acosta-Hughes, B. Forthcoming. *Recalling Lyric in Alexandria. Five Readings*. Princeton.

Austin, C. 2007. "Nuits chaudes à Lesbos: buvons avec Alcée, aimons avec Sappho." In Bastianini and Casanova 2007:115–126.

Bastianini, G., and Casanova, A., eds. 2007. *Atti del convegno internazionale di studi "I papiri di Saffo e di Alceo": Firenze 8-9 giugno 2006*. Studi e Testi di Papirologia n.s. 9. Florence.

Bettarini, L. 2007. "Note esegetiche alla nuova Saffo: i versi di Titono (fr. 58,19–22 V.)." *Zeitschrift für Papyrologie und Epigraphik* 159:1–10.

———. 2008. "Saffo e l'aldilà in *P.Köln* 21351, 1–8." *Zeitschrift für Papyrologie und Epigraphik* 165:21–31.

Burzacchini, G. 2007. "Saffo Frr. 1, 2, 58 V. tra documentazione papiracea e tradizione indiretta." In Bastianini and Casanova 2007:83–114.

Danielewicz, J. 2006. "Bacchylides fr. 20A, 12 S.-M. and Sappho, P.Köln fr. I–II, 12." *Zeitschrift für Papyrologie und Epigraphik* 155:19–21.

Di Benedetto, V. 1985. "Il tema della vecchiaia e il fr. 58 di Saffo." *Quaderni Urbinati di Cultura Classica* n.s. 19:145–163.

———. 2005. "La nuova Saffo e dintorni." *Zeitschrift für Papyrologie und Epigraphik* 153:7–20.

Esposito, E. 2005. *Il Fragmentum Grenfellianum (P.Dryton 50): Introduzione, testo critico, traduzione e commento*. Eikasmos studi 12. Bologna.

Ferrari, F. 2005. "Contro Andromeda: recupero di un'ode di Saffo." *Materiali e Discussioni per L'analisi dei Testi Classici* 55:13–30.

Führer, R. 2007. "Zum neuen Sappho-Papyrus." *Zeitschrift für Papyrologie und Epigraphik* 59:11.

Gallavotti, C. 1947. *Saffo e Alceo*. Collana di studi greci 10. Naples.

Gronewald, M., and Daniel, R. W. 2004a. "Ein neuer Sappho-Papyrus." *Zeitschrift für Papyrologie und Epigraphik* 147:1–8.

———. 2004b. "Nachtrag zum neuen Sappho-Papyrus." *Zeitschrift für Papyrologie und Epigraphik* 149:1–4.

———. 2005. "Lyrischer Text (Sappho-Papyrus)." *Zeitschrift für Papyrologie und Epigraphik* 154:7–12.

———. 2007a. "Griechische Literarische Texte: 429. Sappho." *Kölner Papyri*. Band 11. (eds. Ch. Armoni, M . Gronewald, K. Maresch, et al.) 1–11. Papyrologica Coloniensia 7. Paderborn.

———. 2007b. "Griechische Literarische Texte: 430. Lyrischer Text (Sappho-Papyrus)" *Kölner Papyri.* Band 11. (eds. Ch. Armoni, M . Gronewald, K. Maresch, et al.) 12–19. Papyrologica Coloniensia 7. Paderborn.

Gulick, Ch. B., trans. 1941. *Athenaeus. The Deipnosophists.* Vol. 7. Loeb Classical Library. Cambridge MA.

Hardie, A. 2005. "Sappho, the Muses and Life after Death." *Zeitschrift für Papyrologie und Epigraphik* 154:13–32.

Hunt, A. S. 1922. "New Classical Fragments. 1787. Sappho, Book IV." *The Oxyrhynchus Papyri Part XV* (ed. B. P. Grenfell and A. S. Hunt) 26–46. London.

Janko, R. Forthcoming. "Tithonus and Eos in the New Sappho (fr. 58, 11–23), with a note on Horace *Odes* I 22." *Symposium Lesbium: Poetry, Wisdom and Politics in Archaic Lesbos: Alcaeus, Sappho, Pittachus* (ed. A. L. Pierris) Oxford.

Liberman, G. 2007. "L'édition alexandrine de Sappho." In Bastianini and Casanova 2007:41–65.

Livrea, E. 2007. "La vecchiaia su papiro: Saffo, Simonide, Callimaco, Cercida." In Bastianini and Casanova 2007:67–81.

Lobel, E., ed. 1925. ΣΑΠΦΟΥΣ ΜΕΛΗ: *The Fragments of the Lyrical Poems of Sappho.* Oxford.

Lundon, J. 2007a. "Il nuovo testo lirico nel nuovo papiro di Saffo." In Bastianini and Casanova 2007:149–166.

———. 2007b. "Die fehlende Silbe im neuen Kölner Sappho-Papyrus" *Zeitschrift für Papyrologie und Epigraphik* 160:1–3.

Luppe, W. 2004. "Überlegungen zur Gedicht-Anordnung im neuen Sappho-Papyrus." *Zeitschrift für Papyrologie und Epigraphik* 149:7–9.

Magnani, M. 2005. "Note alla nuova Saffo." *Eikasmos* 16:41–49.

Page, D. L. 1955. *Sappho and Alcaeus: An Introduction to the Study of Ancient Lesbian Poetry.* Oxford. Corrected reprint ed. 1959.

Puglia, E. 2008. "Appunti sul nuovo testo lirico di Colonia." *Zeitschrift für Papyrologie und Epigraphik* 164:11–18.

Rawles, R. 2006. "Musical Notes on the New Anonymous Lyric Poem from Köln." *Zeitschrift für Papyrologie und Epigraphik* 157:8–13.

Turner, E., and Parsons, P. 1987. *Greek Manuscripts of the Ancient World* ed. 2. Bulletin of the Institute of Classical Studies Supplement 46. London.

West, M. L. 2005. "The New Sappho." *Zeitschrift für Papyrologie und Epigraphik* 151:1–9.

Figure 1. Cologne papyrus inv. nr. 21351 (the parts overlapping *P.Oxy.* 1787 fr. 1 are marked with a box).

Figure 2. *P.Oxy.* 1787 fr. 1 (lines overlapping the Cologne Sappho papyrus are marked with a box).

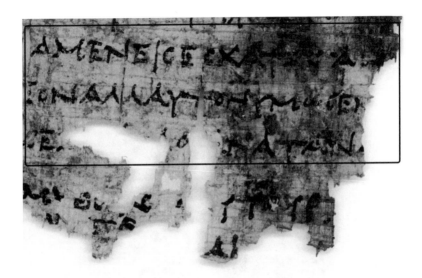

Figure 3. Cologne papyrus inv. nr. 21351, bottom of the second fragment.

Figure 4. Cologne papyrus complete (inv. 21351+21376); the line divides Sappho's verses from the Lyric Poem.

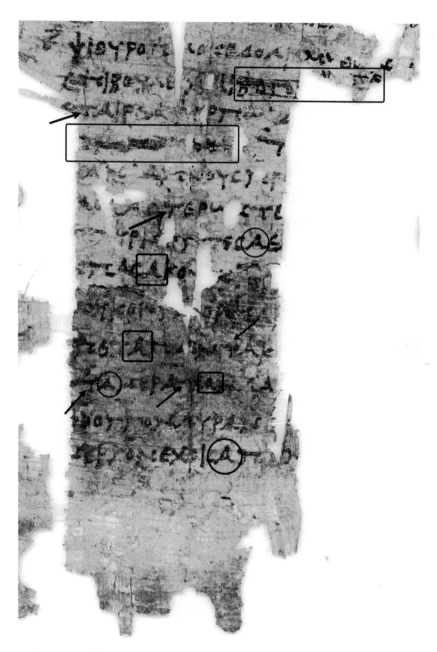

Figure 5. Cologne papyrus inv. 21351+21376, "lyric text"; graphic features: 1. Deletions and corrections in lines 2 and 3 (rectangles); 2. α in two strokes (circles); 3. α, apparently in three strokes (squares). 4. τ (arrows).

Figure 6. Two dicola in the Cologne lyric text (inv. 21376).

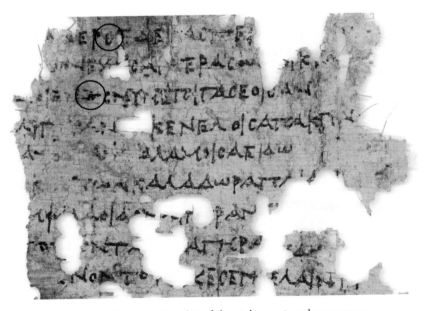

Figure 7. Graphic features in col. I of the Cologne Sappho papyrus.

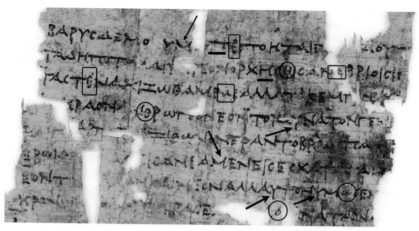

Figure 8. Graphic features in col. II of the Cologne Sappho papyrus. 1. θ and ω, in circles. 2. A particular ω, and some round ε, in squares. 3. Curved π and η, underlined. 5. Rounded υ and μ, marked by arrows.

Figure 9. ω in the Berlin Timotheus papyrus.

Figure 10. A particular α in Sappho's Old-Age poem.

Figure 11. Turner/Parsons 1987 nr. 79 (331/23 BC).

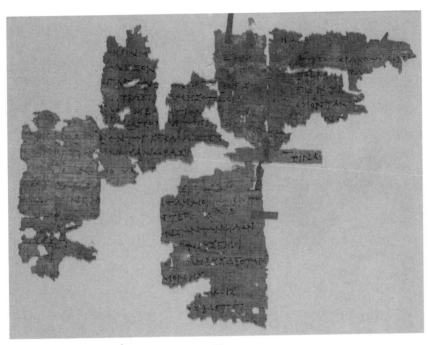

Figure 12. Turner/Parsons 1987 nr. 52.

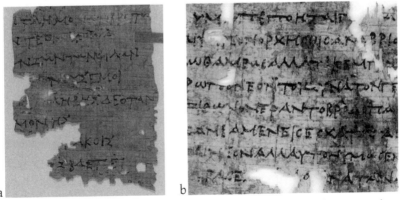

a ⎵ b

Figure 13a-b. Detail of Turner/Parsons 1987 nr 52, facing Cologne Sappho poem.

Figure 14a-b. Detail of a Cologne Sappho poem facing the lyric text.

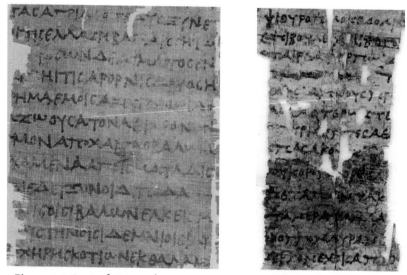

Figure 16. Part of Turner/Parsons 1987 nr. 30 facing the Cologne lyric text.

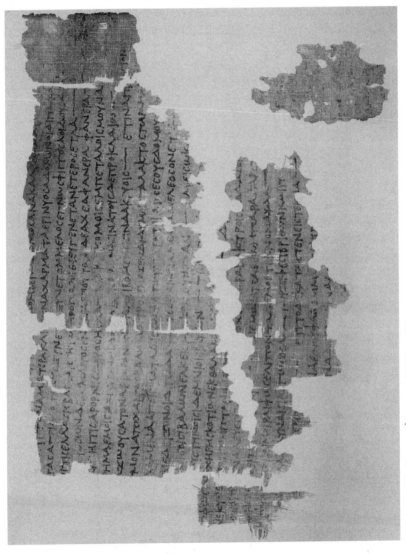

Figure 15. Turner/Parsons 1987 nr. 30.

Figure 17. *P.Oxy.* 1787 fr. 2, with diacritic signs: 1. Sappho fr. 58. 26 Voigt: τὸ λά[. 2. Sappho fr. 59, 1-3 Voigt · Ἐπιν[- - -] | Φίλει . [- - -] | καιν[- - -]. 3. Diacritic signs.

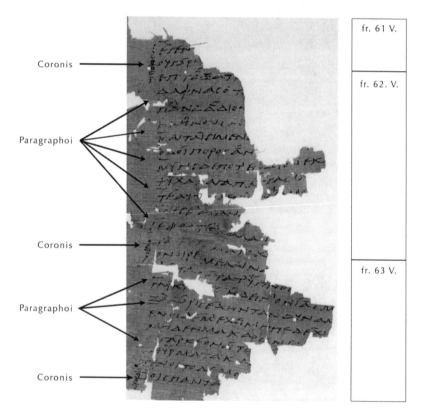

Coronis

Paragraphoi

Coronis

Paragraphoi

Coronis

fr. 61 V.

fr. 62. V.

fr. 63 V.

Figure 18. *P.Oxy.* 1787 fr. 3: coronides and paragraphoi.

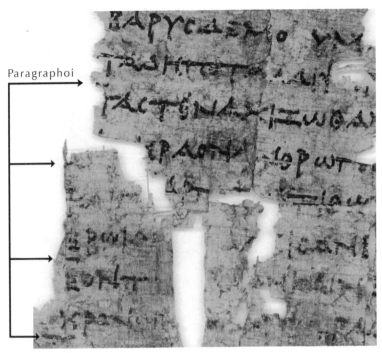

Paragraphoi

Figure 19. Paragraphoi in the Cologne Sappho papyrus.

Figure 20. *P.Oxy.*
1787 fr. 21. 1-2
(coronis).

Figure 21. *P.Oxy.* 1787 fr. 24, 3
(coronis).

Figure 22. Cologne papyrus, line 3:] . νῦν θαλ[ί]ᾳ γε[νέcθω] or γέ[νοιτο]
or πᾴ[ρεcτι] or πὰ[ρ ἄμμι]

Figure 23. Cologne papyrus, line 4: γέρθε δὲ γᾶc γεγ[έcθ]αι or γεγ[οίμαν] or πε[ρίcχοι]

Figure 24. Cologne papyrus, line 5:] . . ν ἔχοιcαν γέραc or Μοίcει]ον ἔχοιcαν γέραc or [κῆ μοιcοπόλων ἔc]λον ἔχοιcαν γέραc

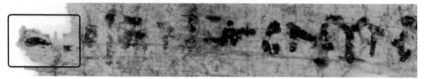

Figure 25. Cologne papyrus, line 6:] . οιεν or πάνται δέ με θαυμά]ζοιεν or ψῦχαι κέ με θαυμά]ζοιεν

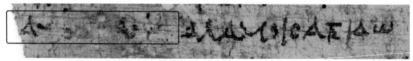

Figure 26. Cologne papyrus, line 8 A+B.

Figure 27. Cologne papyrus, line 18.

4

The New Sappho Poem
(*P.Köln* 21351 and 21376)
Key to the Old Fragments

André Lardinois

THE EGYPTIAN DESERT CONTINUES TO REVEAL TO US ITS TREASURES. The most spectacular find in recent years is probably the Milan papyrus, containing over one hundred new epigrams of the Hellenistic poet Posidippus, published in 2001.[1] No less spectacular is the collection of twenty-five papyrus fragments that the German university of Cologne obtained in 2002. On close inspection it became clear that among these fragments were the remains of at least one and probably two poems of Sappho.[2] This essay will focus on the second of the two Sappho poems found on the Cologne papyrus, the so-called Tithonos poem. I will first discuss the reconstruction of this poem. Next, I will show how the structure of the Tithonos poem can help to elucidate the structure of some older Sappho fragments, especially fragments 16 and 31. Finally, at the end of the paper I will suggest a possible performance context for the new poem.

---

[1] Bastianini and Gallazzi 2001, re-edited in Austin and Bastianini 2002. This essay is a combination of two papers I delivered at the APA: "A New Sappho Papyrus (*P.Köln* 21351): Key to the Old Fragments" (APA Montreal 2006) and "The New Sappho Poem: Where does it end?" (APA San Diego 2007). I wish to thank the original audiences, also listeners at the universities of Ghent, Iowa and Oxford, as well as Jan Maarten Bremer, Irene de Jong, Richard Rawles and the anonymous referees for their helpful comments and suggestions. I further would like to thank Debby Boedeker for her comments and for sharing with me her forthcoming article, and the two editors for bringing this volume together.

[2] Gronewald and Daniel 2004a and 2004b. More recently, Gronewald and Daniel (2005) have published the continuation of the third fragment, but this continuation will not concern us here, since it does not appear to contain work by Sappho. Cf. the contributions of Hammerstaedt and Obbink to this volume.

A Reconstruction of the New Sappho Poem: Where Does It End?

A new papyrus often raises as many questions as it resolves. This holds true for the Cologne papyrus as well. While this papyrus considerably helps to supplement an older poem of Sappho, known previously from the Oxyrhynchus papyri (fr. 58), it also raises new questions about the poem's ending, because the Cologne papyrus only overlaps with lines 11 to 22 of the Oxyrhynchus papyrus. The Italian scholar Gallavotti had already suggested that with the address to the *paides* in line 11 of the Oxyrhynchus papyrus a new poem began—a suggestion that now seems to be confirmed by the Cologne papyrus.[3] We should in the case of the Oxyrhynchus papyrus therefore speak of at least two fragments: fragment 58a, which runs till line 10, and fragment 58b that begins in line 11. But where does fragment 58b end? Most editors of the Oxyrhynchus papyrus, starting with Lobel, have assumed that lines 23–26 also belong to the poem, but these lines do not appear on the papyrus from Cologne.

The question of the poem's ending is closely related to the way its beginning is reconstructed. I will therefore first discuss the different supplements that have been proposed for the opening lines. According to Gronewald and Daniel, the speaker, whom they identify as Sappho, makes a first-person statement about her own poetic activities to a group of girls in the first two lines of the poem: φέρω τάδε Μοίσαν ἰ]οκ[ό]λπων κάλα δῶρα, παῖδες / [λάβοισα πάλιν τὰ]ν φιλάοιδον λιγύραν χελύνναν ('I bring these lovely gifts of the violet-bosomed Muses, girls, picking up again the clear, melodious lyre').[4] A similar reading is proposed by Joel Lidov in this volume: νῦν δὴ μ' ἔτι Μοίσαν ἰ]οκ[ό]λπων κάλα δῶρα, παῖδες / [φίλημμι δὲ φῶνα]ν φιλάοιδον λιγύραν χελύνναν ('Now there are still for me the lovely gifts of the violet-bosomed Muses, girls, and I love the song-loving voice of the melodious lyres').[5] West, however, has suggested that Sappho addresses the young women in a second person statement and commands them with the words: Ὕμμες πεδὰ Μοίσαν ἰ]οκ[ό]λπων κάλα δῶρα, παῖδες / [σπουδάσδετε καὶ τὰ]ν φιλάοιδον λιγύραν χελύνναν ('You for the lovely gifts of the violet-bosomed Muses, girls, be zealous and for the clear

---

[3] Gallavotti 1957:113. Cf. Di Benedetto (1985:147) and Page (1955:129), who quotes the fragment starting from this line.

[4] Gronewald and Daniel 2004a:7. Given Sappho's involvement in the setting up of young women's choruses and her use of the word elsewhere in her poetry for girls (e.g. frr. 49.2, 113, 132.1) it is most likely that the word παῖδες here refers to young women as well.

[5] See Lidov's contribution to this volume, pp. 93-94.

melodious lyre').[6] He postulates a sharp contrast between the poetic activities of the young women and Sappho's inability to dance, on which she comments in the following two lines.

I find the reading of Gronewald and Daniel, especially in the form proposed by Lidov, more appealing than that of West. Sappho is after all singing the song and playing the lyre, while the girls she addresses are probably dancing. By commenting on the gifts of the Muses she is bringing, Sappho emphasizes the fact that she may no longer be able to dance "like fawns" (or "like the girls"—the indirect reference to the girls helps to explain the plural form of νεβρίοισιν), but she is still capable of singing and playing the lyre. This distinction will turn out to be significant, as we shall see. I do accept the contrast West postulates between the first and second couplet, but this is a contrast not between the young women, who are dancing and paying attention to the music, and Sappho, who is not, but between Sappho's own singing and playing of the lyre and her inability to dance.[7]

The biggest question, however, surrounding the new Sappho poem is the way it ended: more specifically whether or not it originally continued with the four lines that follow in the Oxyrhynchus poem. These four lines were assumed to belong to the poem by Edgar Lobel in his edition of the Oxyrhynchus fragment,[8] and he was followed by all subsequent editors. In Campbell's text and translation they read as follows:

]ι̣μέναν νομίσδει
]αις ὀπάσδοι
ἔγω δὲ φίλημμ' ἀβροσύναν, ...] τοῦτο καί μοι
τὸ λά[μπρον ἔρος τὠελίω καὶ τὸ κά]λον λέ[λ]ογχε.

(he / she) thinks
might give
but I love delicacy... this and love has obtained
for me the brightness and beauty of the sun.[9]

---

[6] West 2005:4. σπουδάσδετε in West's reconstruction of the line does not have to be read as an imperative, but could also represent a declarative statement in the second person plural indicative. West, however, in his translation opts for an imperative, following Di Benedetto (2004:5–6), who wishes to read two imperatives in the opening two lines.

[7] Cf. Rawles 2006:4 and Lidov in this volume.

[8] Lobel 1925:26.

[9] Campbell 1982[1990]:100–101. The last two lines are supplemented on the basis of a citation in Athenaeus 687b.

As Deborah Boedeker points out in her contribution to this volume, a different translation of the last line is possible, connecting τὠελίω with ἔρος instead of with τὸ λάμπρον καὶ τὸ κάλον: "and love of the sun has obtained for me (provides me with) brightness and beauty". Love of the sun is a common Greek metaphor for love of life and Athenaeus, who quotes the line, interprets Sappho's words in just this way (τοῦ ζῆν ἐπιθυμία).[10] I believe the ambiguity to be deliberate and that one should construct τὠελίω both with ἔρος and with τὸ λάμπρον καὶ τὸ κάλον: "love of the sun / life has obtained for me the brightness and beauty [of the sun / life]".[11] Constructing τὠελίω both with ἔρος and with τὸ λάμπρον καὶ τὸ κάλον would agree with the idea expressed in the opening priamel of Sappho fr. 16, namely that the most beautiful thing on earth is whatever one loves: the speaker's love of life makes it for her an object of beauty.

If we add these four lines the tone of the poem changes considerably. Sappho would not just resign herself to her situation of being old, but actually present an alternative. She would admit that she is no longer beautiful herself, but she can enjoy the beauty and brightness of other things. The same would apply to the beautiful gifts of the Muses she mentions at the beginning of the poem: note the possible echo between τὸ κάλον in the last line of the continuation and the κάλα δῶρα in the opening line of the poem. Sappho may be old and unable to dance, but she is still capable of making music: she is singing the song and playing the "melodious lyre" mentioned in line 2. To these activities of the speaker the word ἀβροσύναν in line 15 could refer. Furthermore, if Lidov's reconstruction of the first two lines of the poem is correct (see above), the speaker's love (φίλημμι) of the sound of the clear-sounding lyres in line 2 would be echoed by her love (φίλημμ') of ἀβροσύναν in line 25, and this verb, together with κάλα δῶρα (1) and τὸ κάλον (26), would create a ring-composition, linking beginning and end of the poem.

So these four lines would certainly fit the Tithonos poem. But do they belong to it or not? As regards the ending of the new Sappho poem three possibilities have been advanced over the past three years:

---

[10] Athenaeus 687b. For a somewhat different translation of the passage, see Hammerstaedt in this volume.

[11] A similar construction is found in Sappho fr. 96.15–17, where the genitive Ἄτθιδος should be connected both with the preceding participle ἐπιμνάσθεισ(α) and the following noun ἰμέρωι: πόλλα δὲ ζαφοίταισ' ἀγάνας ἐπιμνάσθεισ' Ἄτθιδος ἰμέρωι... βόρηται ("going to and fro, remembering gentle Atthis she is consumed by desire [for Atthis]").

1) The Cologne papyrus only copied part of the poem: it misses the last four lines that are found in the Oxyrhynchus papyrus and originally belonged to the poem.[12]

2) We have to assume that the poem in the Oxyrhynchus papyrus also ends at line 22 and that the next four lines belong to a new poem.[13]

3) There existed in the Hellenistic period two versions of the poem, one ending on the myth of Tithonos, as in the Cologne papyrus, and another continuing the poem with four more lines, as in the Oxyrhynchus fragment.[14]

At first sight the second possibility, which argues that lines 23 to 26 of the Oxyrhynchus papyrus do not belong to the poem, appears to be most likely. Why would the scribe of the Cologne papyrus have only copied part of the poem and not the whole thing? There is little in the Oxyrhynchus papyrus to indicate that lines 23–26 belong with the previous poem, although there are no positive indications that they do not belong either. In most editions of this fragment a coronis is printed after line 26, but this coronis was only a conjecture of Lobel and does not appear on the papyrus itself. In Lobel and Page's Sappho edition it was printed between brackets, but in Voigt's edition the brackets disappeared and the coronis became fixed.[15]

Still, I am not entirely convinced that the continuation of the Oxyrhynchus papyrus does not belong to the poem. West refers to Lobel's conjecture as a "naughty coronis",[16] but Lobel, in my opinion, did have some reason to postulate the end of the poem after line 26. If one looks carefully at *P.Oxy.* 1787 fr. 2, which preserves traces of the first letters of line 26,[17] one can see that below these letters a line is drawn, which is slightly longer than the paragraphos that appears two lines lower on the papyrus. This length of the line is not conclusive and the stroke could represent just as well the end of a paragraphos

---

[12] Gronewald and Daniel 2004a, Puelma and Angiò 2005b, Edmunds 2006, Burzacchini 2007:98–110 and Livrea 2007.

[13] Di Benedetto 2004, Luppe 2004, Janko 2005, West 2005, Bernsdorff 2005, Rawles 2006, Austin 2007 and Ferrari 2007:179–80.

[14] This suggestion is advanced by Boedeker in this volume and in Boedeker forthcoming. Cf. Yatromanolakis 2007:344n259 and 360.

[15] Lobel and Page 1955:41; Voigt 1971:78.

[16] West 2005:4.

[17] See Figure 17 in Hammerstaedt, this volume. One can also consult pictures of the Oxyrhynchus papyri, including the small *P.Oxy.* 1787 fr. 2, on the Oxford Oxyrhynchus website: http://www.papyrology.ox.ac.uk/P.Oxy/papyri/the_papyri.html.

as the cross bar of a coronis, as Jürgen Hammerstaedt argues in this volume. However, I believe that the relative length of the line gave Lobel the idea that it was part of the cross bar of a coronis and not the end of a paragraphos. If a coronis did appear on the papyrus here, it would mean that some poem ended at line 26, and one would either have to assume that it marked the end of a very short four-line poem or that the scribe who wrote the Oxyrhynchus papyrus considered lines 23–26 to be part of the Tithonos poem. The former possibility (a four-line poem) has recently been argued by Di Benedetto,[18] but, for reasons given below, I find the latter option (four lines belonging to the Tithonos poem) more likely.

Another reason why Lobel may have thought that lines 23–26 on the Oxyrhynchus papyrus were part of the Tithonos poem is the quotation of lines 25 and 26 in Athenaeus. Athenaeus, as we have seen, believes that these lines refer to Sappho's desire for life, a meaning which fits the contents of the new Sappho poem and suggests that the words do come from a poem about human mortality. It is certainly possible that the Tithonos poem was followed by another poem with a similar subject matter in the Oxyrhynchus papyrus, but it is also possible that these four lines formed the conclusion in the Oxyrhynchus edition of the poem.

More recently, Mario Puelma and Francesca Angiò have argued that Posidippus in one of his newly found epigrams alludes to the Tithonos poem, including the last four lines of the Oxyrhynchus papyrus.[19] Similarly, Enrico Livrea has discovered possible allusions to Sappho's poem, including the four-line extension of the Oxyrhynchus papyrus, in Callimachus' *Aetia* fr. 1.32–40 Pfeiffer and in Cercidas fr. 7 Powell.[20] Posidippus' epigram 52 A-B speaks about a young girl who grows old while watching the grave of her father and the beautiful sun (τὸν καλὸν ἠέλιον) in the last line of the epigram. There are several reminiscences of the Sappho poem in this epigram, including old age that reaches the girl eventually, just as it seizes the speaker and Tithonos in the Sappho poem.[21] Puelma and Angiò further point out that the epithet καλός is very

---

[18] Di Benedetto 2006.

[19] Puelma and Angiò 2005b.

[20] Livrea 2007. Jan Maarten Bremer has drawn my attention to the second stasimon of Euripides' *Heracles*, esp. lines 637–686, which also seem to draw on Sappho's poem.

[21] Danielewicz (2005), adopting an emendation of Ewen Bowie in line 3, argues that the girl is not a living person, but a representation on the base of the sundial. If so, the parallel with Tithonos would be even more striking: like Tithonos, the girl has been immortalized (as an art object), but still old age reaches her. Bowie's reading is, however, far from certain: see Puelma and Angiò 2005a:19–20n18.

unusual for the sun and reminiscent of the last line in the Oxyrhynchus continuation, where Sappho speaks about the brightness and beauty of the sun. This allusion, of course, would gain in strength if the epithet in the last line of Posidippus' epigram would echo the last line of Sappho's poem, at least in the version Posidippus possessed. What Puelma and Angiò have overlooked is that the likelihood of an allusion to a Sappho poem in this epigram is confirmed by the preceding epigram in the collection. In the last line of this epigram (51 A-B) a group of girls is asked to sing "songs of Sappho" (Σα[πφῶι' ἄισμ]ατα) at the grave of a young girl. Posidippus would subsequently allude to just such a song in his next epigram, thus connecting his epigrams in subtle ways that are becoming gradually clearer.[22]

Finally, Lowell Edmunds has pointed out in Edmunds 2006 and in his contribution to this volume that it is highly unusual, though not entirely unprecedented, for archaic Greek songs to end on a paradigmatic story and not to return to the speaker or the present situation. One would, for example, expect the speaker to return to the *paides*, who are addressed in the opening lines and remain present throughout the poem. I already referred above to the possible allusion to the girls in the plural νεβρίοισιν in line 6; I also believe that the age of her addressees helps to explain the speaker's use of the imperfect ἔφαντο in line 9: "they used to say" (sc. before you girls were born). As a parallel one can point to Phoenix's use of the imperfect ἐπευθόμεθα, with which he introduces the paradigmatic story of Meleager to his young disciple Achilles in *Iliad* 9.254.[23] A return to the girls at the end of the poem would be accomplished by reading the imperative ἴστε δὲ in the lacuna of line 25, as suggested by Di Benedetto.[24]

My own work on the fragments of Solon has convinced me that the textual transmission of archaic Greek poetry throughout the classical and early Hellenistic periods was much less stable than is generally assumed.[25] I therefore consider it most likely that Sappho's poem survived in two versions, as Boedeker

---

[22] See the various essays in Acosta-Hughes et al. 2004 and in Gutzwiller 2005, as well as Gutzwiller's original study of Hellenistic Greek epigram (Gutzwiller 1998). The reading Σα[πφῶι' ἄισμ]ατα in the last line of Posidippus' epigram 51 is, of course, a conjecture, but a very plausible one: the gap does not allow for many other possible readings and there are more references to Sappho's songs in Posidippus' epigrams, including epigrams 55 and 122 A-B. Lapini (2005:239) suggests reading Σα[πφοῦς ἄισμ]ατα, which is perhaps preferable, because, as one of the anonymous referees pointed out to me, it avoids hiatus at the midline of the pentameter. This reading would not alter the meaning of the line, however.

[23] Cf. Edmunds 2006:24.

[24] Di Benedetto 2006:5.

[25] Lardinois 2006. Faraone (2006) has come to the same conclusion after examining the fragments of Tyrtaeus.

also argues in this volume and in more detail in her forthcoming article: one ends on the myth of Tithonos, as in the Cologne papyrus, and the other continues the poem with four more lines, as in the Oxyrhynchus fragment. We should not forget that the Cologne papyrus pre-dates the Alexandrian editions of Sappho's poetry, on which the Oxyrhynchus papyrus is based and of which there may well have been more than one.[26] We seldom have the remains of more than one edition of early Greek poetry from antiquity, but when we do, they regularly differ from one another.[27] We therefore may not want to assume too readily that different copies of early Greek poetry would have been the same in antiquity, especially before the canonical editions of the Alexandrian scholars. Perhaps we should even adopt the opposite assumption and expect them to diverge, as is, for example, the case with different editions of medieval poetry.[28] I believe that the four-line continuation on the Oxyrhynchus papyrus was part of the original poem but, in later versions, had become detached from it, perhaps, as Boedeker suggests, in order to present the poem as a reflection on old age, suitable for performance at a symposium but without the positive twist Sappho had provided it.[29]

A Comparison between the New Poem and Sappho frr. 16 and 31

With or without the continuation on the Oxyrhynchus papyrus the Tithonos poem reveals a clear structure. Lines 1–2 address a group of girls (παῖδες), who are probably dancing while the speaker is singing and playing the lyre. The following four lines represent the first-person speaker in a difficult situation: she has grown old and, as a result, she is no longer able to dance. The speaker complains about her situation, but at the same time reconciles herself to it, because, as she says, it is impossible for any human not to grow old. She illus-

---

[26] Yatromanolakis 1999 and Liberman 2007:41.

[27] Examples are the so-called "wild papyri" of Homer's epics and the different versions of Theognis' poetry preserved in the *Theognidea*, on which see, respectively, Haslam 1997 and Bowie 1997. Ucciardello (2005) argues that different copies of Ibycus' poetry, with their own linguistic variations, must have circulated in antiquity.

[28] See e.g. Haustein 1999 and Bein 1999a on the variations in the medieval editions of the German lyrical poet Walther von der Vogelweide. I owe these references to my colleague in Dutch medieval literature, Johan Oosterman. Boedeker in this volume refers to the principle of "*mouvance*" advanced by "new philologists" in medieval studies and Nagy's application of this idea to the transmission of the Homeric epics (Nagy 1996: esp. 7–38).

[29] See Boedeker's essay in this volume. For old age as a sympotic theme, see e.g. Campbell 1983:215–220 and Slings 2000:432–434. Note the parallels that have been drawn between this poem of Sappho and Anacreon fr. 395 PMG or Mimnermus frr. 2 and 4 West (Gronewald and Daniel 2004a:3).

trates this gnomic thought with a mythological example: the story of Tithonos, who married the Dawn goddess and was made immortal but nevertheless grew old. If we add the four lines of the Oxyrhynchus papyrus the first person speaker of the poem not only resigns herself to her situation but presents an alternative as well: no longer beautiful herself, she can nevertheless enjoy the beauty and brightness of other things, like the sun.

This structure of the new poem can be used to clarify the structure of some older fragments of Sappho that are less well preserved. First of all there is fragment 31, the famous fragment that begins with the words φαίνεταί μοι κῆνος. In this fragment the first person speaker enumerates a series of afflictions she endures while looking at a girl who is talking to a man and laughing. She is even at the point of dying, or so she says in lines 15 and 16. This long list of symptoms is itself reminiscent of the list of complaints Sappho enumerates in the Tithonos poem.[30] And, just as in the new Sappho poem, the speaker of fragment 31 resigns herself to her situation. So much is clear from the half line preserved of the last strophe: ἀλλὰ πὰν τόλματον ("but all can be endured"). The remainder of this line suggests that Sappho illustrated this gnomic thought with the example of a poor man (πένητα), but here the citation of the poem in the text of Longinus unfortunately breaks off. We therefore do not know if Sappho in fragment 31 also offered an alternative to her feelings, as she does in the continuation of the Oxyrhynchus papyrus.[31]

It is commonly accepted that Sappho 31 continued with a gnomic statement in line 17, in which she resigns herself to her situation. In the case of Sappho fragment 16, however, the possible continuation of the poem, after line 20, is disputed and mostly rejected.[32] Most commentators (and almost all translators) assume that this poem ends with Sappho's wish to see Anactoria in line 20, and that with line 21 a new poem begins. There is not much room, however, for a complete new poem, because at the beginning of line 32 traces of a coronis are preserved, so we know that a poem ended here.[33] Moreover, I believe that the new Sappho papyrus offers some evidence that a new poem did not begin in line 21, but that the Anactoria poem continued. It has long been recognized that lines 21 and 22 of fragment 16 preserve traces of a gnomic saying: some-

---

[30] Cf. West 2005:6.

[31] For possible reconstructions of the closing stanza of Sappho's poem, see West 1970:312–313, Rösler 1990, Lidov 1993 and, more recently, D'Angour 2006, who suggests that Sappho ended the poem on an extended, gnomic thought.

[32] Pfeijffer 2000:1n1 with earlier references. Among those who accept the continuation of the poem after line 20 are Howie 1977, Aloni 1997:25–26 and Bierl 2003.

[33] Cf. Hutchinson 2001:167.

thing, we are told, is not possible (οὐ δύνατον γένεσθαι) for a human being or human beings (ἀνθρώπωι or ἀνθρώποις). This gnomic statement bears a close resemblance to the one we find halfway the new Sappho poem, where the words οὐ δύνατον γένεσθαι also appear at line end and a general human being (ἄνθρωπον) is presented as subject.

Jakob Sitzler proposed the following reconstruction of the gnomic statement in lines 21–22 of fragment 16: ἀλλ' ἄραν] μὲν οὐ δύνατον γένεσθαι / παῖσ]αν ἀνθρώπ[ωι, π]εδέσχην δ' ἄρασθαι ("but it is not possible that every wish / for a human is fulfilled, but to pray to partake in...").[34] If this reconstruction is even half correct, the speaker in fragment 16 would not only utter a gnomic statement in lines 21–22, but would indicate by it that she resigns herself to her situation. With this gnomic continuation, fragment 16 shows a structure very similar to the one we detected in the Tithonos poem and in fragment 31. The first person speaker first describes a painful situation: she would like to see Anactoria, but cannot do so, because Anactoria is not there. In the continuation of the poem, starting with the gnomic statement in lines 21–22, she then resigns herself to this situation: she realizes that she is asking for the impossible and that she has to settle for something less, perhaps to partake in memories of Anactoria, something with which Sappho consoles herself in other poems as well.[35]

One of the few commentators who has dared to propose a possible reconstruction of fragment 16 beyond line 22 is the British scholar J.G. Howie.[36] Howie postulates that the speaker after line 22 told a new myth, which would provide her with an alternative example from the figure of Helen, mentioned in the first half of the poem, and would have introduced a more modest wish. Howie's suggestion that another myth appeared in the second half of fragment 16 gains some plausibility from the fact that the second half of the new Sappho poem also contains a paradigmatic story that helps the speaker to reconcile herself to her situation. It would also help to counterbalance the somewhat daring comparison of the first person speaker (and Anactoria) to the figure of Helen in the first half of the poem.

The structures of fragments 16, 31 and 58 thus reveal a remarkable similarity. In all three poems, the speaker first sketches a painful or difficult situation. She complains, but then resigns herself to this situation with the help of a gno-

---

[34] Sitzler in his review of Lobel 1925, quoted by Voigt 1971 *ad* fr. 16.21s.
[35] For the theme of memory in Sappho's poems, see Burnett 1983:277–313 and Lardinois 2008. Cf. Sappho frr. 94 and 96.15–16.
[36] Howie 1977.

mic thought and a mythical or general example. Finally, she may have offered herself an alternative, as she appears to be doing in fragment 16 and in the continuation of the Tithonos poem in the Oxyrhynchus papyrus.

The Performance Context of the New Sappho Poem

The structure of fragments 16, 31 and 58 resembles that of consolation speeches, such as we find, for example, in the *Odyssey*.[37] Reinhold Merkelbach has called fragment 16 a consolation poem or, even better, a consolation song (*"ein Trostlied"*).[38] In such a song the first-person speaker recognizes the difficulty of her situation, but calls on herself and probably her audience to take heart. In fragments 16 and 31 the speaker has to distance herself from a young woman—a theme we encounter more often in Sappho's poetry.[39] In the new Sappho poem the situation is different: here the speaker bids her youth and her beauty farewell.

This brings me to the possible performance context of these poems. I have argued elsewhere that fragments 16 and 31 were probably performed at wedding banquets.[40] The performer of these songs praises the beauty and erotic appeal of the bride, while at the same time expressing something of her own sorrow and that of friends and family of the bride in having to let go of her. In the case of the new Sappho poem the performance context is harder to gauge, although I could imagine the song as being performed at a wedding banquet as well. At the wedding feast the assumed advanced age of the singer could be contrasted playfully with the youth of the girls, dancing to her song, on the one hand, and with the blooming adolescence of the bride and groom on the other. The comparison of the first-person speaker with the unhappy Tithonos would also contrast with the usual comparisons of bride and groom with great heroes and heroines in other wedding songs,[41] while at the same time, perhaps, entailing a warning for the happy couple that they too, in time, will grow old.[42]

The opening of the Tithonos poem bears a resemblance to fragment 26 of Alcman, as was noted already by Claude Calame.[43] In this fragment Alcman addresses a group of young women and complains that his limbs no longer can

---

[37] See Howie 1977, esp. 223–227.

[38] Merkelbach 1957:13.

[39] On the age of the women named in Sappho's poetry, see Lardinois 1994.

[40] See my 2001 article.

[41] See Hague 1983:133–135. Cf. Sappho frr. 23, 31.1, 44.34, 105b and 111.

[42] Rawles (2006:5) analyzes the Tithonos story in terms of the possible significance it would have for the young women addressed in the first line of the poem, including their marriages.

[43] Calame 1983:474.

carry him. Antigonus of Carystus, who quotes the fragment, claims that Alcman spoke these lines "weak from old age and unable to whirl with the choruses and the girls' dancing" (ἀσθενὴς ὢν διὰ τὸ γῆρας καὶ τοῖς χοροῖς οὐ δυνάμενος συμπεριφέρεσθαι οὐδὲ τῇ τῶν παρθένων ὀρχήσει):

οὔ μ' ἔτι, παρσενικαὶ μελιγάρυες ἰαρόφωνοι,
γυῖα φέρην δύναται· βάλε δὴ βάλε κηρύλος εἴην,
ὅς τ' ἐπὶ κύματος ἄνθος ἅμ' ἀλκυόνεσσι ποτήται
νηδεὲς ἦτορ ἔχων, ἁλιπόρφυρος ἰαρὸς ὄρνις.

No longer, honey-toned, strong (or: holy)-voiced girls
can my limbs carry me. If only, if only I were a cerylus,
who flies along with the halycons over the flower of the wave
with resolute heart, strong (or: holy) sea-blue bird."[44]

Alcman's poem is written in dactylic hexameters, a meter we know to have been used for wedding songs, including Sappho's.[45] Since Alcman was reputed to have composed wedding songs, I would not be surprised if his song was performed at the wedding banquet as well.[46]

This interpretation of the performance context of the poem is speculative, I know, but one thing is certain: the poem suggests that Sappho performed her poetry in public or semi-public settings and not in the privacy of her own home. Sappho may have been the singer of the song, but she was probably supported by a group of young girls, the *paides* mentioned in line 1, who were dancing while she was singing. The public performance context of Sappho's poetry, for which I have argued elsewhere,[47] is being confirmed by one of the new epigrams of Posidippus as well. This is epigram number 51, to which I already referred earlier. According to the reconstruction of Battezzato,[48] it reads as follows:

'δακρυόεσσα[ι ἔπεσθε, θε]οῖς ἀνατείνατε πήχεις'
τοῦτ' ἐπὶ πα[ιδὸς ἐρεῖτ' αὐ]τόμαται, Καρύαι,

---

[44] Antigonus of Carystus *Marvels* 23, quoted by Campbell 1988 *ad* Alcman fr. 26.

[45] Sappho frr. 104a.1, 105a and c.

[46] For evidence that Alcman composed wedding songs, see Contiades-Tsitsoni 1990:46–63. For references to solo and group performances at wedding banquets, see Lardinois 1996:151n4. Acosta-Hughes (forthcoming) has noted some possible reminiscences of the Tithonos poem in Theocritus' *Idyll* 18, his so-called wedding song for Helen.

[47] Lardinois 1996.

[48] Battezzato 2002.

Τειλεσίης, ἧς [νεῖσθε πρὸ]ς ἠρίον· ἀλλὰ φέρουσαι
εἴαρι πορφυρέ[ου φύλλ' ἐς ἀ]γῶνα νέμους
θῆλυ ποδήν[εμοι ἔρνος] ἀείδετε, δάκρυσι δ' ὑμέων
κολλάσθω Σα[πφῶι' ἄισμ]ατα, θεῖα μέλη.

"[Follow on] tearfully, lift up your arms to the [gods]",
   this [you will say] spontaneously, o Karyai, for the [child]
Telesia, to whose tomb [you come]. But bringing
   in spring to the contest [leaves] from the purple glade,
sing with wind-swift feet the virgin [shoot], and to your tears
   let there be joined Sa[ppho's son]gs, divine melodies.

This epigram of Posidippus imagines a group of girls, named Karyai, dancing at the grave of a girl named Telesia and singing songs of Sappho, assuming the restoration is correct.[49] What better songs could these girls be singing there than consolation poems of Sappho?

Bibliography

Acosta-Hughes, B., et al., eds. 2004. *Labored in Papyrus Leaves: Perspectives on an Epigram Collection Attributed to Posidippus (P.Mil.Vogl. VIII 309).* Hellenic Studies 2. Washington DC.

———. Forthcoming. *Recalling Lyric in Alexandria. Five Readings.* Princeton.

Aloni, A. 1997. *Saffo. Frammenti.* Florence.

A-B. See Austin and Bastianini 2002.

Austin, C., and Bastianini, G., eds. 2002. *Posidippi Pellaei Quae Supersunt Omnia.* Milan. (= A-B)

Austin, C. 2007. "Nuits chaudes à Lesbos: buvons avec Alcée, aimons avec Sappho." In Bastianini and Casanova 2007:115–126.

Bastianini, G., and Gallazzi, C., eds. 2001. *Epigrammi: P.Mil.Vogl. 8. 309.* With C. Austin. Papiri dell' Università degli studi di Milano 8. Milan.

Bastianini, G., and Casanova, A., eds. 2007. *Atti del convegno internazionale di studi "I papiri di Saffo e di Alceo": Firenze 8-9 giugno 2006.* Studi e Testi di Papirologia n.s. 9. Florence.

Battezzato, L. 2002. "Song, Performance, and Text in the New Posidippus." *Zeitschrift für Papyrologie und Epigraphik* 43'31–42.

---

[49] See n22 above.

Bein, Th. 1999a. "Fassungen – iudicium – editorisches Praxis." In Bein 1999b:72–90.

———, ed. 1999b. *Walther von der Vogelweide: Textkritik und Edition.* Berlin.

Bernsdorff, H. 2004. "Schwermut des Alters im neuen Köln Sappho-Papyrus." *Zeitschrift für Papyrologie und Epigraphik* 150:27–35.

Bettarini, L. 2005. "Note linguistiche alla nuova Saffo." *Zeitschrift für Papyrologie und Epigraphik* 154:33–39.

Bierl, A. 2003. "'Ich aber (sage): das Schönste ist, was einer liebt!': Eine pragmatische Deutung von Sappho Fr. 16 LP / V." *Quaderni Urbinati di Cultura Classica* 74:91–124.

Boedeker, D. Forthcoming. "Sappho Old and New (P.Köln 21351 and 21376, and P.Oxy. 1787): An Overview of Texts and Contexts." *Symposium Lesbium: Poetry, Wisdom and Politics in Archaic Lesbos: Alcaeus, Sappho, Pittacus* (ed. A. Pierris). Oxford.

Bowie, E. 1997. "The Theognidea: A Step Towards a Collection of Fragments?" *Collecting Fragments/Fragmente sammeln* (ed. G. W. Most) 53–66. Göttingen.

Burnett, A. 1983. *Three Archaic Poets: Archilochus, Alcaeus, Sappho.* Cambridge MA.

Burzacchini, G. 2007. "Saffo Frr. 1, 2, 58 V. Tra documentazione papiracea e tradizione indiretta." In Bastianini and Casanova 2007:83–114.

Calame, C. 1983. *Alcman: Introduction, texte critique, témoignages, traduction et commentaire.* Rome.

Campbell, D. A., ed. 1982. *Greek Lyric I.* Cambridge MA. Corrected second edition 1990.

———. 1983. *The Golden Lyre: The Themes of the Greek Lyric Poets.* London.

———, ed. 1988. *Greek Lyric II.* Cambridge MA.

Contiades-Tsitsoni, E. 1990. *Hymenaios und Epithalamion: Das Hochzeitslied in der frühgriechischen Lyrik.* Stuttgart.

D'Angour, A. 2006. "Conquering Love: Sappho 31 and Catullus 51." *Classical Quarterly* 56:297–300.

Danielewicz, J. 2005. "Posidippus Epigr. 52 Austin-Bastianini (P. Mil. Vogl. VIII 309, col. VIII 25–30)." *Zeitschrift für Papyrologie und Epigraphik* 151:30–32.

Di Benedetto, V. 1985. "Il tema della vecchiaia e il fr. 58 di Saffo." *Quaderni Urbinati di Cultura Classica* n.s. 19:145–163.

———. 2004. "Osservazioni sul nuovo papiro di Saffo." *Zeitschrift für Papyrologie und Epigraphik* 149:5–6.

———. 2006. "Il tetrastico di Saffo e tre postille." *Zeitschrift für Papyrologie und Epigraphik* 155:5–18.

Edmunds, L. 2006. "The New Sappho: ἔφαντο (9)." *Zeitschrift für Papyrologie und Epigraphik 156:23–26.*

Faraone, C. A. 2006. "Stanzaic Structure and Responsion in the Elegiac Poetry of Tyrtaeus." *Mnemosyne* 59:19–52.

Ferrari, F. 2007. *Una mitra per Kleis: Saffo e il suo pubblico.* Biblioteca di Materiali e discussioni per l'analisi dei testi classici 19. Pisa.

Gallavotti, C. 1957. *Saffo e Alceo: Testimonianze e frammenti. Vol 1: Saffo* rev. ed. 3. Naples.

Gronewald, M., and Daniel, R. W. 2004a. "Ein neuer Sappho-Papyrus." *Zeitschrift für Papyrologie und Epigraphik* 147:1–8.

———. 2004b. "Nachtrag zum neuen Sappho-Papyrus." *Zeitschrift für Papyrologie und Epigraphik* 149:1–4.

———. 2005. "Lyrischer Text (Sappho-Papyrus)." *Zeitschrift für Papyrologie und Epigraphik* 154:7–12.

Gutzwiller, K. 1998. *Poetic Garlands: Hellenistic Epigrams in Context.* Berkeley.

———, ed. 2005. *The New Posidippus: A Hellenistic Poetry Book.* Oxford.

Hague, R. 1983. "Ancient Greek Wedding Songs: The Tradition of Praise." *Journal of Folklore Research* 20:131–143.

Haslam, M. 1997. "Homeric Papyri and the Transmission of the Text." *A New Companion to Homer* (eds. I. Morris and B. Powell) 55–100. Leiden.

Haustein, J. 1999. "Walther von der Vogelweide: Autornähe und Überlieferungsvarianz als methodisches Problem." In Bein 1999b:63–71.

Howie, J. G. 1977. "Sappho Fr. 16 (LP): Self-Consolation and Encomium." *Papers of the Liverpool Latin Seminar 1* (ed. F. Cairns) 207–235. Liverpool.

Hutchinson, G. O. 2001. *Greek Lyric Poetry: A Commentary on Selected Larger Pieces.* Oxford.

Janko, R. 2005. "Sappho Revisited." *Times Literary Supplement* December 23.

Lapini, W. 2005. "Posidippo, Ep. 51 Austin-Bastianini." *Philologus* 149:233–243.

Lardinois, A. 1994. "Subject and Circumstance in Sappho's Poetry." *Transactions of the American Philological Association* 124:57–84.

———. 1996. "Who Sang Sappho's Songs?" *Reading Sappho: Contemporary Approaches* (ed. E. Greene) 150–172. Berkeley.

———. 2001. "Keening Sappho: Female Speech Genres in Sappho's Poetry." *Making Silence Speak: Women's Voices in Greek Literature and Society* (eds. A. Lardinois and L. McClure) 75–92. Princeton.

———. 2006. "Have we Solon's verses?" *Solon of Athens: New Historical and Philological Approaches* (eds. J. H. Blok and A. P. M. H. Lardinois) 15–35. Leiden.

————. 2008. "'Someone, I Say, Will Remember Us': Oral Memory in Sappho's Poetry." *Orality, Literacy, Memory in the Ancient Greek and Roman World* (ed. A. MacKay) 79–96. Mnemosyne Supplement 298. Leiden.

Liberman, G. 2007. "L'édition alexandrine de Sappho." In Bastianini and Casanova 2007:41–65.

Lidov, J. B. 1993. "The Second Stanza of Sappho 31." *American Journal of Philology* 114:503–535.

Livrea, E. 2007. "La vecchiaia su papiro: Saffo, Simonide, Callimaco, Cercida." In Bastianini and Casanova 2007:67–81.

Lobel, E., ed. 1925. ΣΑΠΦΟΥΣ ΜΕΛΗ: *The Fragments of the Lyrical Poems of Sappho.* Oxford.

Lobel, E., and Page, D. L., eds. 1955. *Poetarum Lesbiorum Fragmenta.* Oxford. (= L-P)

L-P. See Lobel and Page 1955.

Luppe, W. 2004. "Überlegungen zur Gedicht-Anordnung im neuen Sappho-Papyrus." *Zeitschrift für Papyrologie und Epigraphik* 149:7–9.

Merkelbach, R. 1957. "Sappho und ihre Kreis." *Philologus* 101:1–29.

Nagy, G. 1996. *Poetry as Performance: Homer and Beyond.* Cambridge.

Page, D. L. 1955. *Sappho and Alcaeus: An Introduction to the Study of Ancient Lesbian Poetry.* Oxford. Corrected reprint edition 1959.

Pfeijffer, I. L. 2000. "Shifting Helen: An Interpretation of Sappho, Fragment 16 (Voigt)." *Classical Quarterly* 50:1–6.

Puelma, M., and Angiò, F. 2005a. "Die Sonnenuhr und das Mädchen." *Zeitschrift für Papyrologie und Epigraphik* 151:15–29.

————. 2005b. "Sappho und Poseidippos: Nachtrag zum Sonnenuhr-Epigramm 52 A.-B. des Mailänder Papyrus." *Zeitschrift für Papyrologie und Epigraphik* 152:13–15.

Rawles, R. 2006. "Notes on the Interpretation of the 'New Sappho'." *Zeitschrift für Papyrologie und Epigraphik* 157:1–7.

Rösler, W. 1990. "Realitätsbezug und Imagination in Sapphos Gedicht ΦΑΙΝΕΤΑΙ ΜΟΙ ΚΗΝΟΣ." *Der Übergang von der Mündlichkeit zur Literatur bei den Griechen* (eds. W. Kullmann and M. Reichel) 271–287. Tübingen.

Slings, S. R. 2000. "Symposion and Interpretation: Elegy as Group-Song and the So-Called Awakening of the Individual." *Acta Antiqua Academiae Scientiarum Hungaricae* 40:423–434.

Ucciardello, G. 2005. "Sulla tradizione del testo di Ibico." *Lirica e Teatro in Grecia. Il Testo e la sua ricezione* (ed. S. Grandolini) 21–88. Naples.

V. See Voigt 1971.

Voigt, E.-M., ed. 1971. *Sappho et Alcaeus: Fragmenta.* Amsterdam. (= V)

West, M. L. 1970. "Burning Sappho." *Maia* 22:307–330.

———. "The New Sappho." *Zeitschrift für Papyrologie und Epigraphik* 151:1–9.

Yatromanolakis, D. 1999. "Alexandrian Sappho Revisited." *Harvard Studies in Classical Philology* 99:179–195.

———. 2007. *Sappho in the Making: The Early Reception.* Hellenic Studies 28. Washington DC.

5

Tithonus in the "New Sappho" and the Narrated Mythical Exemplum in Archaic Greek Poetry

Lowell Edmunds

carminis finem statueram, nunc dubito
—M.L. West[1]

AT PRESENT, SOME THINK THAT THE TWELVE LINES OF THE "NEW SAPPHO" are a complete poem; some think that the poem must have continued, as it appears to do in the Oxford papyrus (*P.Oxy.* 1787).[2] One way to approach the question of completeness is to focus on the Tithonus exemplum, and to compare it with the typical use of the narrated mythical exemplum in archaic Greek poems.[3] If the "New Sappho" is complete in twelve lines, then it ends with an exemplum. How likely is it that an exemplum will conclude a poem?

The question of such a conclusion has already been addressed apropos of the "New Sappho" by Hans Bernsdorff.[4] He wishes to establish what he calls the "open" conclusion as a stylistic feature of archaic Greek lyric.[5] But, as he has to admit at the outset, in archaic monody there exists only one possible case of a complete poem ending with a mythical narrative. It is Alcaeus fr. 44.[6] Bernsdorff thus has to look elsewhere, and he chooses Pindar and Horace.

---

[1] *IEG²*, on Simonides fr. 20.12.

[2] I am grateful to Michele Caprioli for corresponding with me about this paper.

[3] "Narrated" refers to the telling of a story or some part of a story. My category of exemplum thus excludes references to a god or hero which are limited to a name and epithet and/or relative clause. The word "mythical" refers to traditional stories about gods and heroes.

[4] Bernsdorff 2005. Stehle, this volume, n3, takes the twelve lines of the new Sappho as a complete poem. (Though Stehle's article is about time, she does not discuss the odd imperfect in line 9, on which see Edmunds 2006.)

[5] Bernsdorff 2005:2n5 on the term "open": it is from Walter Wili.

[6] All references to Sappho and Alcaeus are to Voigt's edition.

In Pindar, he finds three "open" endings, two in odes (*Olympian 4*; *Nemean 1*) and one in a paean (4). In my opinion, Pindar is the wrong place in which to look. Dionysius of Halicarnassus took Pindar and Sappho to represent opposite kinds of style, and Horace is likely to be reflecting this view in *Odes* 4.2.[7] Although both Pindar and Sappho are "lyric" poets, they differ in time, place, dialect, meters, and performance venue, thus also, I assume, in the use of the mythical exemplum. In this last respect, some differences are immediately obvious. First, the opening and closing formulas of the Pindaric mythical narrative are strikingly different from those in monody.[8] Second, the myth in Pindar tends to be more allusive and to be complexly related to the historical reality to which it refers. (The mythical exemplum in tragedy, too, tends to stand in a complex relation to the action.[9]) As for Horace, as one who hoped to play the *Lesboum barbiton* (*Odes* 1.1.34), he seems a more likely candidate for comparison with Sappho. It is unclear, however, why his practice in one epode (13) and four odes (1.7; 1.8; 3.11; 3.27) is probative for Aeolic monody. Note that, in each of these poems, Horace concludes not with narrative, as a twelve-line "New Sappho" would conclude, but with quotation of a character in the narrative, whose words directly or indirectly make the point that Horace wishes to make.

My comparanda for the Tithonus exemplum are in archaic poems for solo performance. I will also discuss the narrated mythical exemplum in speeches in Homer, for reasons to be explained later.[10]

First, Sappho and Alcaeus. The former provides at most two exempla. In fr. 16, Helen leaves Menelaus and her daughter and so forth. If J.G. Howie is right, the poem did not end at line 20 but continued to line 33, where there

---

[7] As Hunter 2007:217–219 argues.

[8] Edmunds 2006:n2: The typical opening in Pindar is relative pronoun + aorist + ποτε + aorist participle (or a subset of these). See Bonifazi 2004, who points out that "γάρ is the particle that introduces mythical sections without a relative pronoun" (47), citing two places in Pindar and referring to de Jong 1997. The typical closing is the notorious break-off, with return to the first-person: Race 1990:41–57.

[9] For example, a character may contest the relevance of a myth to him- or herself. Zagagi 1980:32–46 studies places in tragedy in which a character whom the chorus has attempted to comfort with a mythical exemplum contests the appropriateness of the exemplum by insisting that "his own situation has surpassed ... the unhappy events of the myth in question" (33).

[10] For an inventory of narrated mythical exempla, I started with Oehler 1925. I am not, however, the new Oehler whom we need. Canter 1933 might be useful for purposes other than mine. He gives an inventory of exempla arranged by topic (206–219), with a few comments, e.g. on comparative frequency in Greek and Latin, on their usage.

is a coronis.[11] If that was the end of the poem, one can assume that there was a return to the gnome with which the poem begins or to the circumstances which occasioned that gnome. In fr. 17, a prayer or cult hymn[12] to the Hera of Lesbos,[13] Sappho, having evoked Hera's support of the Atreidae, returns to her petition with νῦν δὲ κ[άμοι (11; cf. fr. 1.25 καὶ νῦν). Someone might say that the closing petition is obligatory in a prayer and therefore has no bearing on the question of how the "New Sappho," which is not a prayer, ended.[14] The formal markers, however, and, one might say, the style of prayer or cult hymn were hardly restricted to ritual occasions but were broadly shared across genres. For example, sixteen of Pindar's epinicians begin with cult hymns.[15]

For Sappho, then, there are perhaps two examples, in one of which Sappho returns from the myth to the present. In Alcaeus, four relevant examples appear. In the sequence of Voigt numbers, the first is fr. 38A, in which Alcaeus exhorts Melanippus to get drunk with him. He uses Sisyphus as an example of the futility of human attempts to escape death and returns to his exhortation with ἀλλ' ἄγι (10). Fr. 42 is the curious twelve-line (four Sapphic strophes) *synkrisis* of Helen and Thetis. It begins ὡς λόγος and it ends by rounding off the *synkrisis* without an application of the myths. If this poem, with its "open" conclusion, is complete, then it is a parallel to the "New Sappho" understood as a complete poem, which happens also to be twelve lines long. But, from the time of its publication, opinions have differed about the completeness of Alcaeus fr. 42, and one would have to say that it is a parallel not to a twelve-line "New Sappho" but to *the problem of* a twelve-line "New Sappho."[16] Even if Alcaeus fr. 42 is complete, it is possible that it could function as a complete poem only within a sympotic context, in which it was part of a chain, attempting to cap

---

[11] Howie 1977. (Please note the conditional form of this proposition.) See Bierl 2003:121n112 for a list of publications since Howie's which take the view that fr. 16 continued after the sixth strophe.

[12] See Race 1992:28 and n49 on the term "kletic hymn," which could also be used of Sappho fr. 17. He does not distinguish between kletic hymn and prayer. On the distinction between cult hymn and rhapsodic hymn, see Miller 1986:1–5; Race 1992:28–31.

[13] Hera of Lesbos: cf. Alcaeus fr. 129.6; Sappho test. 59 (from the *Palatine Anthology* 9.189).

[14] Race 1982:10–14 on the request at the end of the hymn, at which point "the hymnist tries to establish the closest connection between him and the god." Race 1992:19n17 for bibliography on hymnal openings. Race 1992:28–29 (diagram) shows clearly that the poet or singer returns at the end, with a salutation or a request, to the divinity named or addressed at the outset.

[15] Race 1992:30.

[16] Complete: The majority opinion. See Rösler 1980:223 and n269 for references. Maronitis 2004:79–80 gives a formalistic argument for unity. Campbell 1982:259: "16 is certainly the last line." Incomplete: see references in Rösler 1980:224n270. Rösler's own arguments for incompleteness: 224–227; 233–235 (would have been ten strophes long).

the preceding symposiast's effort.[17] Another fragment of Alcaeus which some have considered complete is 44.[18] The myth here is modeled on the episode in the *Iliad* in which Achilles asks his mother to intercede with Zeus on his behalf (1.348–427; 493–516). Though sense can be made of the poem only in line 6, and the beginning of the poem is thus uncertain, a coronis at line 8 shows where the poem ended. It ended with the myth. Fr. 44 is thus a secure example of what Bernsdorff calls the "open" conclusion, and the only secure example in Sappho and Alcaeus he can point to.[19] The fourth and last example from Alcaeus is fr. 298 with the myth of Cassandra and Ajax's impiety, apparently preceded and followed by reference to the impiety of Pittacus, betrayer of his companions.[20] Pittacus is referred to in line 47. For Alcaeus, then, we have one example of a myth concluding a poem (fr. 44), two examples of a return from the myth to the present situation (frs. 38A, 298), and one *non liquet* (fr. 42).

Elegy contains many mythical exempla but only a few that are narrated and thus relevant to the present question. Mimnermus' lines on the sun are a description and not a narrative (fr. 12). They are from *Nanno* and thus presumably had some particular contextual frame. The two fragments on Jason and the Golden Fleece are from a narrative (frr. 11–11A), and it sounds as if the narrative is being used as an argument for something, but context is completely lacking.[21] In the priamel in Theognis 699–718, the foils—heroes and mythical figures—are concise and unnarrated, with one exception, Sisyphus. His story is amplified to the length of five couplets (703–12).[22] The priamel as a whole is framed by a gnome (men consider wealth the greatest *aretê*, 699–700, 717–718).[23] Another narrated mythical exemplum in Theognis, this time two

---

17 For the sympotic destination of fr. 42: Jurenka 1914:229; Rösler 1980:221 (fr. indicates the "non-political conversational material of the *hetaireia*"); cf. Page 1955:280n1; Vetta 1981:486–487.

18 Page 1955:282: "ends abruptly in the eighth line, leaving the sequel to the memory of the audience."

19 Bernsdorff 2005:2 cites Meyerhoff 1984:52–53.

20 Thus already Tarditi 1969:86–96. Taalman Kip 1987:125: " ... [W]e cannot even guess how Alcaeus made the switch from myth to reality at the end of the fragment. We can only say something about the way the myth is introduced. If we assume (as I think we must) that this happens at v. 4, we may ascertain that the conclusion of the story comes first, serving as a link between reality and the story proper."

21 The context in Strabo 1.2.40 does not help.

22 Faraone 2005a and 2005b has recently written about the unit of five couplets as a characteristic building-block of elegy, which he calls a "stanza." In both articles, he refers to Weil 1862, the first to perceive these units. Weil called them "strophes" and also spoke of response. He devoted less than a page (8) to Theognis and referred only to lines 1135–1150, without noticing the "choral" introductions to the mythical exempla in lines 703–712 and 1123–1128.

23 See Henderson 1983 on the framing of the exemplum.

couplets long, occurs in a pederastic poem (1341–1350).[24] The myth, which is about Ganymede, is part of an *argumentum ex Iove*.[25] Zeus did it. Why shouldn't I? Theognis introduces the myth with ἐπεί ποτε καί and ends by addressing someone named Simonides: οὕτω μὴ θαύμαζε. In another poem, Theognis compares his sufferings to those of Odysseus (1123–1128). It is not clear that this poem, which ends with talk of vengeance on the suitors, is complete.[26] I suggest that what we have points to a missing conclusion in which Theognis returned to one of his favorite themes, namely, vengeance on his enemies.[27]

The only example in Theognis—the only example in all of elegy—of an "open" ending is the poem in which Theognis, addressing a boy, compares his pursuit of him to Atalanta's suitors' pursuit of her (1283–1294). He introduces the exemplum with ὥς ποτέ φασιν. He concludes: she came to know Aphrodite in spite of her refusal. In a sympotic context, the point of the exemplum is so clear that it is perhaps more effective if left unexpressed: as even Atalanta yielded, so you will yield to me. This poem, too, however, is surrounded by controversy. There are those, like West, who say that it is an amalgam of two poems; there are those who say that it is a single, complete poem.[28]

To conclude on elegy, there is now the remarkable mythical narrative concerning Telephus which constitutes the "new Archilochus" (*P.Oxy.* 4708). Dirk Obbink in his publication of the fragment suggests that the story may be an exemplum and shows how it could have functioned as such.[29]

The largest and I would say most useful set of narrated mythical exempla is found in the speeches in Homer. But what justifies using these speeches as comparanda for Sappho? There are three reasons. In the first place, mythical exempla have the same introductory elements in these speeches as are found

---

[24] On the attribution of these lines to Euenos of Paros, either the contemporary of Socrates or an older one, which was proposed by four different scholars between 1907 and 1934, see Vetta 1980:121–123.

[25] Cf. Theognis 1345–1350 (discussed in this paper); Aristophanes *Clouds* 1079–1082 (Weaker recommends *argumentum ex Iove* if Pheidippides is accused of adultery); Euripides *Trojan Women* 948–950 (Helen uses this argument); Plato *Euthyphro* 5e–6a (Euthyphro uses it apropos of prosecuting his father); etc.

[26] Campbell 1982:339n1 sums up the position of the doubters: "Many assume that the poem is incomplete."

[27] For this theme: Edmunds 1985:103.

[28] Amalgam: West 1974:165–167; *IEG*² app. crit. on 1288–1294; Vetta 1975; Vetta 1980:81–82. Not an amalgam but self-consistent: Ferrari 1989:316–320; Gerber 1991:213–214; Gerber 1999:371n4. With clairvoyance denied West and Vetta (and earlier scholars cited by Vetta), an anonymous reader tells me: "The Atalanta exemplar in Theognis 1287–1294 is perfectly comprehensible as it is." He or she provides no explanation.

[29] In Gonis and Obbink 2005:20–21.

in monody and elegy. Second, the speeches belong to a set of rhetorical genres, and some of these genres, for example, prayer, lament, and supplication, are shared with poetry.[30] Third, as rhetorical utterances, the speeches in Homer are, like poems or songs, performance genres.[31]

Much research has been devoted to narrated mythical exempla in Homer, which are customarily referred to as "paradeigmata."[32] Scholars have classified them in various ways, discussed their functions, and the distortions or inventions which appear in the myths themselves. My question is a simple, formal one: do speakers return from a narrated myth to the situation which prompted the telling? The answer is yes. M. M. Willcock made the relevant point in an article in 1964: paradeigmatic speeches in Homer have a ring-compositional structure, with the myth in the middle.[33] The same is true of the few paradeigmata in the Homeric Hymns, one of which happens to be about Tithonus.[34] The same is true also of the ainos, of which we have fifteen examples in archaic and classical poetry which survive in their entirety.[35]

Earlier, I mentioned introductory elements as a shared feature of exempla in monody and epic speeches. The same is true of the elements by which the speaker

---

[30] Martin 1989:44: "the major rhetorical genres available for the heroic performers are prayer, lament, supplication, commanding, insulting, and narrating from memory." Further, "these discourse types constitute poetic 'genres' outside epic" (94). Martin shows the lyric basis of Hector's speech at *Iliad* 7.235–241. He cites (n81) Nagy's *Pindar's Homer* (at that time forthcoming) in order to distinguish his own point ("a relation to lyric") from Nagy's chronology of hexameter, which begins in shorter meters of the kind which we call "lyric."

[31] Martin 1989:37 (*muthoi* are public; performance before an audience); 160 ("performance" a more inclusive term for "speeches"); 225 (historical basis of the speeches: "performance of self"). The use of mythical exempla in Athenian oratory has been seen as continuous with the practice of the Homeric heroes: Gotteland 2001:11. Cf. Thomas 2000:257 on Antiphon DK 87 B54 in particular and sophists' use of myth. I have not seen Demoen 1997.

[32] Andersen 1975 and 1978; Austin 1966:300–304 (discusses the mythical exemplum in relation to a larger "paradigmatic logic" informing historical digressions in the *Iliad*); Braswell 1971; Heubeck 1954; Pedrick 1983. For older discussion, see Heubeck 1954:23n33. *Pietatis causa*, I cite also Fraenkel 1927 and Jaeger 1945:40–43 (see also Index s.v. "Example").

[33] Already Heubeck 1954:25: "*normhafte Dreistufenaufbau*."

[34] *Homeric Hymn to Apollo* 300–375 (Typhoeus) is a rare example of a narrated mythical excursus (not an exemplum) in the poet's own voice. Note transition formulas at 307 and 375. Cf. West on Hesiod *Theogony* 22. In the *Homeric Hymn to Hermes* 414–462 the poet introduces into his narrative a cosmogonic song sung by Hermes which succeeds in softening the anger of Apollo at the theft of his cattle. The examples most relevant to the question of the mythical exemplum in the new Sappho are Aphrodite's precedents for her union with Anchises: Tros (*Homeric Hymn to Aphrodite* 200–217) and Tithonus (*Homeric Hymn to Aphrodite* 218–238). The latter story also explains why the mortal Anchises cannot become her husband. Note transition formulas at 202 and 218.

[35] Holzberg 2002:20. In nine of the fifteen, the speaker draws the moral from the tale.

rounds off the exemplum and returns to the present. Here are a few instances: In Iliad 20, Aeneas concludes his genealogical discourse to Achilles: ἀλλ᾽ ἄγε μηκέτι ταῦτα ... (244). In *Iliad* 24, Achilles concludes the Niobe exemplum: ἀλλ᾽ ἄγε δὴ καὶ νῶϊ ... (618). Compare the way Alcaeus turns from the Sisphyus exemplum to his exhortation to Melanippus: ἀλλ᾽ ἄγι ... (fr. 38A.10). Achilles' concluding formula in the speech to Priam is really a combination of two formulae which can occur separately. With καὶ νῶϊ one can compare νῦν δὲ κ[ἄμοι in Sappho fr. 17.11 (cf. fr. 1.25 καὶ νῦν). A favorite way to round off a paradeigma in Homer is with a phrase introduced by ὥς, e.g ὥς καὶ ἐγώ, and one can compare in Theognis the phrase οὕτω μὴ θαύμαζε which I have already cited.[36]

To move toward a conclusion, a survey of the evidence for the narrated mythical exemplum in archaic monody and elegy shows only a single indubitable case of an "open" conclusion, against a few cases of an A-B-A structure, where A is the present situation and B is the myth. Alcaeus fr. 42 has the "open" conclusion, which may be owing to its place in a sympotic chain. As for the Theognidea, lines 1287–1294 (on Atalanta) would also be an example of an "open" ending if it were certain that these lines constitute a single poem. Another exemplum in Theognis is followed by an explicit return to the situation which prompted the myth. In Homer, the speaker who uses a paradeigma will regularly apply it to the present situation. In Alfred Heubeck's formulation, the argument of the paradeigma in Homer is either "Thus someone acted then, thus you should act now" or "Thus it happened once before, take warning."[37]

The preponderance of the evidence, such as it is, especially if one admits speeches in Homer, as I think that one can, leads one to expect a return from the myth to the present, an A-B-A structure. One would expect Sappho, then, to return from Tithonus to her present situation, and one notes in lines 23–24 of the Oxyrhynchus papyrus present tenses which would indicate a return to the present time of the enunciation. Further, one notes καί μοι, which resembles a rounding-off formula. I cited an example of this formula from Sappho fr. 17.11. Penelope, too, uses it at Odyssey 19.524 to round off the story of Pandareus' daughter, the nightingale, and return to her own situation.

Penelope's myth illustrates something else. As I said in the abstract of the presentation from which this paper has emerged, "The narrator finds a particular point of contact between the myth and the situation to which he or she applies

---

[36] Theognis 1349 οὕτω μὴ θαύμαζε. Cf. ὥς at *Iliad* 11.762; 14.328; 18.120; 19.134; 23.643. For the imperative cf. *Iliad* 1.274; 15.31.

[37] Heubeck 1954:23–24. (I have somewhat simplified the second kind of argument.)

it." The tertium comparationis is never in doubt or left as allusion or riddle.[38] In the "New Sappho," Tithonus clearly illustrates the gnome that mortals inevitably grow old. If this exemplum has some further, different meaning, this idea will be found not in the myth itself but in Sappho's perspective on the myth. The peculiar imperfect ἔφαντο suggests that Sappho's perspective has indeed changed, presumably because of self-understanding that post-dates the perspective of the subjects of ἔφαντο. She knows something that they didn't know.

What ought to be in concluding lines is some kind of self-consolation, as the first editors of the "New Sappho" thought.[39] Alex Hardie has put together, from other fragments of Sappho (including, obviously, the one in the Cologne papyrus) and from a vast array of related material, the elements that one would expect to find in the conclusion, even though Hardie appears to believe, in spite of himself, that the twelve lines are a complete poem. These elements are devotion to the Muses in the form of song and dance, with related eschatological hopes, all as part of the choric education with which the poem begins.[40]

My reading is a historicizing one. It aims at establishing the outline of the poem that Sappho's audience might have expected. There is another kind of reading, equally important, which I would call a possible reading. For example, when Richard Janko in an article in the *Times Literary Supplement* explains the Tithonus exemplum as in itself consolatory he gives a reading which might have become possible at some point in antiquity and is possible for us.[41] Likewise, when Bernsdorff cites Horace for the practice of Sappho, I think that he is really talking about a way of reading Sappho which he learned from Horatian innovation in the use of the mythical exemplum. The later poet enables new ways of reading the earlier poet.[42]

This distinction I have made between the way or ways we can read the "New Sappho" and the way the twelve lines would have appeared to Sappho's audience needs further discussion, as an anonymous reader's reaction to this

---

[38] *Pace* Rawles 2006:3.

[39] Gronewald and Daniel 2004b:3-4.

[40] Hardie 2005. Cf. Nagy 1973:177: "As a coda to this poem, the last two verses amount to a personal and artistic manifesto."

[41] Janko 2005. (Cf. Hardie 2005:28n100.) Rawles 2006:7 assumes the concept of what I am calling a possible reading: "A reading of the poem which absorbed the element of the story in which Tithonus is metamorphosed into a cicada is necessarily conjectural, since it cannot be certainly demonstrated that this element was available to Sappho and her audience. It can at best be shown that it is compatible with what we do know and with how the poem may in any case be read."

[42] As Borges said, " ... [E]ach writer *creates* his precursors": Borges 1964[1952]. For discussion of this idea see Edmunds 2001:159–163.

paper shows. He or she states: "We moderns have no trouble making sense of the twelve-line poem and its final mythical exemplar. Sappho's audience would have been more equipped to do so as well." In this way, he or she collapses the distinction between reception contemporary with Sappho and later reception such as Janko's. The deductive form of his or her argument, of the modus ponens type, is not the usual one in discussion amongst classicists, but it happens to be convenient for illustrating what I consider a mistaken point of view. It can be restated thus:

> If we moderns can make sense of the twelve-line "New Sappho," then Sappho's audience could make sense of it, too.
>
> We can make sense of it.
>
> Therefore Sappho's audience could make sense of it.

In this kind of argument, as everyone knows, everything depends on the truth of the premises. The first premise here is, I submit, untenable. It assumes that the mind will always, across millennia, respond to the same poetic work in the same fundamental way. A counter-argument from common sense suffices. The workaday classicist constantly discovers not the fundamental similarity of the ancient to the modern mind but its alterity. One could also point to the current vogue of reception studies, which is showing how the meaning of ancient texts has differed in different times and places. A stronger counter-argument against the idealist, transhistorical pretension of the syllogism I have analyzed can be found in Hans-Georg Gadamer's *Truth and Method*. On his account, the understanding of an ancient text comes about not in spite of but because of and within our historical distance from that text.

Postscript

Several speakers besides me at the two Sappho panels held in San Diego in 2007 addressed the question of the completeness of the "New Sappho." Dee Clayman described the Cologne papyrus as the remains of a Hellenistic florilegium on old age, mortality and song, comparing the roughly contemporary "New Posidippus" (*P.Mil.Vogl.* VIII 309) with its thematic arrangements under nine headings. The "New Sappho" might be a truncated edition of the poem, she said, enough for the compiler's purposes. André Lardinois, too, compared the "New Posidippus," and said that, in the unstable conditions of archaic poetry, two different versions might have been transmitted. Both he and Clayman were thinking materialistically, so to speak, i.e. of transmission in writing. Gregory Nagy, thinking in terms of performance, spoke of the ending of the archaic poem as always already fungible. Deborah Boedeker, too, argued for the possibility of different versions in performance. The position I have taken in this paper can be reconciled with the positions of Clayman and Lardinois, I believe. As for Nagy's and Boedeker's view, one would have to imagine, for the twelve-line "New Sappho," a performance context in which the audience, if I am right about the precise point of contact between performer and his or her situation, is content with Tithonus as an exemplum illustrating the old saw about the inevitability of aging. The only way around this conclusion, or to counter this conclusion, is to argue that the Tithonus myth, as in the twelve-line "New Sappho," contains a latent, positive, consolatory idea. So Richard Janko argued in his *TLS* article,[43] and so, but finding a different idea, did Joel Lidov, though Lidov stopped short of saying that the "New Sappho" is a complete poem, preferring "complete poetic statement." To repeat, I myself do not expect a mythical exemplum in such a context to be a riddle or to be allusive. (The myth in Pindar is another story.)

Bibliography

Andersen, Ø. 1975. *Paradeigmata: Beiträge zum Verständnis der Iliad*. Diss., University of Oslo .

———. 1978. *Die Diomedesgetalt in der Ilias*. Symbolae Osloensis Supplement 25. Oslo.

Austin, N. 1966. "The Function of the Digressions in the *Iliad*." *Greek, Roman, and Byzantine Studies* 7:295–312. Reprinted 1978: *Essays on the Iliad: Selected Modern Criticism* (ed. J. Wright) 70–84. Bloomington, IN.

Bastianini, G., and Casanova, A., eds. 2007. *Atti del convegno internazionale di studi "I papiri di Saffo e di Alceo": Firenze 8–9 giugno 2006*. Studi e Testi di Papirologia n.s. 9. Florence.

Bernsdorff, H. 2005. "Offene Gedichtschlüsse." *Zeitschrift für Papyrologie und Epigraphik* 153:1–6.

---

[43] It is not my purpose in this paper to argue against such interpretations. It seems necessary, however, to point out that reliance on Hellanicus fr. 140 Fowler = FGrH 4 F 140 as an early authority for metamorphosis of Tithonus into a cicada is risky. This fragment, from a scholiast on *Iliad* 3.168, runs: "Day (Ἡμέρα) fell in love with Tithonus, son of Laomedon, brother of Priam, by whom she had a son Memnon, and, after she had regaled him with a long life, she changed him into a cicada." One has to agree with Jacoby 1957:466: *"mehr as die genealogie wird H nicht gehörchen."* The scholiast offers not an alternate version of the myth but nonsense.

Bierl, A. 2003. "'Ich aber (sage), das Schönste ist, was einer liebt!' Eine prag-
matische Deutung von Sappho Fr. 16 LP/V." *Quaderni Urbinati di Cultura
Classica* 74:91–124.

Bonifazi, A. 2004. "Relative Pronouns and Memory: Pindar Beyond Syntax."
Harvard Studies in Classical Philology 102:41–68.

Borges, J. L. 1964. "Kafka and his Precursor." *Other Inquisitions, 1937–1952*. Trans.
R. L. C. Simms. 106–108. Austin TX. Originally published 1952: *Otras inqui-
siciones, 1937–1952*. Buenos Aires.

Braswell, B. K. 1971. "Mythological Innovation in the *Iliad*." *Classical Quarterly*
n.s. 21:16–26.

Campbell, D. A., ed. 1982. *Greek Lyric I*. Cambridge MA. Corrected second edition
1990.

Canter, H. V. 1933. "The Mythological Paradigm in Greek and Latin Poetry."
American Journal of Philology 54:201–224.

de Jong, I. J. F. 1997. "ΓAP Introducing Embedded Narratives." *New Approaches to
Greek Particles* (ed. A. Rijksbaron) 175–185. Amsterdam Studies in Classi-
cal Philology 7. Amsterdam.

Demoen, K. 1997. "A Paradigm for the Analysis of Paradigms: The Rhetorical
Exemplum in Ancient Imperial Greek Theory." *Rhetorica* 15.2:125–158.

Edmunds, L. 1985. "The Genre of Theognidean Poetry." In Figueira and Nagy
1985:96–111.

———. 2001. *Intertextuality and the Reading of Roman Poetry*. Baltimore.

———. 2006. "The New Sappho: ἔφαντο (9)." *Zeitschrift für Papyrologie und
Epigraphik* 156:23–26.

Faraone, C. A. 2005a. "Exhortation and Meditation: Alternating Stanzas as a
Structural Device in Early Greek Elegy." *Classical Philology* 100:317–336.

———. 2005b. "Catalogues, Priamels, and Stanzaic Structure in Early Greek
Elegy." *Transactions of the American Philological Association* 135:249–265.

Ferrari, F. 1989. *Teognide: Elegie*. Milan.

Figueira, T., and Nagy, G., eds. 1985. *Theognis of Megara: Poetry and the Polis*. Bal-
timore.

Fraenkel, H. 1927. Review of R. Oehler, *Mythologische Exempla in der älteren
griechischen Dichtung* (Aarau 1925). *Gnomon* 3:569–576.

Fraenkel, H. 1962. *Early Greek Poetry and Philosophy*. Oxford.

Gerber, D. E. 1991. "Early Greek Elegy and Iambus 1921–1989." *Lustrum* 33:7–
225.

———, ed. 1999. *Greek Elegiac Poetry from the Seventh to the Fifth Centuries BC*. Loeb
Classical Library. Cambridge MA.

Gonis, N., et al., eds. 2005. *The Oxyrhynchus Papyri 69*. London.

Gotteland, S. 2001. *Mythe et rhétorique: les exemples mythiques dans le discours politique de l'Athènes classique*. Paris.

Gronewald, M., and Daniel, R. W. 2004a. "Ein neuer Sappho-Papyrus." *Zeitschrift für Papyrologie und Epigraphik* 147:1–8.

———, 2004b. "Nachtrag zum neuen Sappho-Papyrus." *Zeitschrift für Papyrologie und Epigraphik* 149:1–4

Hardie, A. 2005. "Sappho, the Muses and Life after Death." *Zeitschrift für Papyrologie und Epigraphik* 154:13–32.

Henderson, W. H. 1983. "Theognis 702–712: The Sisyphus-exemplum." *Quaderni Urbinati di Cultura Classica* n.s. 15:83–90.

Heubeck, A. 1954. *Der Odyssee-Dichter und die Ilias*. Erlangen.

Holzberg, N. 2002. *The Ancient Fable: An Introduction*. Trans. C. Jackson-Holzberg. Bloomington IN.

Howie, J. G. 1977. "Sappho Fr. 16 (LP): Self-Consolation and Encomium." *Papers of the Liverpool Latin Seminar 1* (ed. F. Cairns) 207–235. Liverpool.

Hunter, R. 2007. "Sappho and Latin Poetry." In Bastianini and Casanova 2007:213–225.

Jacoby, F. 1957. *Die Fragmente der griechischen Historiker* ed. 2. vol. 1a. Leiden.

Jaeger, W. 1945. *Paideia* ed. 2. vol. 1. Trans. G. Highet. New York.

Janko, R. 2005. "Sappho Revisited." *Times Literary Supplement* December 23.

Jurenka, H. 1914. "Neue Lieder der Sappho und des Alkaios." *Wiener Studien* 36.201–243.

Maronitis, D. N. 2004. *Homeric Megathemes: War—Homilia—Homecoming*. Trans. D. Connolly. Lanham MD.

Martin, R. 1989. *The Language of Heroes: Speech and Performance in the "Iliad."* Ithaca.

Meyerhoff, D. 1984. *Traditioneller Stoff und individuelle Gestaltung: Untersuchungen zu Alkaios und Sappho*. Hildesheim.

Miller, A. M. 1986. *From Delos to Delphi: A Literary Study of the Homeric Hymn to Apollo*. Leiden.

Nagy, G. 1973. "Phaethon, Sappho's Phaon, and the White Rock of Leukas." *Harvard Studies in Classical Philology* 77:162–177.

Oehler, R. 1925. *Mythologische Exempla in der älteren griechischen Dichtung*. Aarau.

Page, D. L. 1955. *Sappho and Alcaeus: An Introduction to the Study of Ancient Lesbian Poetry*. Oxford. Corrected reprint 1959.

Pedrick, V. 1983. "The Paradeigmatic Nature of Nestor's Speech in *Iliad* 11." *Transactions of the American Philological Association* 113:55–68.

Race, W. H. 1982. "Aspects of Rhetoric and Form in Greek Hymns." *Greek, Roman, and Byzantine Studies* 23:5–14.

———. 1990. *Style and Rhetoric in Pindar's Odes*. American Classical Studies 24. Atlanta.

———. 1992. "How Greek Poems Begin." *Yale Classical Studies* 29:13–38.

Rawles, R. 2006. "Notes on the Interpretation of the 'New Sappho'." *Zeitschrift für Papyrologie und Epigraphik* 157:1–7.

Rösler, W. 1980. *Dichter und Gruppe: Eine Untersuchung zu den Bedingungen und zur historischen Funktion früher griechischer Lyrik am Beispiel Alkaios*. Munich.

Slater, W. J. 1996. Review of M. M. Willcock, *Pindar Victory Odes: Olympians 2, 7 and 11, Nemean 4, Isthmians 3, 4 and 7* (Cambridge 1995). *Bryn Mawr Classical Review* 96.02.03.

Taalman Kip, A. M. van Erp. 1987. "Alcaeus: 'Aias and Kassandra'." *Some Recently Found Greek Poems* (eds. J. M. Bremer, A. M. van Erp Taalman Kip, and S. R. Slings) 95–127. Mnemosyne Supplement 99. Leiden.

Tarditi, G. 1969. "L'asebeia di Aiace e quella di Pittaco." *Quaderni Urbinati di Cultura Classica* 8:86–89.

Thomas, R. 2000. *Herodotus in Context: Ethnography, Science, and the Art of Persuasion*. Cambridge.

Vetta, M. 1975. "Forma e immagini del teognideo (Theogn. 1283–94)." *Prometheus* 1:209–224.

———, ed. 1980. *Theognis: Elegiarum liber secundus*. Rome.

———. 1981. "Poesia e simposio (A proposito di un libro recente sui carmi di Alceo [= Rösler 1980])." *Rivista di Filologia e di Istruzione Classica* 109:483–495.

Weil, H. 1862. "Über Spuren strophischer Composition bei der griechischen Elegikern." *Rheinisches Museum* 17:1–13.

West, M. L. 1974. *Studies in Greek Elegy and Iambus*. Berlin.

Willcock, M. M. 1964. "Mythological *Paradeigma* in the *Iliad*." *Classical Quarterly* n.s. 14:141–154.

Zagagi, N. 1980. *Tradition and Originality in Plautus: Studies of the Amatory Motifs in Plautine Comedy*. Hypomnemata 62. Göttingen.

6
No Way Out?
Aging in the New (and Old) Sappho

Deborah Boedeker

I WILL NOT REHEARSE IN DETAIL the brief but exciting history of the "New Sappho" Cologne papyrus that was published in 2004 by Michael Gronewald and Robert Daniel, familiar as it is to readers of this volume.[1] Suffice it to say that *P.Köln* 21351 (with 21376), dated to the early third century BCE (Gronewald and Daniel 2004a:1), provides our earliest surviving text of Sappho, and to note that twelve of the 33 lines attested on this papyrus appear also in the much later *P.Oxy.* 1787, frr. 1–2. The latter was first published in 1922 (Grenfell and Hunt 1922:26–46, with Plate II) and is transmitted in modern editions as Sappho frr. 58–59 LP/V.[2] The Cologne and Oxyrhynchus texts of the repeated lines complement each other to the extent that it is now possible to read or restore them almost in their entirety; for convenience, I will call this composite 'Passage X'.

These twelve lines, considered by some experts to represent a complete poem, are preceded in the Cologne papyrus by eight very fragmentary but apparently Sapphic lines in the same meter (Passage A), without any indication of a break in the text. They are followed by thirteen lines (Passage B), separated from what precedes by a koronis, and apparently written in a different hand. On metrical and linguistic grounds, Passage B could scarcely have originated with Sappho, as was maintained already by the original editors (Gronewald and Daniel 2004a:1, 2005), and has been confirmed by other scholars as well (e.g. West 2005:1; Rawles 2006; Hammerstaedt in this volume). In the Oxyrhynchus

---

[1] I thank the panel organizers and volume editors for their intellectual enterprise and collegiality; and my fellow contributors, especially Dee Clayman, Lowell Edmunds, André Lardinois, and Dirk Obbink, for lively discussions about the new Sappho.
[2] In what follows, except as noted, all references to the text of Sappho will be from Voigt 1971, and the translations are my own.

papyrus, written about five centuries later (third century CE), Passage X is preceded by ten lines (Passage M) and followed by seven (Passage N) that are not attested in the Cologne papyrus—all of them in the same meter and Aeolic dialect. The following table schematically represents these segments of the two papyri.

P.Köln 21351 + 21376	P.Oxy. 1787, frr. 1–2 = Sappho frr. 58–59
Passage A (8 lines)	Passage M (= Sappho fr. 58.1–10)
Passage X (12 lines, attested in both Cologne and Oxyrhynchus papyri)	
[Koronis] Passage B (13 lines: not aeolic)	Passage N (= Sappho fr. 58.23–26 + fr. 59)

Sapphic *mouvance?*

As mentioned above, the Oxyrhynchus fragments are printed in modern editions as Sappho frr. 58 and 59. A 16-line segment of this text, fr. 58.11–26, has generated a great deal of critical attention as a complete poem that reveals the speaker's values, in which beauty, love, and refinement (*abrosuna*) trump the hardships of old age and perhaps even death itself.[3] All these interpretations depend on the relationship between X and the first four lines of N:

> X: I am aging, alas, as all humans must, even Tithonus.

> N: But I cherish *abrosuna* and, thanks to Eros, I have obtained the brilliance and beauty of the Sun (or: thanks to *eros* of the Sun, I have obtained brilliance and beauty).

Passage X taken by itself is a starker poem than XN,[4] one that perhaps better satisfies modern sensibilities. In Martin West's words, "The final phrase gives a

---

[3] E.g. Di Benedetto 1985; Nagy 1973; Lieberman 1995. Preisshofen 1971:59–60 alone, as far as I am aware, considers the beginning of fr. 58 (Passage M in my scheme) to be part of the same poem.

[4] For convenience I will occasionally refer to the 16-line text Sappho fr. 58.11–26, with its first twelve lines now expanded by the Cologne papyrus, as XN, even though this excludes the very

poignant edge to the whole... [Tithonus] lived on, growing ever more grey, frail, and decrepit, while ever beholding, and measuring himself against, the unfading beauty of his consort—even as Sappho grows old in the face of a cohort of protégées who, like undergraduates, are always young" (West 2005:6).

Whether Passage X is rightly considered a complete poem, however, has been questioned on several grounds. First, the original editors labeled its ending (ἀθάνατον ἄκοιτιν 'immortal wife') "*sehr abrupt;*" they assumed that for some reason the rest of the poem (by which they meant fr.58.23–26) was omitted in the Cologne papyrus (Gronewald and Daniel 2004a:2). Lowell Edmunds has put this suggestion to the test, arguing (against Bernsdorff 2005:2–4) that the reference to Tithonus attested at the end of X would be an unusual conclusion to an archaic poem that begins with an I-you deictic situation, as this one does with Sappho addressing the *paides*. Edmunds' survey of archaic poetry and fifth-century tragedy indicates that it would be much more usual for the poet to come back, in his words, "either to the starting point of the deictic framework (I-you) of the opening or to some reassertion of herself by Sappho," rather than to end, as does Passage X, with a distal mythological reference, in this case to Tithonus (Edmunds 2006:24; see also Edmunds, this volume). Fr. 58.23–26, which seems to return to the speaker's perspective (perhaps as contrasted with that of Tithonus), would provide an ending far more typical of archaic poetic structure than do the last lines of Passage X. André Lardinois (in this volume) further argues that ending a poem with the *abrosyna* passage would conclude the reflection on old age with a note of self-consolation that is found also in two other Sappho poems, frr. 16 and 31.[5]

Second, Mario Puelma and Francesca Angiò (2005; *contra*, Di Benedetto 2006:10) have proposed that a recently-published Hellenistic epigram appears to allude to the combined Sappho text XN (i.e. to both fr. 58.11–22 and fr. 58.23–26), noting that the final couplet of Posidippus 52 A-B mentions both "old age" (γῆρας[6]) and "the beautiful Sun" (κάλον ἠέλιον; cf. τὸ λάμπρον ἔρως ἀελίω καὶ τὸ κάλον λέλογχε, Sappho fr. 58.26):

ἀλλὰ σὺ γῆρας ἵκοῦ, κούρη· παρὰ σήματι τούτωι
σωρὸν ἐτέων μέτρει τὸν καλὸν ἠέλιον.

---

fragmentary final three lines of Passage N. (See West 2005:7–9 for a possible reconstruction of the 7-line Passage N, i.e. fr. 58.23–26 and fr. 59, which he calls "the ἀβροσύνα poem;" Di Benedetto 2006:5–11, on the other hand, insists that fr. 58.23–26 is a separate 4-line poem.)

[5] See Preisshofen 1977:59 for an earlier (pre-"New Sappho") brief mention of the consolatory theme in these texts.

[6] Now securely attested twice, in lines 3 and 12 of Passage X, cf. also ἀγήραον in line 8.

> But you, maiden, arrive at *old age*; alongside this tomb,
> for a mass of years, measure the *beautiful sun.*
>
> Posidippus 52.5–6 A-B (my translation)

Lardinois (this volume) not only finds this epigram's allusion to Sappho fr. 58 plausible, but astutely observes that in the immediately preceding epigram (Posidippus 51 A-B), a group of females is asked to sing "songs of Sappho"[7] at a young girl's grave, a reference that, he believes, strengthens the likelihood of another Posidippean nod to Sappho in 52 A-B.

All this discussion of the different endings of Passage X and fr. 58 is aimed, at least implicitly, at recovering what Sappho originally wrote. I will resist focusing primarily on that question in this paper, however, despite its appeal and significance. In light of the textual evidence at hand, and at this relatively early point in our reflections on the New Sappho, I will instead consider whether the Cologne and Oxyrhynchus papyri reflect two different performance versions of a song attributed to Sappho—attested both as X (or perhaps AX) in the Cologne papyrus and as XN (or even MXN, as Preisshofen proposed) in the Oxyrhynchus. In other words, I want to entertain the possibility that this well-crafted,[8] memorable set of six couplets[9] on old age could have been performed both by itself and as part of a longer song or songs.[10]

Recent scholarship has focused on a variety of partial analogs to this phenomenon, found in other poetic works both ancient and medieval. Textual variations in manuscripts of medieval poetry and prose are explained as reflecting variations in the oral performance of those works. "New philologists" consider such divergences, nicely termed *mouvance* (see e.g. Zumthor 1994), as intrinsic to some medieval poetic traditions, rather than trying to reconstruct an "original" text from which all others are derived.[11] Gregory Nagy, moreover, argues that the Homeric epics were performed by oral poets well into the Hellenistic period, and that they too consisted not of an original

---

[7] Accepting the editors' restoration Σα[πφῶι' ἄισμ]ατα at 51.6.

[8] On the balanced structure of Passage X see Janko 2005.

[9] Although the lines are isometric, they are divided into couplets by short horizontal marks to the left of the column in the papyrus.

[10] See also Boedeker, forthcoming. Nagy, this volume, also argues for a multiform song suited to different performance contexts. I am encouraged to see that Yatromanolakis 2007:360n341 (end of note) similarly suggests that this 12-line passage "might perhaps be a performative version of a longer song... a composition that included lines 23–26 of fragment 58V."

[11] For a lucid synopsis of some recent scholarship on *mouvance* in medieval manuscripts, on the relationship between oral performances and written texts, and on other focuses of the "new philology," see Baisch (n.d.). I am grateful to Regina Höschele for pointing me to this resource.

text with its variants, but rather of the multiforms one would expect for a song that is continually being recomposed in performance. Nagy attributes to this practice the textual variants that are attested in scholia, in later citations, and in papyrus fragments of the epics, and argues that "canonical" textual editions of the *Iliad* and the *Odyssey* were fixed only by Hellenistic scholars (Nagy 1996; *contra*, Powell 1997).

Independently from arguments about performance and textualization of Homeric epic, we know that works attributed to Sappho (and other archaic poets) were reperformed in various contexts.[12] In light of this performance tradition, a degree of *mouvance* is readily conceivable for her songs as well. What we see with Passage X in the Cologne and Oxyrhynchus papyri is not the same, however, as the kind of variation seen in the Homer citations. Rather than variant readings of words, or the inclusion or omission of a line or two, we have a twelve-line passage that is repeated almost verbatim, as far as we can see in the extant texts, in two different poetic contexts.[13] (This much is true even if Passage X is a complete poem in itself, since it is surrounded by different lines in the two papyri.)

Repeated passages exist also in the corpora of other archaic Greek poets, including Solon, Theognis, and Alcaeus.[14] For a very brief example, consider the Theognidean couplet:

Νεβρὸν ὑπὲξ ἐλάφοιο λέων ὣς ἀλκὶ πεποιθώς
ποσσὶ καταμάρψας αἵματος οὐκ ἔπιον·

---

[12] A charming anecdote attributed to Aelian, for example, tells of Solon, determined to learn a song of Sappho he had heard his nephew sing at a drinking party: Stobaeus *Florilegium* 3.29.58. (This anecdote, and the larger question of reperforming and recomposing archaic lyrics at symposia, is discussed at length by Yatromanolakis 2007:52–164 *passim*, esp. 85–88, and 341–34.) If the texts we have in the two papyri diverge because of local performance traditions such as this one, however, it is likely that the dialect would diverge as well. Hence we must assume that at some point both versions of Passage X were "corrected" for the Aeolic dialect. Interestingly, attention to such matters may have predated Ptolemaic patronage of scholarship. Isagoras (*Letter* 8.4) indicates that the exiled Agenor of Mytilene was working in fourth-century Athens on the *historia* of Lesbian poetry: see Nagy 2004:40 (citing Nagy 1996:192–193).

[13] The sections of Passage X that appear in both the Cologne and Oxyrhynchus papyri are virtually identical, except for the rendering of nasals before stops, e.g. τί κεν ποείην in *P.Oxy.* 1787, fr. 2.16, vs. τί κεμ ποείην in *P.Köln* 21351 fr. 2.15.

[14] As Benjamin Acosta-Hughes kindly reminds me, a different kind of textual "replication" may be found in the Callimachean *Coma Berenices*. The *Coma* probably circulated both in a shorter version (*Aetia* fr. 110), and as a longer independent poem, reflected in the famous translation of Catullus 66, where lines 15–38 and 79–88 do not correspond to anything in the (fragmentary) Greek lines. For an early proposal of this hypothesis see Pfeiffer 1928:339.

> Like a lion confident in its strength, with my claws I seized
> a fawn from under the hind, but did not drink its blood.

As a statement of action begun but not completed, these lines appear as Theognis 949–950, in a context that is possibly political and certainly gnomic; they appear again in an erotic context in 1278cd. However this is to be explained by the convoluted history of the Theognidean corpus,[15] the couplet evidently was (at some point) transmitted and read in two different textual contexts.

The Sapphic lines in question can also make sense in more than one configuration, as both their earlier and more recent (i.e. post-"New Sappho") admirers have taught us, but they make a *different* sense depending on whether X is considered as an independent poem, as it might be in the Cologne papyrus, or as part of a longer composition, as it has long been thought to be in the Oxyrhynchus papyrus.

The main purpose of this paper is to consider this dual possibility from the perspective of a single line, one of the most striking in the passage (and one which the Cologne papyrus greatly expanded for us):

ἀγήραον ἄνθρωπον ἔοντ' οὐ δύνατον γένεσθαι

for one who is human, it is impossible not to grow old

Passage X, line 8

I will first ask how that statement compares with other (at first sight quite different) *adunata* in the corpus of Sappho, and second, how it contributes to a reading of each of the arguably complete poems, X and XN.

Sapphic *adunata*

In Sappho fr. 17, the sons of Atreus "could not" (οὐκ ἐδύναντο, line 8) do something—almost certainly, as Denys Page has argued (1955:58–62), could not sail home from their stopover on Lesbos after the Trojan War (cf. *Odyssey* 3.130ff.)—not until they called on the Lesbian triad Hera, Zeus, and Dionysos. The impossible became possible for them, thanks to successful invocation (cf. κάλεσσαι, Lobel and Page's supplement in line 9) of local gods. This happy ending could be seen as a very benign reprisal of the appeasement of Artemis at Aulis before the Trojan War: in this instance prayer, not human sacrifice, suffices to permit the sailing.

---

[15] See Bowie 1997.

In view of Edmunds' findings with regard to a poem's return to the original deictic situation, it is significant that the story of the Atreids' *adunaton* and prayer is framed by an invocation of Hera in the here and now of the speaker, presumably Sappho. The speaker begins by asking the goddess to appear to her (according to Milne's convincing restoration of line 1), and ends, in good hymnic format, with a request that Hera now come to aid her, "according to the ancient precedent" (κὰτ τὸ πάλ[αιον· fr. 17.12). Despite gaps in the text, the implication is clear that the speaker too faces some difficult situation, and seeks the goddess's help.

Fr. 17 thus resembles in its structure Sappho fr. 1, where Aphrodite is asked to release the character Sappho, once again, from the torments of unrequited love, just as she has done repeatedly in the past. That brilliant, ironically self-deprecating poem raises implicitly the theme of *adunata*, for a god is called upon and asked to bring about something that otherwise the speaker could not achieve, even though it is, she says, what "I most want to happen" (μάλιστα θέλω γένεσθαι, fr.1.17, cf. οὐ δύνατον γένεσθαι, Passage X, line 8). In fr. 1, just as in fr. 17, past invocations were *successful*: "If she runs away, she will soon pursue," the poem's Aphrodite said to its Sappho on an earlier occasion, "and if she does not love, soon she shall love even against her will" (fr. 1.21–24, Campbell trans.). The audience of fr. 1 is led to think that the speaker's prayer will once again be effective.

The other example of a Sapphic *adunaton*, fr. 16.21–22, comes from another one of Sappho's longest and most famous extant texts. The poem begins with the well-known priamel of favorite sights, leading up to the first-person generalization "but I say, the most beautiful thing is whatever one loves" (fr. 16.1–4). This opinion is illustrated by the example of Helen, who left husband and child to sail to Troy (16.5–12)—which reminds the speaker of the lovely but absent Anaktoria (fr. 16.15–20). After this, the text thins out and the meaning becomes less clear, but the phrase οὐ δύνατον γένεσθαι ("not possible to happen": 16.21) is followed after a short gap by ἀνθρωπ[. . . π]εδέχην δ' ἄρασθαι ("human being... pray to share...": 16.22). Here too, a human impossibility is juxtaposed with, and perhaps overcome by, prayer.

Passage X, like frr. 1, 16, and 17, also presents a situation affecting the speaker. Here, she claims that the physical effects of old age have given her a heavy *thymos* (Passage X, line 5).[16] After saying that she often laments those symptoms, she asks rhetorically, "But what might I do?" (Passage X, line 7),

---

[16] See Lidov, "Acceptance or Assertion?", this volume, for a different interpretation of this phrase.

and in the following line declares that no human being is able to avoid old age (ἀγήραον... οὐ δύνατον γένεσθαι). As proof of this statement, the speaker offers Tithonus, who was not saved from old age even by the love of the goddess Dawn.

This conclusion, however, is counter to the pattern that seems to prevail in the other fragments of Sappho that mention or allude to *adunata*, in which the impossible is remedied (or at least remediable) by a god's response to prayer. Is it possible that a remedy for this *adunaton* lurks even in Passage X? Richard Janko has suggested that Tithonos' everlasting old age might be mitigated somehow by his immortal song (Janko 2005). A partial reprieve of the mythical *comparandus* might in turn suggest that the speaker-poet too would not simply grow old and die. But this reading assumes that the audience would draw on a particular extra-Sapphic variant of the story, which is attested only later, in which Tithonus becomes a cicada whose sound (unlike all the rest of him) does not fade away.[17] On balance, it seems to me more likely that Tithonus is here meant to serve as the extreme case, proving that no human can escape old age. Enamored Dawn made her Trojan prince immortal, and remains his immortal wife, but *gêras* seized him even so.

In another way too, the *adunaton* in Passage X is different from that in Sappho fr. 17 (and perhaps fr. 16 as well). It refers not to something "impossible" in present circumstances (such as the Atreids' inability to sail from Lesbos), but to a general, permanent limitation of human nature: old age, the example of Tithonus shows, is more inescapable than death itself. In a twist from the version of this myth attested in the *Homeric Hymn to Aphrodite* (223–224), here no blame is imputed to Dawn for "forgetting" to ask Zeus for Tithonus' agelessness as well as immortality; Passage X implies that there was nothing anyone could do about it.

A similar, general limitation on human nature may be attested in another Sappho fragment, if any one of several plausible supplements in line 12 is correct:[18]

>]όδος μ[έ]γαν εἰς Ὄλ[υμπον
> ἀ]νθρω[π]αίκ.[
>
> [There is no] road to great Olympus
> for mortals...
>
> Sappho fr. 27.12–13 (trans. Campbell)

---

[17] For discussion of the variant, see Janko 2005.
[18] For suggested supplements, see Voigt 1971:54.

To the sentiment of this restored reading we can compare Pindar *Pythian* 10.27–30:

> ὁ χάλκεος οὐρανὸς οὔ ποτ' ἀμβατὸς αὐτῷ·
> ὅσαις δὲ βροτὸν ἔθνος ἀγλαΐαις ἁ-
>   πτόμεσθα, περαίνει πρὸς ἔσχατον
> πλόον· ναυσὶ δ' οὔτε πεζὸς ἰὼν <κεν> εὕροις
> ἐς Ὑπερβορέων ἀγῶνα θαυμαστὰν ὁδόν.

> He cannot mount the bronze sky,
> but of all the glories that our mortal race attains,
> he sails to the utmost point;
> whether you go in ships or on foot, you would not discover
> the wondrous road to the contest-ground of the
>   Hyperboreans.
>   Pindar *Pythian* 10.27–30 (my translation)

The victor's father, happy though he is, cannot reach the fabled Hyperboreans—but immediately (lines 31–45) we learn that once upon a time Perseus did get there, being led by Athena (ἀγεῖτο δ' Ἀθάνα, *Pythian* 10.45). Again, what is "impossible" for mortals is attained with help from a god.

These *adunata,* moreover, are qualitatively different from the examples of hybris, such as "let no one of mortals fly to Olympus or try to marry the Cyprian queen Aphrodite...", attested in a parthenion of Alcman (fr. 1.16–20 Page). Unlike the impious actions in the Alcman fragment, the *adunata* in the Sappho (and Pindar) examples just cited are not presented as wicked, but simply as unachievable by mortals—at least without divine assistance.

Adunata in the New Sappho

This theme relates in divergent ways to the *adunaton* of the New Sappho, depending on whether we consider Passage X by itself or together with Passage N (fr. 58.23–26). Taken by itself, Passage X teaches that aging is baneful but cannot be avoided. These twelve lines would make a poignant sympotic song on grim old age, a topic attested in a number of archaic lyrics and elegies, including Mimnermus frr. 1, 2, and 4 W, Anacreon fr. 395 P, and Alcaeus fr. 50 V.[19] Such poems as these, whatever their archaic origins, could well have been among the poetic "classics," as Nagy has called them, learned by elite fifth- and

---

[19] On old age in archaic and classical Greek poetry, including Sappho fr. 58, see Preisshofen 1977, Di Benedetto 1985, and especially Falkner 1995, with bibliography. Brandt 2002 offers a broad

fourth-century Athenian youths, presumably for performance in symposia, as attested in Aristophanes and Plato (Nagy 2004:41). Such a performance tradition, in Athens and elsewhere, could explain how Passage X (or possibly even AX[20]) eventually made its way to the Cologne papyrus, in a poetic context different from that of the Alexandrian edition of Sappho's collected works, which is generally accepted as the basis of the Oxyrhynchus version.[21]

What then of the *adunaton* in the Oxyrhynchus Sappho? If we read fr. 58.11–26 (XN) as a continuous passage, it appears that the speaker presents a positive way to deal with the inevitability of aging: she expresses satisfaction with the fine things (*abrosuna*, beauty, brilliance) that Eros or Helios have allotted her. Although she cannot escape old age, the gifts of a god provide compensation. This reading is more in tune with other extant *adunata* in Sappho, in which a god helps with what was humanly impossible.

Perhaps the nearest parallel to this response to old age is found in a passage of the "New Simonides:"

> νήπιοι, οἷς ταύτηι κεῖται νόος, οὐτὲ ἴσασιν
> ὡς χρόνος ἔστ' ἥβης καὶ βιότοι' ὀλίγος
> θνητοῖς. ἀλλὰ σὺ ταῦτα μαθὼν βιότου ποτὶ τέρμα
> ψυχῆι τῶν ἀγαθῶν τλῆθι χαριζόμενος.

> Fools are they whose thoughts are thus! Nor do they know
>   that the time of youth and life is short
> for mortals. But you, learning this at the end of your life,
>   endure, delighting in good things in your soul.
>   Simonides, fr. el. 20.9–12 (ed. and trans. Sider)

These two couplets, advising the addressee to enjoy good things while he can, in the face of inevitable human decline—call to mind the "recompense" pro-

---

study of old age in antiquity. Kirk 1971, surprisingly, ignores Sappho fr. 58. On aging in the New Sappho, see especially Bernsdorff 2005.

[20] It is even possible that Passage A, which features material similar to that attested in Passage X (on which see Hardie 2005, though Hardie considers A and X as separate poems), was transmitted as part of the same song as X. There is no paleographical reason to separate A from X, and the one factor that argues most strongly against that, which is the singular Muse addressed at the very end of A followed by plural Muses restored at the beginning of X, may be misleading, for it is possible to read κάλα, Μοῖσ' in the last line of A, as καλάμοισ' 'reeds' or, as West does (2005:3), as θαλάμοισ' 'chambers'.

[21] Hooker 1976:11, relying on Hephaestion *On Signs* 138, is convinced that there was more than one Alexandrian recension of Sappho (so too Williamson 1995:40). Yatromanolakis 1999:179–180 considers the matter uncertain.

vided by *abrosyna* in XN. Nonetheless, like other archaic fragments on old age, this passage too diverges from the New Sappho, which alone, in the face of an *adunaton*, provides the unflinching acceptance of Passage X *and/or* the god-blessed alleviation of XN.

Whether we read X or XN makes a great difference in how the speaker ultimately faces the inevitability of growing old. As both readings appear to be paleographically and poetically defensible, I have proposed here that the two different contexts in which Passage X appears may come from two different performance traditions. It is conceivable, for example, that X by itself would be deemed suitable for a short sympotic performance on the rather popular topic of old age, whereas XN would be more appropriate for an occasion in which the focus is on divine benevolence.

Indeed, other scholars have found in the text of the New Sappho several themes that might point to such an occasion. Alex Hardie recently emphasized the importance of the Muses in Passages A and X, and elsewhere in Sappho too; he finds that a number of fragments allude to a cult (even "Mysteries") of the Muses by Sappho and other devotees (Hardie 2005). For his part, Lardinois in this volume suggests that XN may have been composed for choral performance at a wedding; this is corroborated by the central importance that Richard Rawles (2006) attributes to the topic of marriage for the girls (*paides*) who are addressed in the New Sappho. It is not difficult to imagine XN performed at an occasion in which the blessings of a god or gods are sought as a remedy or compensation for the eventual hardships of old age, even if a human being cannot bypass those tribulations.

The coexistence of Cologne and Oxyrhynchus Sapphos, in sum, may well give us a glimpse of a more fluid transmission of archaic poetic songs than our texts normally lead us to assume, with different versions suitable for different occasions and audiences.

Bibliography

Baisch, M. n.d. "Altgermanistische Editionswissenschaft." Kompendium der Editionswissenschaften. http://www.edkomp.uni-muenchen.de/CD1/A1/Altgerm-A1-MB.html.

Bernsdorff, H. 2004. "Schwermut des Alters im neuen Köln Sappho-Papyrus." *Zeitschrift für Papyrologie und Epigraphik* 150:27–35.

———. 2005. "Offene Gedichtschlüsse." *Zeitschrift für Papyrologie und Epigraphik* 153:1–6.

Boedeker, D. Forthcoming. "Sappho Old and New (P.Köln 21351 and 21376, and *P.Oxy.* 1787): An Overview of Texts and Contexts." *Symposium Lesbium: Poetry, Wisdom and Politics in Archaic Lesbos: Alcaeus, Sappho, Pittacus* (ed. A. Pierris) Oxford. Based on a paper presented August 8, 2005.

Bowie, E. 1997. "The Theognidea: A Step Towards a Collection of Fragments?" *Collecting Fragments/Fragmente sammeln* (ed. G. W. Most) 53–66. Göttingen.

Brandt, H. 2003. *Wird auch silbern mein Haar: eine Geschichte des Alters in der Antike.* Becks archäologische Bibliothek. Munich.

Di Benedetto, V. 1985. "Il tema della vecchiaia e il fr. 58 di Saffo." *Quaderni Urbinati di Cultura Classica* n.s. 19:145–163.

———. 2005. "La nuova Saffo e dintorni." *Zeitschrift für Papyrologie und Epigraphik* 153:7–20.

———. 2006. "Il tetrastico di Saffo e tre postille." *Zeitschrift für Papyrologie und Epigraphik* 155:5–18.

Edmunds, L. 2006. "The New Sappho: ἔφαντο (9)." *Zeitschrift für Papyrologie und Epigraphik* 156:23–26.

Falkner, T. M. 1995. *The Poetics of Old Age in Greek Epic, Lyric and Tragedy.* Oklahoma.

Gallavotti, C. 1947. *Saffo e Alceo.* Collana di studi greci 10. Naples.

Greene, E., ed. 1996. *Reading Sappho: Contemporary Approaches.* Berkeley.

Grenfell, B. T., and Hunt, A. S., eds. 1922. *The Oxyrhynchus Papyri 15.* London.

Gronewald, M., and Daniel, R. W. 2004a. "Ein neuer Sappho-Papyrus." *Zeitschrift für Papyrologie und Epigraphik* 147:1–8.

———. 2004b. "Nachtrag zum neuen Sappho-Papyrus." *Zeitschrift für Papyrologie und Epigraphik* 149:1–4.

———. 2005. "Lyrischer Text (Sappho-Papyrus)." *Zeitschrift für Papyrologie und Epigraphik* 154:7–12.

Hardie, A. 2005. "Sappho, the Muses and Life after Death." *Zeitschrift für Papyrologie und Epigraphik* 154:13–32.

Hooker, J. T. 1977. *The Language and Text of the Lesbian Poets.* Innsbruck.

Janko, R. 2005. "Sappho Revisited." *Times Literary Supplement* December 23.

Kirk, G. S. 1971. "Old Age and Maturity in Ancient Greece." *Eranos Jahrbuch* 40:123–158.

Liberman, G. 1995. "A propos du Fragment 58 Lobel-Page, Voigt de Sappho." *Zeitschrift für Papyrologie und Epigraphik* 108:45–46.

Lobel, E., ed. 1925. ΣΑΠΦΟΥΣ ΜΕΛΗ: *The Fragments of the Lyrical Poems of Sappho.* Oxford.

Marzullo, B. 1994. "Sapph. fr.58, 25s V." *Philologus* 138.2:189–193.

Nagy, G. 1973. "Phaethon, Sappho's Phaon, and the White Rock of Leukas." *Harvard Studies in Classical Philology* 77:162–177. Revised as: "Phaethon, Sappho's Phaon, and the White Rock of Leukas: 'Reading' the Symbols of Greek Lyric." In Greene 1996:35–57.

———. 1996. *Poetry as Performance: Homer and Beyond.* Cambridge MA.

———. 2004. "Transmission of Archaic Greek Sympotic Songs: From Lesbos to Alexandria." *Critical Inquiry* 31:26–48.

Page, D. L. 1955. *Sappho and Alcaeus: An Introduction to the Study of Ancient Lesbian Poetry.* Oxford. Corrected reprint 1959.

Pfeiffer, R. 1928. "Ein neues Altersgedicht des Kallimachos." *Hermes* 63:302–341.

Powell, B. 1997. Review of Nagy 1996, in *Bryn Mawr Classical Review* 97.3.21.

Preisshofen, F. 1977. *Untersuchungen zur Darstellung des Greisenalters in der frühgriechischen Dichtung.* Hermes Einzelschriften 34. Wiesbaden.

Puelma, M., and Angiò. F. 2005. "Sappho und Poseidippos: Nachtrag zum Sonnenuhr-Epigramm 52 A.-B. des Mailänder Papyrus." *Zeitschrift für Papyrologie und Epigraphik* 152:13–15.

Rawles, R. 2006. "Notes on the Interpretation of the 'New Sappho'." *Zeitschrift für Papyrologie und Epigraphik* 157:1–7.

West, M. L. 1982. *Greek Metre.* Oxford.

———. 2005. "The New Sappho." *Zeitschrift für Papyrologie und Epigraphik* 151:1–9.

Williamson, M. 1995. *Sappho's Immortal Daughters.* Cambridge MA.

Yatromanolakis, D. 1999. "Alexandrian Sappho Revisited." *Harvard Studies in Classical Philology* 99:179–195.

———. 2007. *Sappho in the Making: The Early Reception.* Hellenic Studies 28. Washington DC.

Zumthor, P. 1994. *Die Stimme und die Poesie in der mitteralterlichen Gesellschaft.* Munich.

7

Acceptance or Assertion?
Sappho's New Poem in its Books

Joel Lidov

That time of year thou mayst in me behold,
When yellow leaves, or none, or few do hang
Upon those boughs which shake against the cold,
Bare ruined choirs, where late the sweet birds sang.

SHAKESPEARE'S IMAGE OF THE ABSENCE OF SONG neatly sums up the familiar notion that the essential misery of old age is its distance from the worlds of youthful gaiety. Over twenty years ago, Vincenzo Di Benedetto argued for the literal presence of this motif in Sappho. He posited a pointed contrast between youth and old age in fr. 58V and fr. 21V (both known only from Oxyrhynchus papyri), and inferred in the mention of the Muses' gifts in fr. 58.11 the presence of the theme which denied song to the aged poet, although he cited only one poem, by Horace—Odes 3.15, to an aging *meretrix*—as a parallel for the actual mention of song in this context (the denial of the pleasures of love, of course, is easily paralleled).[1] Di Benedetto reaffirmed his reading shortly after the publication of the Cologne papyrus (*P.Köln* inv. 21351+21356) in which 58.11 is the first of the twelve overlapping lines of the two papyri we call the New Poem. For lines 1 and 2 of the New Poem, where the original editors had suggested supplements that made Sappho represent herself as a musical performer, he proposed instead imperative verbs (1. γεραίρετε...2. χορεύσατε) attributing all the musical activity to the *paides* (Di Benedetto 2004:5–6; Gronewald and Daniel 2004a:7). Di Benedetto's understanding became the basis for M. L. West's commentary on the New Poem:

> The two couplets *clearly* contained an opposition between
> the happy young girls, with *their music and song*, and Sappho

---

[1] 1985:147; he cites F. Stiebitz, "Zu Sappho 65 Diehl," PW 45/46 (1926), cols. 1259–1262.

herself, who is growing old and no longer able to join in *the dancing* ... [my emphases]

...Sappho grows old in the face of a cohort of protégées who, like undergraduates, are always young (2005b:4,6).

And West's supplements for the opening lines modified only the details of Di Benedetto's in order to underscore the opposition they both inferred.

ὔμμες πεδὰ Μοίσαν ἰ]οκ[ό]λπων κάλα δῶρα, παῖδες,
σπουδάσδετε καὶ τὰ]ν φιλάοιδον λιγύραν χελύνναν·

(Cf. Gronewald and Daniel: 1. φέρω...2. λάβοισα). This has now become the common version of the New Poem, taken as the starting point for further articles in ZPE and disseminated in a variety of translations.

I recall this (recent) history to emphasize that the interpretation depends entirely on the supplements. With the second person verbs, Sappho begins by distancing herself from the activity of her companions, and then resigns herself to the human condition (Di Benedetto), and finds consolation for it (West), by reflecting on the fate of Tithonus as a mythological paradigm for the necessity of aging. But the Cologne papyrus does not actually offer any evidence that confirms this interpretation, because, despite all the gains, nothing in the material outside the brackets gives any indication of the verb structure in the first two lines. Certainly, we learn in the poem that the speaker has aged and does not dance (and Alcman 26 PMG, the oft-cited parallel, also says no more than that); but it remains possible that the speaker is emphasizing not the distinction between herself and her addressees, but between singing (which she does) and dancing (which she cannot do).[2] I regard this, in fact, as more probable.

---

[2] Rawles 2006b and Geissler 2005 have explored the possibility of continued singing, but within the limits of West's supplements and the emphasis he introduces on the contrast between Sappho and the *paides*; they depend on finding an allusive relationship to the *Hymn to Aphrodite* to argue that Sappho's continued ability to sing at least mitigates her sense of loss as she compares her diminished abilities to theirs (Geissler stresses the similarity of the *paides* and the Muses). These articles were not available to me when I first developed the thesis of this paper for an oral presentation, but their agreement on the prominence of singing reinforces my conviction that the question of the supplements needs to be reopened. Another recent commentator, Ferrari 2007:179–185 also recognizes that the Singer is still singing and, in contrast to the *paides*, no longer dancing. He retains the focus on the misery of old age, considering the poem a "pathography" (like fr. 31V), in which she accepts its necessity and finds consolation in the implied performance situation: "dalla gioia di poter ancora guidare con la musica e il canto un cora di ragazze adolescenti... (2007:185).

The unusual circumstance of the discovery of the same text in a second papyrus offers the opportunity for a new appraisal of what we should look for when we begin the combined tasks of interpreting and supplementing. For the Cologne papyrus offers not only more words, but a new and different context. Papyrus books themselves constitute ancient contexts. Ancient sources attribute different meters to different books of Sappho, and some papyri that apparently derive from continuous texts present groups of fragments that can conform to a single meter or type. So it is reasonably certain that there was a metrical basis for the arrangement of poems into books in a standard ancient edition.[3] In both sources, the New Poem is preceded by lines in the same meter, but they are not the same lines, so the two papyri are not fragments of copies reproducing the same edition. In this case, therefore, we have the opportunity to take into account the characters of two different contexts. Taken together, they will show that it is more likely that the aging speaker is not expressing resignation or searching for consolation in the common fate of mankind, but rather confidently asserting that her continued devotion to singing assures her of a kind of immortality.

I will begin with the context in the new find. The status of the three poems on the Cologne papyrus has been thoroughly discussed by the original editors and others, especially Alex Hardie (2005) and John Lundon (2007a) (although their discussions proceed from the assumptions of the Di Benedetto / West reading of the New Poem). Despite much that must remain in doubt (for example, whether the poems are complete, or the temporal relation of this papyrus to the Alexandrian edition), for my purposes some points can be reasonably assumed. If the Cologne papyrus represents an alternate metrical edition—even though we have no other reason to think that there was more than one—it would be the end of its book, since the scribe of the New Poem left the remainder of its column blank; it is odd, therefore, although not decisive, that there is no subscription. But it is more likely that this papyrus represents some kind of anthology or partial compilation; the poems of Sappho were popular and would have circulated outside whatever complete edition was available when it was written. What is crucial for establishing the context is the third poem, an anonymous lyric written in the space after the New Poem, in a second, nearly contemporaneous hand. It is not Lesbian; its affinities, which are fully explored by Dee Clayman in this volume, seem to be Hellenistic. However, the association of the three poems does not appear to be unmotivated (which would be possible, as Lundon notes, if it

---

[3] There is a full discussion in Page [1955] 1959:112–116; the most important testimonia are 1, 2, 28–32 Campbell (1982 [1990]). See also Lobel 1925:xii–xv.

were, say, a symposiast's handbook); for the third poem not only shows imitations of Sappho, it shares certain subject matter with the two preceding it. At the least, all three contain references to music and hints of a concern with the underworld or some kind of life beyond the normal limit of death:

P.Köln 1–8: .νέρθε δὲ γᾶς ... ἔχοισαγ γέρας ... ὡς νῦν ἐπὶ γᾶς
...— λιγύραν, —...ἔλοισα πᾶκτιν...ἀείδω;

New Poem: [Μοίσαν]...δῶρα, —... φιλάοιδον λιγύραν χελύνναν
... —myth of Tithonus ἔχοντ' ἀθανάταν ἄκοιτιν

anon. lyric: Hermes? — ...ἄπνους ?... —Orpheus...— [εὖ]
φθογγος λύραν[4]

What the third poem provides, therefore, is a reading of the poems that precede it. Whatever the purpose or origin of the collection (and even if it was part of an edition), to the person who added the third poem, the essential point about old age in the New Poem would have been its connection with the theme of death. This too, of course, is a familiar complaint about old age; indeed, it is easier to find parallels to the connection of age and death than to the separation of age and music.[5] Mimnermus (2.57W) pairs death and old age as the burden of the "black fates" that stand beside us:

...   Κῆρες δὲ παρεστήκασι μέλαιναι,
         ἡ μὲν ἔχουσα τέλος γήραος ἀργαλέου,
         ἡ δ' ἑτέρη θανάτοιο· ...

and Anacreon (50/395.1–2, 7–8 PMG) describes his aging self in terms quite similar to Sappho, and bewails his condition as a sign of impending death:

---

[4] Rawles has suggested (2006a) that the initial line refers to Hermes (rather than Eros, as Clayman and some others take it) but argues for the Hermes of the Homeric Hymn, inventor of the lyre ("breathless" in contrast to the flute), not Hermes *psychopompos*, the escort of the "breathless" to the underworld, as seems to me more likely. Although the evidence allows only speculation on who is meant here, the mention of Orpheus in a Hellenistic poem would imply by itself all the motifs involved.

[5] The evaluation of old age in the poets is studied in detail by Preisshoffen 1977 (see also Brandt 2003:29–38). Both the contrast with youth and the connection with death are typical, and they are not mutually exclusive, although only Mimnermus finds old age worse than death. Old age is commonly associated with the fact of mortality, as one of the markers of the boundary between men and gods.

πολιοὶ μὲν ἡμὶν ἤδη
κρόταφοι κάρη τε λευκόν ...
διὰ ταῦτ' ἀνασταλύζω
θαμὰ Τάρταρον δεδοικώς·

More important for us, however, is that in the first poem (with its mention of being under the earth, having honor, and singing) and in the third (with its mention of Orpheus), music is not only something not lost in old age but even represents a claim on a kind of immortality.[6] So even if the anthologist is quoting only so much as fits his purposes, it seems unlikely that the initial lines of the New Poem represented the poet's resignation from the musical world, in contrast to the *paides*. It is the benefits of music in the face of mortality that seems to have piqued the original compiler's interest.

The Oxyrhynchus papyrus tells a different kind of story. This copy does appears to come from a standard edition of Sappho organized by meter; fragment 58 is one of over 25 items in Voigt's edition (frr. 58–87) that are apparently from the same roll and can be interpreted as in the same meter. But because some partial correlation of meter and content can be observed throughout the corpus of Sappho's poetry, the metrical arrangement may also offer some contextual guidance.

I should stress that I am not arguing that specific meters have specific values or that there are necessary restrictions on what can be said in any meter. But, despite how little actually survives, I do think we can observe some clusters that indicate that for certain kinds of songs or certain types of occasion or performance situations, some meters were typical or at least preferred to others. Conversely, there may have been themes or occasions for which some meters were inappropriate. There are, for example, numerous prayers for divine presence or assistance in the sapphic stanza; of the 19 fragments by Sappho in Voigt that are substantial enough to comment on, seven are prayers and three more may be prayers or contain reports of prayers. Among the 135 items in other meters, only one looks similar (fr. 86). Alcaeus's sapphics have the same tendency: 5 out of 8 are prayers. On the other hand, there appear to be no overt references to the Graces or Muses in the sapphic stanza, no references to the afterlife, and apparently no poems which are self-reflectively

---

[6] Hardie 2005 locates in the poems of the Cologne papyrus and elsewhere in Sappho (especially in 55, to be discussed below, and 147) evidence for the possibility of an actual cult of the Muses, which promised special treatment after death. His treatment of the New Poem is based on West's, but even so, he stresses that its emphasis is on mortality.

concerned with the art of singing.[7] The remnants of the second book were in glyconics with double dactylic expansions (the meter that used to be called aeolic dactyls). Two major examples survive, the description of Andromache's bridal procession and a Hymn to Artemis that is possibly by Sappho; both of these are characterized by extended narrative and a style and content we connect with the Homeric tradition. Looking ahead, in Book 5, which seemed to exhibit more metrical variety, we see that the stanzas in some poems are similar to each other in that they incorporate thrice-repeated glyconics. In the two partially readable fragments of poems of this type, 94 and 96, a woman is being reminded of the joy that remembered pleasures can bring; what remains of a third, fr. 95, contains a motif that also occurs in fr. 94 (but nowhere else), someone who wishes she were dead, and that poem also seems to feature a narrative of the past.

The New Poem, as well as the preceding poem in the Cologne papyrus, would have come from Book 4, which, as best as can be deduced, contained poems written in distichs and perhaps tristichs (see Voigt *ad* fr. 88). It appears that the individual items were short; two consecutive fragments (numbers 62 and 63) have the left margin preserved, and three instances of a coronis mark them off as 12 and 10 lines long, respectively; at 12 lines the New Poem would fit this pattern. The basic meter of both Books 3 and 4 was an aeolic meter with choriambic expansion, rather than the dactylic expansion of Book 2. The meter of the poems in Book 4 was a headless hipponactean with a double-expansion:

$$^\wedge\text{hipp}^{2c} = \quad \times \; - \; \cup \; \cup \; - \; - \; \cup \; \cup \; - \; - \; \cup \; \cup \; - \; \cup \; - \; -$$

It closely resembles the meter of Book 3, which contained only distichs, couplets composed of two identical glyconics with double expansion.

$$\text{gly}^{2c} = \quad - \; \times \; - \; \cup \; \cup \; - \; - \; \cup \; \cup \; - \; - \; \cup \; \cup \; - \; \cup \; -$$

These two meters are related to each other by *epiplokê*; that is, a continuous series of each of them would be the same sequence of longs and shorts—they differ only by being offset by one syllable at the beginning and end. Not much survives of Book 3, but given the metrical similarity and because what does survive seems to be of a piece with the content of Book 4, I will treat the distichs in both books together.

Throughout these fragments we find references to music and to the afterlife, and indications of direct address. We can also pick up an assertive or argu-

---

[7] Fr. 32—αἴ με τιμίαν ἐπόησαν ἔργα / τὰ σφὰ δοῖσαι—could be a possible exception.

mentative tone: people are compared, and there are expressions of strong dis-
approval. The typical features of these fragments are most fully represented in
a poem from Book 3 which we know from several quotations, fr. 55 :

κατθάνοισα δὲ κείσῃ οὐδέ ποτα μναμοσύνα σέθεν
ἔσσετ' οὐδὲ †ποκ'†ὕστερον· οὐ γὰρ πεδέχῃς βρόδων
τῶν ἐκ Πιερίας· ἀλλ' ἀφάνης κἀν Ἀίδα δόμῳ
φοιτάσῃς πεδ' ἀμαύρων νεκύων ἐκπεποταμένα.

But when you die you will lie there and no memory of you
will linger in later time, for you have no share in the roses
that come from Pieria. Unnoticed in Hades' house as well,
you will range among the shadowy dead, flown from our midst."

(tr. A. Miller 1996:58)

The poem is strongly opinionated, in fact censorious, uses direct address and
implies a dialogue context; it refers to poetry and the Muses, and these are
involved in the judgment it passes; and it refers to life after death. Many of the
other fragments are too scrappy to say much about, but I indicate some of the
significant words in the accompanying chart (which excludes fr. 58) We find an
invocation of the Graces in fr. 52, and the correct way to approach them is the
subject of fr. 81; in fr. 56 a *parthenos* is praised for her exceptional *sophia*, which
I would take to mean musical skill. In the half-dozen readable words of fr. 70
we find mention of a chorus, and perhaps harmony. For the dialogic or disputa-
tious element, we see that fr. 71 addresses Mica and condemns her for choosing
the friendship of the house of Penthilus, then says something about singing.
Music is not always involved. Someone is censured for rustic dress in fr. 57. In
fr. 60 we find something about "fighting with me" and "you know well." In fr.
65, Sappho is in the vocative, we see "you," and fame and the underworld are
mentioned. Fr. 62 presents itself as a response to other speakers. Fr. 68 contains
a number of moral judgments: we find "sinful" "does not restrain *koros*", some-
one is described as no longer without guile; "sinful" in fr. 69 and "shameful" or
"ugly" in fr. 64 are among their very few readable words.

Fragments of Sappho, Books 3 and 4 (not including fr. 58)

Frag.	length	censure / comparison	direct address/ dialogue	music or afterlife
53	6 wds			Χάριτες
54	1 line			
55	4 lines	οὐδέ μναμοσύνα σέθεν, ἀφάνης.. φοιτάσης	2nd pers.	βρόδων τῶν ἐκ Πίεριας κἀν Ἀίδα δόμῳ
56	2 lines	οὐδ' ... ἔσσεσθαι ... πάρθενον τεαύταν		σοφίαν
57	=2 lines	ἀγρωΐωτις .... οὐκ ἐπισταμένα		
60	c. 18 wds		ἔμοι μάχεσθαι, σὺ...	
62	c. 20 wds		μύγις...εἰσάιον, ἔφθατε	
63	c. 30 wds		(prayer?)	?μὴ πεδεχην...μηδὲν μακάρων
64	5 wds?	?αἴσχρ[		
65	c. 15 wds		Ψάπφοι σε ?	πάντα κλέος, σ' εννʼ Ἀχερ[οντ...
67	c. 12 wds		2nd pers.	
68	c. 20 wds	αλίτρα, κόρον οὐ κατισχε.[, ἄδολον [μ]ηκέτι		
69	c. 2 wds	ἀλίτρα		
70	c. 8 wds			]αρμονίας (aut n. pr.) χόρον, ... λίγηα.[
71	c. 15 wds	κα[κό]τροπ' ... μέλ[ος] τι γλύκερον	σ' ἔγωὐκ ἐάσω	μέλος ... μελλιχόφων[λίγυραι
72–80	c. 20 wds total			
81	4 lines	ἀστεφανώτοισι δ' ἀπυστρέφονται	2nd pers. imper.	Χαριτες
82	1 line	εὐμορφοτέρα Μ. τὰς Γ.		
86	c. 12 wds			
91	1 line (=60.1?)	ἀσαροτέρας		

(The word count is of words which can be read at all, including conjunctions and particles. Frr. 61, 66, 83–85 are too scrappy even to list. Frr. 58–86 are from *P.Oxy.* 1787; in some cases this is the only clue to their meter. Voigt notes that 64, 65, 73, and 86 may possibly be from tristichs in which the third verse was shorter than the first two.)

The first poem in the Cologne papyrus, with its apparent claim for a singer's fame below the earth, would fit here as well. The unreadable lines in fr. 58 before the New Poem seem to end with "success to/by the mouth," which could also conform. The only fragment that certainly seems to strike a tone different from what I have mentioned is fr. 63, in which someone appeals to Dream, as if to a god, and seems to seek relief from anxiety; but the poem also mentions a concern with "sharing" and "the blessed," presumably a reference to the afterlife.[8]

These scattered examples may not seem like much, but it is important to note that there is in fact very little to read (the second column indicates how much can be read of each). Even if some of the examples appear dubious, it is striking that these key features turn up so readily in so little material. Consider again, that in the Sapphic stanzas, of which there are much more copious remains, discussions of singing as an activity and mentions of the Muses or Graces are rare or missing.[9] Dialogue appears throughout the corpus, but the opinionated and assertive tone is especially peculiar to these fragments, especially in combination with musical activity.[10] The Sappho that I infer in these fragments is the Sappho described by Aelius Aristides (Orat. 28, 51 = Sa. 193 L-P, 55 V *Test.*):

> οἶμαι δέ σε καὶ Σαπφοῦς ἀκηκοέναι πρός τινας τῶν εὐδαιμόνων
> δοκουσῶν εἶναι γυναικῶν μεγαλαυχουμένης καὶ λεγούσης
> ὡς αὐτὴν αἱ Μοῦσαι τῷ ὄντι ὀλβίαν τε καὶ ζηλωτὴν ἐποίησαν
> καὶ ὡς οὐδ' ἀποθανούσης ἔσται λήθη.

> I think you must have heard Sappho too boasting to some of
> those women reputed to be fortunate and saying that the Muses

---

[8] Ferrarri 2007:188 reports a forthcoming study by E. Puglia which introduces the theme of youth too to this fragment by joining fr. 87 (13) LP (not in V) to it, despite a gap of 7 syllables.

[9] The imperative of "sing" occurs in fr. 21 and has been supplied in fr. 22; singing as accompaniment of a wedding procession appears in fr. 27 and 30.

[10] Reproach and baseness certainly seem to be subjects in fr. 3, but the speaker seems to be expressing regret more than any harshness of her own. See Lidov 2002 who argues against the imputation of any reproach to Sappho's brother or to "Doricha" in any of the poems, particularly fr. 3 and 15.

had made her truly blessed and enviable, and that she would not be forgotten even when she was dead. (tr. Campbell)

There are, of course, also references to Eros and Aphrodite among these fragments, in common with all the other books. What we do not find are any hints of a need for resignation in the face of mortality or any expectation that the end of life must necessarily be a dead-end.

Taken together, then, the contexts of the two papyri suggest that we should be looking for a forthright assertion by the speaker—forthright enough to counter any accusation to the contrary—that she enjoys the virtues of a musical life, in particular the expectation of a reward in the afterlife. We should not expect any concession that a person who practices the arts of the Muses will be seriously inferior or lacking in comparison to any one else—whatever the appearances. The speaker of the new poem will be altogether unlike the unfortunately doomed unmusical addressee of fr. 55. Does the text support such a reading?

As I remarked above, the crucial moment for interpretation is the first couplet, because it is there that the poem answers the question of to whom the gifts of the Muses belong. Since παῖδες can be vocative without being the subject, we can look for a supplement in which the gifts of the Muses are what the speaker lays claim to, not what she regrets. That is possible because we can separate singing and lyre-playing, to which age is no barrier, from dancing, to which it is. We could return to the supplements suggested by the original editors (2004a:7), which have been largely ignored in the subsequent discussions:

> φέρω τάδε Μοίσαν ἰ]οκ[ό]λπων κάλα δῶρα, παῖδες,
> λάβοισα πάλιν τὰ]ν Φιλάοιδον λιγύραν χελύνναν·

This at least makes Sappho the lyre-holder, but "bringing" the gifts establishes no line of thought and opens an unanswered question about the context —bring where? They call these lines a prelude, preempting the search for a connection (they assume that the full poem ended with the lines about the love of the sun and constituted a "personal declaration" on the part of the poet). As an example of a more purposeful opening I suggest:

> νῦν δὴ μ' ἔτι Μοίσαν ἰοκ[ό]λπων κάλα δῶρα, παῖδες, (or νῦν μ'
>   ἤδεα Μοίσαν...)
> φίλημμι δὲ φώνα]ν φιλάοιδον λιγύραν χελύνναν·

For the first line: "now I have still the Muses' lovely gifts"[11] or "now the lovely gifts of the Muses are sweet to me", and for the second, "and I love the song-loving voice of the resounding lyres." This sets up the emphasis on the Singer's present condition that is the basis for the contrast between singing and dancing. The opening couplet exemplifies a structural feature that I find characteristic of the first six lines: the first line of each couplet is general—here the Muses' gifts—and the second specifies what is immediately relevant—here the lyre and song.

Two other problems are solved in this example as well. The noun φώναν removes the hard-to-explain definite article of other supplements; and by taking λιγύραν χελύνναν as a genitive plural, it avoids the problem of a doubled adjective for one noun.[12] For the semi-personification of the lyre, compare fr. 118, χέλυ...φωνάεσσα. The plural suggests that the lyres belong to the Muses, singing in harmony; that is, that the singer identifies her song with theirs.

Line 3 begins the explanation for the emphasis on singing in the first couplet. She loves the lyre and song, for she has gotten old. This description fills two couplets:

> νῦν γὰρ μ' ἄπαλον πρὶν] ποτ' [ἔ]ǫντα χρόα γῆρας ἤδη   3
> κατέσκεθε, λεῦκαι δ' ἐγ]ένοντο τρίχες ἐκ μελαίναν·
> βάρυς δέ μ' ὁ [θ]ῦμος πεπόηται, γόνα δ' [ο]ὐ φέροισι,   5
> τὰ δή ποτα λαίψηρ' ἔον ὄρχησθ' ἴσα νεβρίοισι.

> γὰρ Di Benedetto 1985   ἄπαλον e.p.   πρὶν Di Benedetto 2004
> κατέσκ. West 2005   λεῦκαι e.p. P.Oxy. 1787

"For now age has taken hold of my once lovely flesh" (cf. fr. 2 for the repeated initial adverb).[13] The introduction of old age is directed to the goal of explaining something. I stress this point because commentary so far has rushed to describe this as a paratactic symptom-list, like the list of afflictions in the *phainetai moi* fragment, or even in Anacreon's little poem, where his white hair is complemented by his aging teeth. But these lines have more internal struc-

---

[11] For the syntax of an opening with a dative of possession and no copula, cf. Sappho 110 V.

[12] Both difficulties were noted *ad loc.* in the e.p. The genitive was assumed by Diehl and Campbell in their editions of Sappho. The alpha of χελύνναν has a macron in P.Oxy. 1787, but such macrons appear irregularly and are not useful guides; there is a macron over the alpha of an accusative singular in 58.22, and of a genitive plural in 71.3.

[13] The supplement for the start of line 3 printed in the text in the Introduction, ἔμοι δ', supposes a change in topic, from the *paides* to the singer; Di Benedetto's earlier suggestion of the causal particle, not mentioned in the app. crit., seems to me clearer, although an adversative does not alter the logic.

ture than those. The first of these two couplets describes external appearances. Sappho begins, again, with a general statement, that her exterior has been ruined by age. Gronewald and Daniel's supplement ἄπαλον is apt, but not for the reason they give. They cite ἀπαλὸν χρόα from Archilochus 118.1W, where they assume a contrast with Snell's ὄγμοις as a metaphor for "wrinkles" (which they also supply in the next line here).[14] Such a use of the word would make the line specific, smooth skin set against wrinkled, parallel to the contrast of black hair and white in the next line, and so would conform to a reading of the lines as a unstructured list. But ἄπαλος is one of Sappho's own general purpose words for youthful attractiveness, and she uses it as an absolute quality; she applies it not only to hands weaving wreaths (fr. 81.5; cf. Alcaeus 45.5 and inc. auct. 16.2 V= Sappho 93 L-P), and a neck decorated with flowers (fr. 94.16), but also to whole persons: ἀπάλας Γυρίννως (fr. 82a), a child collecting flowers (fr. 122), and sleeping companions (fr. 126).[15] So I take this line to be the general introduction to the youthful appearance that she has lost. In the next line, she is more specific: she has that most notorious visual mark of age, white hair.

The third couplet proceeds from the outward appearance others can see to the physical consequences felt by the singer herself. In its first lines she says, in general terms, that her *thumos* is heavy. This is a physical incapacity, not a psychological affect. *Thumos* in the Lesbians refers to the organ which generates desires that can be acted on and gives impulse to motion. Di Benedetto pointed this out in his notes on the Cologne papyrus,[16] but since it has become common to translate βάρυς... [θ]ῦμος as "heavy-hearted" and give it the value of a state of mind,[17] it will be useful to review the evidence. The *thumos* explains action,

Alcaeus 308b.1–2 V   χαῖρε Κυλλάνας ὸ μέδεις, σὲ γάρ μοι
                       θῦμος ὔμνην,

---

[14] The text is cited by Hephaestion, who gives the nom. sing. ὄγμος, in which case the phrase could be a rude specification of the loss of youthful bloom; see the note of Campbell (1982 [1990]):*ad loc.*

[15] It is not clear whether ἀπάλαν in 94.22V modifies something specific in the following gap or generally characterizes νε]ανίδων in the next line (Theander; v. app. crit). Alcaeus 39a.3V does have γῆρας two lines before ἀπάλων. For further discussion of the word, see also Broger 1996.91–92.

[16] "...è usato a un livello di elementarità animalesca, per indicare l'impulso intimo, lo slancio che induce il movimento" (2004:5).

[17] The psychological interpretation is defended at length by Bernsdorff 2004; he takes it to be an innovation of Sappho's. His argument relies on the emotional uses of forms of βαρὺ στενάχειν in Homer, and on the conception in other poets that anxieties are typical of old age. He does not examine Lesbian uses of θυμός. Hellenistic usage differs.

or is connected to the expectation of action; it is found on either side of prayer:

Sappho 5.3–4 V   κὤσσαϊϝ]οι θύμω<ι> κε θέληι γένεσθαι
πάντα τε]λέσθην, (cf. Sa 1.26–7; 60.5–6)

Alcaeus 129.9–12 V   ....   ἄγ.[ι]τ᾽ εὔνοον
θῦμον σκέθοντες ἀμμετέρα[ς] ἄρας
ἀκούσατ᾽, ἐκ δὲ τῶν[δ]ε μόχθων
ἀργαλέας τε φύγας ῤ[ύεσθε·

When the *thumos* is repressed, a person is unable to act. So the birds afflicted with a cold *thumos* drop their wings:

Sappho 42 V   ταῖσι < – > ψῦχρος μὲν ἔγεντο θῦμος
πὰρ δ᾽ ἴεισι τὰ πτέρα

It is relief from such impairment that Sappho seeks in Poem 1:

Sappho 1.3–4 V   μή μ᾽ ἄσαισι μηδ᾽ ὀνίαισι δάμνα,
πότνια, θῦμον

By the end of the poem she is ready to act. Alcaeus says that something so stirred Helen's *thumos* that she went into motion and followed Paris to Troy:

Alcaeus 283.3–6 V   κ᾽Αλένας ἐν στήθ[ε]σιν [ἐ]πτ[όαισε
θῦμον Ἀργείας· Τροΐω<ι> δ᾽ [ἐ]π᾽ ἄν[δρι
ἐκμάνεισα ξ[ε.]ναπάτα<ι> 'πι π[όντον
ἔσπετο νᾶϊ,

But in contrast, when the same verb is used to describe the disturbance that renders Sappho incapable of action, it does not act on her *thumos*:

Sappho 31.6–7 V   ....   τό μ᾽ ἦ μὰν
καρδίαν ἐν στήθεσιν ἐπτόαισεν,

The general sensation that βάρυς...[θ]ῦμος describes in the New Poem is what we call not a "heavy heart" but a "slowing of the blood" (or a low thyroid-count), and Sappho explicates it immediately as a problem of motion: she cannot move her limbs. That is the general difficulty. In the next line she gets to the point to which the whole description has been building: specifically, she cannot dance. And that is why she emphasizes lyre-playing and singing.

But, as elsewhere in Sappho, the logical development of the argument has become the vehicle for a shifting tenor.[18] The explicit statement of the first three couplets, that the Singer maintains her attachment to song, even as age has deprived her of dance, has turned our attention to the deficits of old age. She makes this topic explicit at the start of the next couplet:

τὰ <μὲν> στεναχίσδω θαμέως· ἀλλὰ τί κεν ποείην;
ἀγήραον ἄνθρωπον ἔοντ' οὐ δύνατον γένεσθαι.

"I often bewail this, but what might I do?" στεναχίζω is a striking word choice here. Greek gives us στένω, the frequentative στενάζω, its poetic lengthened form στενάχω, and this further lengthened form στεναχίζω. The word is frequent in Homer, where it is clearly very emphatic, and occurs in no other archaic or classical author. What has moved Sappho, a writer who rarely uses a long word where a short one will do, and who avoids otiose syllables, to adopt this blatant epicism? To use such a word here is to call attention to the manner of speech itself. In addition, the whole phrase has something formulaic about it. Compare the lament for Adonis, fr. 141:

κατθνάσκει, Κυθέρη', ἄβρος Ἄδονις· τί κεν θεῖμεν;

"Adonis is dying, what might we do?" and the cry of the Furies when they think that Athena's judgment has utterly vanquished them: στενάζω· τί ῥέξω; (Aeschylus *Eumenides* 788). It is the cry not of someone confronting gray hair and arthritis, but confronting death or ruin. On the one hand the language is disproportionate to what has been described, perhaps humorously exaggerated; on the other, it brings us to the true subject of the poem.[19] The gnome on the inevitability of old age, which completes the couplet, is a reminder not only of the necessity of losing our youth but of the inevitability of death. It is in this context that the role of Dawn must be appreciated. For from this invocation of mortality at its center, the poem now works back to its beginning. Tithonus too did not move his limbs, but he was carried to the ends of the earth by a god's favor (with a repeated use of φέρω):

---

[18] I have in mind particularly the way the example of Helen in fr. 16 serves logically to illustrate the gnome and applies to Sappho's desire for Anactoria, but rhetorically it also serves to make Helen a paradigm for the beauty of Anactoria, described in the final surviving stanza; see Pfeijffer 2000.

[19] Ferrari 2007:181 points out the correspondence of στεναχίσζω and Anacreon's ἀνασταλύζω (395.7, quoted above); note that in Anacreon also the verb introduces the theme of death as the problem of old age.

καὶ γάρ π̣[ο]τ̣α Τίθωνον ἔφαντο βροδόπαχυν Αὔων
ἔρῳ [....]ε̣ἰσανβάμεν' ἐς ἔσχατα γᾶς φέροισα[ν,

And when gray old age took from Tithonus his youthful looks, he too still had an immortal companion:

ἔοντα [κ]ά̣λ̣ο̣ν καὶ νέον, ἀλλ' αὖτον ὔμως ἔμαρψε
χρόνωι π̣ό̣λ̣ι̣ο̣ν γῆρας, ἔχ[ο]ντ' ἀθανάταν ἄκοιτιν.

The final position establishes Dawn as a parallel to the Muses in the first line. The participle ἔχοντ' should not be read concessively ("even though he had…"; ὔμως contrasts with the previous verbs), as would be required by the logic of the consolatory interpretation; that degree of emphasis on a concessive meaning would be difficult without a particle—καί or περ—and lacks a parallel in Sappho.[20] Rather, the emphasis shifts from the loss to what Tithonus has and will always have. In other versions of the story, in particular the one related by Aphrodite in the Hymn to Aphrodite, Tithonus is marked by the continuing sound of his voice (237) in the context of his weakness and his rejection from Aphrodite's bed. Although the hymn is the nearest parallel to Sappho temporally and marks Tithonus as in between the human and divine, we need not assume that Aphrodite's speech there (explaining to her lover, somewhat illogically, why she will not marry him) determines a negative image of Tithonus for the whole early tradition; the formulaic references in Homer (Iliad 11.1–2=Odyssey 5.1–2) describe him as Dawn's continuing bed mate. Nor should we assume a necessary opposition between elderly voices and the capacity for song. The value of the voice of the aged was also an available tradition. The old men of Iliad 3 are likened to cicadas (to which Tithonus is also likened in the fifth century), which become emblems of the Muses in the opening of the Phaedrus.[21] The Old Men of the Agamemnon make clear that singing is what is left when strength and mobility are gone (72–75, 104–109):

---

[20] The only concessive participle I have found in Sappho is 1.24, κωὐκ ἐθελοίσα—which not only has the particle, but is also not needed for the basic logic of the conditional sentences to which it is attached; it abbreviates *volens nolens* as a supplementary emphasis. The necessity of the concessive meaning is stressed by West (2005b:6) to avoid banality under his interpretation. As Rawles (2006b:2) points out, in West's reading it is the similarity of the "feelings and emotions" supposed for Tithonus and Sappho that are the grounds for the paradigm.

[21] Preisshoffen 1977:13–19 provides a nuanced analysis of the myth of Tithonos in the Hymn, where he is situated between the good fortune of immortalized Ganymede and the long-lived but mortal dryads. Preisshoffen emphasizes the myth's importance for the theme of the necessity of mortality. King 1989 offers a structuralist study of the myth, in which all versions come

ἡμεῖς δ' ἀτίται σαρκὶ παλαιᾷ
τῆς τότ' ἀρωγῆς ὑπολειφθέντες
μίμνομεν ἰσχὺν
ἰσόπαιδα νέμοντες ἐπὶ σκήπτροις.

κύριός εἰμι θροεῖν ὅδιον κράτος αἴσιον ἀνδρῶν
ἐντελέων· ἔτι γὰρ θεόθεν καταπνεύει
πειθώ, μολπᾶν ἀλκάν, σύμφυτος αἰών·

In content, the 12 lines of the New Poem assert positively what fr. 55 asserted negatively: having a share in the world of music—the roses of Pieria, the song even if not the dancing—assures one of continuing companionship, even in the afterlife. The singer makes an assertion, and the tone is confident.

Is the New Poem a complete poem? It has a beginning, middle and end, and the general structure of ring composition. But there are also readings that incorporate the lines that follow in the Oxyrhynchus copy (as Boedeker and Lardinois illustrate in this volume)—two fragmentary lines that allow for a variety of connections with the New Poem, and two completed by a quotation in Athenaeus; objections have also been raised to making the end of the poem coincide with the end of a paradigmatic myth. I think that the root of the problem, in this case, is the notion of a poem that stands by itself. I would prefer to say that these 12 lines are a complete statement. The second person address and the context of Book 4 suggest that there is a dialogic situation; the poet affirms what another might deny or devalue.[22] In fact, the lines from Athenaeus that are part of what follows in the Oxyrhynchus papyrus assert the value of the here and now, and could well be a contrastive reply to these lines. But it could also be the statement of the person who is censured in fr. 55, just as the New Poem could be a response to the kind of anxiety expressed by the speaker

into play simultaneously. She observes that the Hymn's specification of his voice (237 φονὴ ῥεῖ ἄσπετος) may reflect what is in other versions a contrast between old age and the continuing song of the cicada. The Hellenistic use of the myth, in which the transformation to a cicada figures prominently, is explored by Acosta-Hughes and Stephens 2002:251–253 and Geissler 2005:11–12.

22 Di Benedetto (2006:11) argues that the four lines following the New Poem in the Oxyrhynchus papyrus (=58.23–26), which contain the quotation from Athenaeus, could be an independent composition and suggests that it may be part of a dialogue. But Lowell Edmunds (2006), in addition to observing the absence of a return from the myth to the occasion, has pointed out that there is no parallel for the use of the imperfect ἔφαντο to introduce an exemplum. A dialogue might provide a specific reference for the past tense, but in the absence of either a generic model or a certain local explanation, the problem of the poem's occasion or genre can only remain open.

of fr. 63, who appears to fear not having a share in the blessed. So I propose that what we are looking at are songs for performances that involved some kind of give and take, whether between the chorus and the *chorodidaskalos* negotiating their roles or between choral members (or leaders) enacting a rivalry, in which relatively short compositions were exchanged in a kind of lyric conversation.[23] As relatively independent units, they may have been combined in any number of ways. Whatever their original arrangement, they could have been rearranged for re-performance. If they were composed for the same type of occasion—in other words, belong to a single genre—the similarities among the songs might have suggested different ways of grouping them to subsequent performers, readers, or editors. Certainly, the Alexandrian standard edition of Sappho may have collected such items without regard for their sequence in any actual performance. If the poems were composed for an occasion in which the participants used both the meters of Books 3 and 4, the system of collection, based on meter, would have separated them. (Sappho fr. 137 V, the exchange between Sappho and Alcaeus quoted by Aristotle, while probably apocryphal, suggests the possibility that Athenian readers could have found dialogue using related meters.)

Such exchanges may have a direct descendant in the bucolic *amoebaea* of Theocritus, but there is now another possible confirmation of the existence of dialogic exchanges. In a poem mourning the death of the *parthenos* Nikomache, disappointing her many suitors, Posidippus tells how Fate took, among her other delights, Nikomache's continuing exchange of Sapphic song or conversation at the loom.

> πάντα τὰ Νικομάχης καὶ ἀθύρματα καὶ πρὸς ἑῷαν
> κερκίδα Σαπφῴους ἐξ ὀάρων ὄαρους
> ᾤχετο Μοῖρα φέρουσα προώρια· ...
>
> (Posidippus 55.1–3 A-B)

All Nicomache's delights, all her conversations à la Sappho,
  one after the other, at the sound of the morning shuttle,
Fate has taken away prematurely.

> (C. Austin)

---

[23] On the leadership roles within a choral performance, see Calame 2001:.43–74.

The editors refer the words generally to feminine talk about love and other subjects.[24] But Posidippus may be suggesting a more specifically literary activity, if my assumption about the contents of Books 3 and 4 is correct, for there could be no better description of such a collection then to call it Σαπφῴους ἐξ ὀάρων ὄάρους, conversations in song by Sappho about the rewards of a life in which the Muses and Graces and what they concern themselves with play a major part, composed for performance by or with young women.[25]

Bibliography

Acosta-Hughes, B., and Stephens, S. A. 2002. "Rereading Callimachus' Aetia Fragment 1." *Classical Philology* 97:238–255.

Bastianini, G., and Gallazzi, C., eds. 2001. *Epigrammi: P.Mil.Vogl. 8. 309*. With C. Austin. Papiri dell' Università degli studi di Milano 8. Milan.

Bergk, T., ed. 1878–82. *Poetae Lyrici Graeci*. Leipzig.

Bernsdorff, H. 2004. "Schwermut des Alters im neuen Köln Sappho-Papyrus." *Zeitschrift für Papyrologie und Epigraphik* 150:27–35.

Brandt, H. 2003. *Wird auch silbern mein Haar: eine Geschichte des Alters in der Antike*. Beck's archäologische Bibliothek. Munich.

Broger, A. 1996. *Das Epitheton bei Sappho und Alkaios: eine sprachwissenschaftliche Untersuchung*. Innsbrucher Beiträge zur Sprachwissenschaft. Innsbruck.

Calame, C. 2001. *Choruses of Young Women in Ancient Greece: Their Morphology, Religious Role, and Social Function* ed. 2. Trans. D. Collins and J. Orion. Lanham MD.

Di Benedetto, V. 1985. "Il tema della vecchiaia e il fr. 58 di Saffo." *Quaderni Urbinati di Cultura Classica* n.s. 19:145–163.

———. 2004. "Osservazioni sul nuovo papiro di Saffo." *Zeitschrift für Papyrologie und Epigraphik* 149:5–6.

———. 2006. "Il tetrastico di Saffo e tre postille." *Zeitschrift für Papyrologie und Epigraphik* 155:5–18.

Edmunds, L. 2006. "The New Sappho: ἔφαντο (9)." *Zeitschrift für Papyrologie und Epigraphik* 156:23–26.

---

[24] Bastianini and Gallazzi 2001 *ad loc*. That view is defended by Pretagostini 2003. But given the combination of death and Sapphic singing, it is tempting to see an even more specific allusion in πρὸς ἕῳαν.

[25] I am grateful to Dirk Obbink, Dee Clayman, Ellen Greene, and Marilyn Skinner for organizing the two Sappho panels in January 2007, and to my fellow panelists and subsequent readers, whose contributions gave me the opportunity to improve the original oral version of this paper.

Ferrari, F. 2007. *Una mitra per Kleis: Saffo e il suo pubblico.* Biblioteca di Materiali e discussioni per l'analisi dei testi classici 19. Pisa.

Geissler, C. 2005. "Der Tithonosmythos bei Sappho und Kallimachos: Zu Sappho fr. 58 V, 11–22 und Kallimachos, Aitia fr. 1 Pf." *Göttinger Forum für Altertumswissenschaft* 8:105–114.

Gronewald, M., and Daniel, R. W. 2004. "Ein neuer Sappho-Papyrus." *Zeitschrift für Papyrologie und Epigraphik* 147:1–8.

Hardie, A. 2005. "Sappho, the Muses and Life after Death." *Zeitschrift für Papyrologie und Epigraphik* 154:13–32.

King, H. 1989. "Tithonos and the *tettix.*" *Old Age in Greek and Latin Literature* (ed. T. M. Falkner and J. de Luce) 68–89. SUNY Series in Classical Studies. Albany.

Lidov, J. B. 2002. "Sappho, Herodotus, and the *Hetaira.*" *Classical Philology* 97:203–237.

Lobel, E., ed. 1925. ΣΑΠΦΟΥΣ ΜΕΛΗ: *The Fragments of the Lyrical Poems of Sappho.* Oxford.

Lundon, J. 2007. "Il nuovo testo lirico nel nuovo papiro di Saffo." *I papiri di Saffo e di Alceo* (ed. G. Bastianini and A. Casanova) 149–166. Studi e Testi di Papirologia, N.S. 9. Florence.

Miller, A. M., trans. 1996. *Greek Lyric: An Anthology in Translation.* With introduction and notes. Indianapolis.

Page, D. L. 1955. *Sappho and Alcaeus: An Introduction to the Study of Ancient Lesbian Poetry.* Oxford. Corrected reprint 1959.

Pfeijffer, I. L. 2000. "Shifting Helen: An Interpretation of Sappho, Fragment 16 (Voigt)." *Classical Quarterly* 50:1–6.

Pretagostini, R. 2003. "L'epigramma per Nicomache (Posidippo, *P.Mil.Vogl.* VIII 309, IX 1–6)." *Il papiro di Posidippo un anno dopo. Atti del convegno internazionale di studi: Firenze 13–14 giugno 2002* (ed. G. Bastianini and A. Casanova) 121–128. Florence.

Preisshofen, F. 1977. *Untersuchungen zur Darstellung des Greisenalters in der frühgriechischen Dichtung.* Hermes Einzelschriften 34. Wiesbaden.

Rawles, R. 2006a. "Musical Notes on the New Anonymous Lyric Poem from Köln." *Zeitschrift für Papyrologie und Epigraphik* 157:8–13.

———. 2006b. "Notes on the Interpretation of the 'New Sappho'." *Zeitschrift für Papyrologie und Epigraphik* 157:1–7.

West, M. L. 2005. "The New Sappho." *Zeitschrift für Papyrologie und Epigraphik* 151:1–9.

8
The Meter and Metrical Style
of the New Poem

Joel Lidov

P. OXY. 1787, INCLUDING SAPPHO 58 V—AND SO THE "NEW POEM"—has been
assigned to Book Four of the Alexandrian edition of her works since its
first publication (*Ox. Pap.* XV:26; cf. Lobel 1925:xii). Because the assign-
ment is a conjecture, this is a good moment to review the status of the ques-
tion, and at the same time to observe, and try to appreciate, an apparent pecu-
liarity in Sappho's use of the meter in this poem. First, however, I will attempt
to place the meter into the context of what we have of the work of Sappho and
Alcaeus.

The Metrical Type of the New Poem

The meter seen in the New Poem had been known from complete examples
provided by four quotations: Sa. 58.26 V, 81.4–8 V, 82a V, 91 V. The last two
are from Hephaestion *Enchiridion* 7.5 (p. 36.15–16 C = Sappho 154 V Test.) who
calls it *aiolikon* and says that "Sappho used it often (πολλῷ αὐτῷ ἐχρήσατο)."
In general, such statements should be taken with a grain of salt. The ancient
metricians, who liked to identify the "first discoverer" of each metrical form,
also often named the "frequent user"; it is likely that both identifications
were driven by a desire to explain the often inconsistent nomenclature. In
this case, Hephaestion associates the *aiolikon* with an Aeolic poet.[1] Sappho's
use of the form is now also confirmed in several of the lines restored by the

---

[1] Liberman (2002:I.cviii) aptly prefaces his collection of metrical testimonia for Alcaeus with
a general notice from Aelius Theon (*Progymnasmata* 73 p. 32 Patillon-Bolognesi): ὥσπερ
Ἀριστοφάνειόν τι μέτρον καὶ Σαπφικὸν καὶ Ἀλκαϊκὸν καὶ ἄλλο ἀπ' ἄλλου λέγεται, οὐχ ὡς
τούτων τῶν ποιητῶν μόνων ἢ πρώτων ἐξευρηκότων τὰ μέτρα, ἀλλ' ὅτι αὐτοῖς ἐπὶ τὸ πλεῖστον
ἐχρήσαντο ("so a certain meter [is called] aristophanean or sapphic or alcaic, and another is
called after another poet, not because these poets alone [used] or first found the meters, but
because they made most use of them").

combination of the old and new papyri, and the number of fragments in *P.Oxy.* 1787 makes it clear that in this case we can take Hephaestion literally.

Modern handbooks mostly describe it (in the terminology established by Bruno Snell) as an acephalous hipponactean with a double choriambic expansion, or *^hipp*²ᶜ:

$$\times — \smile\smile — — \smile\smile — — \smile\smile — \smile — \overline{\smile}$$

It belongs to a larger group of metrical forms, or cola, which in modern usage are also often called aeolic. Individual aeolic forms allow no variations that would change the syllable count (contraction or resolution), but a few examples suggest that they can tolerate internally an exchange in the order of a long and short syllable. This is consistent with the theory that they represent more conservatively than other forms the derivation of Greek meters from an Indo-European syllable-counting system. More specifically, this form belongs with a group of cola that are most easily described in terms of the relation of each to the glyconic (or glyconean, *gl*): $\times\times — \smile\smile — \smile —$. The hipponactean is one syllable longer than a glyconic, the pherecratean one syllable shorter. The extra syllable of the hipponactean can be long or short, but as the final syllable of a verse line, it is conventionally assumed to be long. Here the hipponactean has only one indeterminate syllable at the start, and so is called acephalous, on the assumption that two syllables are normal in the aeolic basis. Since in fact one syllable bases are a normal variant, there would be some advantage in using West's term hagisichorean (1982:30) to avoid the impression that the verse is somehow felt to be foreshortened, but I will retain the traditional term in this discussion. The acephalous hipponactean and the glyconic are both eight syllables long, and there is no reason to give one formal priority over the other (although the glyconic may descend from an earlier prehistoric stage). It is probably more useful to retain the emphasis on syllable-count and think of them as eight-syllable forms of the same type that have different endings: one blunt, $— \smile —$ and one pendant, $\smile — —$.

Aeolic forms of this type can be expanded by repetition(s) of the internal sequence of two short syllables: choriambic expansion when the whole sequence $— \smile\smile —$ is repeated and dactylic expansion when $— \smile\smile$ is repeated. Lines could also be expanded externally by a full or partial iambic metron ($\times — \smile —$, $— \smile —$, $\smile — —$) before or after the specifically aeolic segment, but there are only a couple of examples in the Lesbian poets of internal and external expansion of the same verse. Given that the iambic metra and the aeolic forms can merge seamlessly, how one divides a verse line between them and identifies the exact aeolic form involved generally depends on the theoretical assumptions behind the analysis.

Aeolic forms, especially the various expanded forms, make up the great bulk of what has been recovered of Lesbian poetry. Poems of unexpanded *gl* are not found, but in Sappho, stanzas variously formed from unexpanded glyconics and expanded ones are found together in one papyrus (*P.Berol.* 9722); in Alcaeus there is evidence of several such stanzas from a variety of sources. Simple $^\wedge hipp$ is found in four lines attributed to Sappho (168b V), but the attribution is disputed. Expanded forms are much more common. Examples of dactylic expansion of glyconic, especially, and of pherecratean are found for both poets, and choriambic expansion of glyconic—in particular, gl^{2c}—is well represented in both. Sappho also has choriambic expansion of pherecratean, and of course, $^\wedge hipp^{2c}$. There is no firm evidence that Alcaeus ever used $^\wedge hipp^{2c}$, although two of his fragments (48 V, 61 V) have line ends that are compatible with it. Alcaeus, in fact, has very few examples of hipponacteans at all; the ones that do occur are the product of uncertain analyses.[2]

The description I have just given follows one entirely modern theory, and I have tried to set it out it in a way that is compatible with a description in terms of Indo-European derivation.[3] Other modern descriptions have put more emphasis on the choriamb as the distinctive element (making dactylic expansion secondary); some have focused on the mix of dactylic and trochaic feet (and make choriambic expansion secondary); some follow more closely ancient authorities. All of these latter are from the late Hellenistic or Roman imperial period and offer entirely different groupings. Hephaestion, for example, in the passage cited above, calls the meter of the New Poem an acatalectic major ionic tetrameter. The corresponding glyconic form is an acatalectic antispastic tetrameter (10.6, p. 34.11–12 C). Other contemporary theories would have described both in terms of internal segments that could be related to the more familiar forms of iambic or dactylic poetry. Forms with dactylic expansion were usually related to dactylic verse, rather than to other forms of aeolic. If we want to know what Sappho or Alcaeus would have thought of the relation of the various meters to each other, we can only infer it from how they combined them in stanzas.

---

[2] Other types of meter—dactylic, ionic, and iambo-trochaic—also occur in both poets. Since many of these occur in citations from ancient metricians, who were more interested in cataloguing types than in describing a body of work, it is difficult to know just how large a role non-aeolic forms play.

[3] For a history of the aeolic forms, see Nagy 1996.

Most of the metrical forms we know occur as single lines; that is, we know more line types than stanza types, especially in the case of Sappho's poetry. This may be in part because ancient authorities tended to quote only single lines, even in cases in which we know that the lines are parts of stanzas. But, as will be discussed below, a series of identical lines arranged in couplets seems to have been a frequent form of composition. The stanza types that do survive—and there are more for Alcaeus than Sappho—are especially valuable for the negative evidence they give (the examples are most easily seen in Voigt's "Conspectus" for each poet; see also West 1982:31–33). There is no stanza which combines both choriambic and dactylic expansion, although there are stanzas which combine each with the simple forms or (more rarely) with externally expanded forms. The use of the contrast between blunt and pendant endings to set off sections of verse—for example glyconic and pherecratean—familiar from the versification of Anacreon and throughout dramatic lyric, is not found in the Lesbian poets; with the exception of the alcaic stanza, they use one or the other type of ending consistently in a stanza.[4] Variations between lines in a stanza are largely achieved by the amount of internal or external expansion.[5] To put this positively, by maintaining uniformity in construction, they were able to make a variety of distinctive song types out of a smaller variety of often similar materials. And within the limits of the state of our evidence, the New Poem, written entirely in $^{\wedge}hipp^{2c}$, appears to exhibit a metrical form that is distinctively Sappho's.

I will consider below the particular similarity of the New Poem with others written in repeated lines and with the corresponding metrical type gl^{2c}.

The Arrangement of Meters in Books

While it is generally assumed that the Alexandrian edition of Sappho arranged the poems by meter, the evidence associating different metrical patterns with different books is quite sparse (unless otherwise cited, see Sappho 226–234 V and Sappho T29–T36 Campbell with his notes). No ancient source actually says that the poems of Sappho were arranged by meter, but the descriptions that say certain meters were found in certain books leads to this conclusion.

---

[4] One analysis of Alcaeus 130b V yields pendant *hipp* together with blunt *gl* and *gl^c*, as well as an exceptional combination of the latter with $^{\wedge}gl^c$. But the alternate analysis, combining only expanded and unexpanded *gl*, conforms much more on all counts to Alcaeus's practice elsewhere.

[5] There is some very slight evidence for asynartete verse in the Archilochean style, with contrasting lines (see section D in each Conspectus in Voigt); such verse forms may also account for some of the isolated iambo-trochaic lines cited in antiquity.

In addition, the papyri that show multiple poems in the same (or very similar) meters or stanzas (*P.Berol.* 5006, 9722; *P.Oxy.* 1231+2166(a), 1787) suggest a metrical arrangement. And in the case of the first three books the ancient sources tells us that each of them contained poems of a single metrical type. Since any hypotheses we make about the distribution of meters in the remaining books need to take account of all of them, my discussion of Book Four here is necessarily somewhat simplified.[6]

There is no evidence whatsoever, direct or indirect, for Book Four. As Page explained, the assignment of the meter used in the New Poem to Book Four was based on the observation that *P.Oxy.* 1787 contains fragments of "a considerable number of poems, ... The evidence, as far as it goes, indicates that these manuscripts come from a book wholly or largely homogeneous in metre; if so, it appears reasonable to assign to it the fourth place in the series, since the first three books were metrically homogeneous whereas the fifth was not" (1955:114–115). In fact, there are not enough lines assigned to this papyrus (or in this meter) to guarantee that they constitute a book "wholly or largely" in one meter (nor do they guarantee enough columns), not even one half the size of the 1320 lines recorded by the colophon to Book One, but we can safely say that there were many poems in this meter which apparently belonged to one book. I emphasize this because of a potential complication in the idea of a "book." Hunt reported in his original edition of *P.Oxy.* 1787 (*Ox. Pap.* XV:126–127) that fragments of other poetry in the same hand were found with these. Now that we possess one (albeit much earlier) papyrus combining poems in this meter with non-Lesbian poetry, the possibility that *P.Oxy.* 1787 does not represent a book roll from an edition of Sappho, but some other kind of compilation, seems less far-fetched.[7] I shall proceed, however, on the assumption that there

---

[6] I hope to present a fuller discussion elsewhere. Most of the difficulties concern Book Five, and are not immediately relevant to the discussion of the meter of the New Poem. Page offers a summary discussion of the evidence for distribution of meters (1959.112–116). Liberman 2007 provides a fuller presentation, with a spare critique and his own hypotheses; I am in agreement with him on many points. Yatromanolakis 1999 surveys the evidence for the number of books and, against Page, reaffirms Wilamowitz's conclusion that there only eight books and that the last was referred to as "*Epithalamia*"; Liberman argues for nine books in eight rolls. I shall assume that there were eight books, and not review the question further here.

[7] This is also the case with *P.Oxy.* 1788, from the same find but in a different hand; the aeolic fragments were assigned to Alcaeus by the first editors (=Alcaeus 115–128a V) on the basis of their style and of their variety in meter and content, on the assumption that they all came from one book of one poet. Subsequent discussions have all been based on the same assumption (see Liberman 2007:55–56n59, with reference to previous literature, where he withdraws his earlier ascription to Sappho). But there exists the possibility that they are from a collection, and are by more than one author.

are a sufficient number of poems in the same meter to represent a selection from a single book, even if the roll whose fragments we possess is not actually from a complete edition.

In addition to the book-by-book evidence for metrical patterns, we can also consider the possibility that stanza structure played a role in the arrangement of poems into books. In the Greek sources,[8] poems are distinguished on the basis of whether they are written in lines or in *systems* (i.e., stanzas). The latter can be composed of similar or dissimilar metra. Sappho Book Two is cited in the *Peri Poematon* as an example of poems composed in stanzas in similar metra (1.1, p. 63.7–8 C). This is then further explained under the rubric of "common" *systems*, and the example given this time is poems such as those in Sappho Books Two and Three: these are in stanzas because they are marked off every two lines and the total number of lines is always even (that is, they are written in couplets, or *distichs*), but since the lines are identical, they could also be said to be written in lines (1.2, p. 63.15–24 C). *Paragraphoi* that represent such markings are in the papyri for Book Two, in which all the poems are in the meter gl^{2d}. And both the Oxyrhynchus and Cologne papyri have *paragraphoi* that mark off distichs in the poems we are now attributing to Book Four, even though that book is not cited as part of the example. However, since the author of *Peri Poematon* was only using Sappho as an example—not describing her edition—he did not need to include Book Four when he cited Two and Three. But there may have been another reason to omit it. *P.Oxy.* 2290 = Sa. 88 V contains lines that are compatible with $^{\wedge}hipp^{2c}$. The papyrus fragment contains the right edge of a column and every third line appears to be distinctly shorter—although not very much shorter—suggesting that it contained three-line stanzas (see Voigt's apparatus and the note *ad loc.* added in Lobel-Page 1963.67). Some poems from *P.Oxy.* 1787 appear to follow the same pattern; in that case, Book Four would have contained at least that one other type of stanza form.[9]

---

8 Stanzas are discussed in the *Peri Poematos* and *Peri Poematon* that are found with the mss. of Hephaestion *Enchiridion* (they can be assumed to epitomize the same source; see van Ophuijsen 1993); the latter contains the fuller treatment of this topic. There is nothing of additional significance in the Latin sources.

9 What survives for the first two lines of the supposed stanza of Sa. 88 V is, at most, the first seven of the last nine syllables, ...]◡−−◡◡−◡[−×. For the third line, the end survives, ...]◡◡−◡−×. As Voigt indicates, it is likely that the third line is one choriamb shorter. In *P.Oxy.* 1787, the same pattern is possible for Sappho73 V, and (more doubtfully) 64a V and 86 V (note especially line 4); in Sappho 65 V, there is a paragraphos after line 9, and confusing traces of what would be another both two and three lines earlier. Gallavotti 1957 gathers these fragments as a set of poems separate from the ones in distichs (nos. 72–75 in his edition).

I suggest that a series of considerations affected the distribution of meters. Books One to Three contained poems in the only three meters in which there was enough material to fill a book. That would be consistent with the fact that no source associates other books with a single meter. Beginning with Book Four, then, different meters were combined in each book.[10] One source, the single piece of evidence for the meter of Book Seven, indirectly suggests that within each book poems were still grouped by meter.[11] Unfortunately, this passage is corrupt: Hephaestion *Enchiridion* 10.5, p. 34.7–8 C reads: ...ᾧ μέτρῳ ἔγραψεν ᾄσματα καὶ Σαπφὼ ἐπὶ † τῆς τοῦ ἑβδόμου· (the mss. vary in regard to the extra article), "a meter in which Sappho also wrote songs at † the of the seventh Book." It appears to indicate that the use of this meter characterized one part of the book.[12] If we accept that as a general rule of arrangement, the next question is, what governed the selection of meters to be combined into a single book. The possible combination of two and three-line stanzas in *P.Oxy.* 1787, and the collection of similar stanzas in *P.Berol.* 9722 (whatever book they belonged to) suggest that perceived metrical similarity determined the groupings. At the same time, the order of the books themselves might reflect a movement from those with uniform lines to stanzas with similar lines of varying length to more mixed stanzas. Although Book One may owe its position to the special prominence of the sapphic stanza, it may also have been seen to use continuous identical lines in a *system*, since the "*epodos*" that concludes the sapphic stanza may not have been considered a line in the same sense as the previous ones.[13]

---

[10] As Liberman 2007:49 observes, the inclusion of more than one meter in the book would also be consistent with the difference between Hephaestion's language introducing ^hipp²ᶜ, Σαπφὼ πολλῷ αὐτῷ ἐχρήσατο (*Enchiridion* 11.5 [p. 36.15–16 C] = Sa. 154 V Test.), and the formula that he uses for the meters of Books Two and Three, ᾧ τὸ δεύτερον (τρίτον) ὅλον Σαπφοῦς γέγραπται, *Enchiridion* 7.7 [23.15 C], 10.6 [34.12 C] = Sappho 227, 229 V).

[11] This is a separate conclusion from Lobel's hypothesis that the poems of the same metrical form were arranged alphabetically (1925:xv).

[12] A word such as τελευτῆς (Bergk) or ἀρχῆς (Westphal ap. Bergk) may be missing, or a confusion over an abbreviation of, e.g., τέλους (Bergk) may be behind the error.

[13] The ancient practice of writing the poem out in three identical and one different line would seem to satisfy the definition of a poem in stanzas of dissimilar metra (and if it did, one could then wonder why the example was not used, given the examples from Sappho for stanzas in similar metra). And certainly some Latin sources simply describe it as four "verses" (e.g., Diomedes Thrax 1.519, 521 Keil). But Dionysius Halicarnassensis in *De compositione verborum* 19, discussing sources of variety in composition, remarks, that Sappho and Alcaeus "composed small strophes, without much variety in the few cola, and used very few epodes"(μικρὰς ἐποιοῦντο στροφάς, ὥστ' ἐν ὀλίγοις τοῖς κώλοις οὐ πολλὰς εἰσῆγον μεταβολάς, ἐπῳδοῖς τε πάνυ ἐχρῶντο ὀλίγοις). The masculine epodos here (in distinction from the feminine, used a few lines earlier, to indicate the third strophe of a triad) seems likely not to refer to Archilochean epodes as a

Book Three included lines with double choriambic expansion, but only of the form *gly*²ᶜ; since there were in addition poems in lines with double expansion in the form ^*hipp*²ᶜ, it is reasonable to think that they would have been assigned to Book Four. It is reasonable because the general similarity of the two lines seems obvious—they have the same number of syllables and the same relationship to each other as the hendecasyllables of the sapphic and alcaic strophe—and the pattern of couplets continues.[14] A variant three-line stanza, using the same long line twice, could have been part of the same book if metrical similarity was a determining criterion. Perhaps this book could have also contained the fifteen-syllable *pher*²ᶜ (which shares the further similarity of a pendant ending with ^*hipp*²ᶜ); that verse pattern is illustrated by Sappho 140 V, the mourning for Adonis (it may share thematic affinities with the New Poem; the original editors [Gronewald and Daniel 2004] made an explicit connection between the New Poem and Phaon/Adonis, and, at the least, the irreparability of death is common to both sets of lines).

In the absence of direct evidence of any sort, anything we say about Book Four is subject to doubt. There is also no evidence for Book Six, and in fact we have no explicit reason to exclude any meter from any book after Book Three. But until more evidence is discovered, the criteria I have described at least confirm the reasonableness of assuming that the New Poem belongs to Book Four and give us some sense of its place in the whole. If this is the case, the reader of the ancient edition of Sappho encountered poems in each of the

---

genre but to what gives those their name, the epode which *Peri Poematon* 7.2 (71.2–3 C) defines as "something extra (περιττόν τι) attached to a long line." That could easily be a description of the last segment of the sapphic stanza; epodus is also used for it by Marius Victorinus (Aphthonius), 6.161–162 Keil. From that point of view, the separation of the fourth "line" serves less to mark it as a colon than to preserve the similarity of the other three—an exception that tests the rule defining stanzas of similar metra, but does not break it (although it would certainly disqualify Book One from being used as an example).

[14] The similarity would not have been obvious according to the theories of the *Encheiridion*, mentioned earlier, by which the meter of Book Three is antispastic, and that of the New Poem major ionic. The treatment of the latter as a version of the same type as the former involves a category of variation not recognized in that handbook but familiar to other ancient authorities (Atilius Fortunatianus 6.296–297 Kiel specifically applies it to derive the sapphic from the alcaic hendecasyllable by the transfer of one syllable). I am assuming that the editors of the Alexandrian edition would have been pragmatically influenced by the fifteen syllables the two forms have in common (on the pragmatism of Alexandrian colometry in general, see Parker 2001). Without that assumption the argument is weaker, and depends more on the assumption—made by Page, but which I consider unjustified—that we know that Book Five contained an even greater variety of stanza types, and for that reason should follow the book represented by *P.Oxy.* 1787. I propose in my interpretative essay, in this volume, that the similarity is also substantive.

first four books—half the edition—that were in repetitions of single, long verse forms. First, the externally expanded 11-syllable line of the sapphic stanza filled Book One, and this was followed by even longer lines with internal expansion written mostly in couplets: the fourteen-syllable lines of glyconics with double-dactylic expansion in Book Two, and the sixteen-syllable lines of glyconics and of acephalous hipponacteans, both with double choriambic expansion, in Book Three and much of Book Four.

Metrical Style in the New Poem

I turn now to how Sappho used the verse form in the New Poem. In her *Conspectus Metrorum* Voigt indicates that the lines with double choriambic expansion tend to have a word-end between the choriambs. This is true for *gl²ᶜ* (also called the major asclepiad) in both Sappho's and Alcaeus's practice,[15]

$$\times\times—\cup\cup—\;\vdots\;—\cup\cup—\;\vdots\;—\cup\cup—\cup\overline{\cup}$$

and Sappho's treatment of *^hipp²ᶜ* is similar:

$$\times—\cup\cup—\;\vdots\;—\cup\cup—\;\vdots\;—\cup\cup—\;\vdots\;\cup—\overline{\cup}$$

Voigt marks a word-end preference when word-end occurs in at least half of the instances. Such counting depends on many assumptions, not least on how a "word" is to be defined and how to treat partial or uncertain lines. I have not tried to double-check her counts, but they can certainly be accepted as broadly indicative, and in themselves they are not surprising. (Horace turned the division between choriambs into a rule in his asclepiads.) Thus, the line which Hephaestion first quotes (Sappho 83a V) to illustrate the meter that also occurs in the New Poem can be taken as a model:[16]

εὐμορφότερα | Μνασιδίκα | τὰς ἀπάλας | Γυρίννως

As a matter of style, however, we expect that Sappho will not follow this pattern rigidly; one of the characteristics of her composition is variety.[17] And when

---

[15] The first syllable is always long in Alcaeus's poems and usually long in Sappho's; the second is usually long in Alcaeus's. Alcaeus also has a bridge within the second choriamb.

[16] Encheiridion 11.5 (36.17 C). He also quotes Sapho 91 V, ἀσαροτέρας οὐδάμα πωξἰρανα, σέθεν τύχοισαν. which begins with a short syllable, and has no break (with synizesis) between the second and the third choriamb; by his ionic analysis the initial short would be a variation from the norm worth mentioning.

[17] As Jim Powell, one of her best translators, puts it: "Sappho's secret consists largely in keeping her caesura moving: in her sapphics the caesura (a pause in mid-verse) seldom falls in the same place in two consecutive lines" (Powell 1993:38)·

variety is absent, it is typically absent for a reason. This can be seen most clearly in Book One, where she normally avoids long sequences with word-ends (or with no word-ends) in any one given position but does have continuous word-ends in two passages. Both of these have a strongly unified and marked character: in every line but the last of fr. 31 V there are word-ends after the fourth position—where they are, in addition, unexpected, since there tends to be a bridge in that position in other poems—and, less remarkably, in Poem 1.18-25 V, the epiphany of Aphrodite, word-ends fall unvaryingly in the position after the fifth syllable (see Lidov 1993:510–513). We can use two four-line fragments, Sappho 55 V in major asclepiads and Sappho 81.4–7 V in this meter, as samples of her style of composition in a verse with extended choriambic expansion. In the following schemes, broken lines indicate word-ends formed by appositives, and light type textually uncertain passages.[18]

Sappho 55:

```
   1    2    3    4    5    6    7    8    9    10   11   12   13   14   15   16
1  —    ◡    —    ◡ ⦙ ◡  |  —'—    ◡ ⦙ ◡    —  |  —    ◡    ◡    —  |  ◡    —
2  —    ◡ '—    ◡ ⦙ ◡  '  –†|  —    ◡    ◡  |. —⦙—  |  ◡    ◡    —  |  ◡    —
3  —⦙—⦙—    ◡    ◡    — |, —'◡    ◡    —  | —⦙◡    ◡    —  |  ◡    —
4  —    —    —  | ◡ ⦙'◡    —    —    —  | ◡    ◡    —  |  ◡    ◡    —    ◡    —
```

κατθάνοισα δὲ κείσηι οὐδέ ποτα μναμοσύνα σέθεν
ἔσσετ᾽ οὐδὲ †ποκ᾽ -†ὕστερον· οὐ γὰρ πεδέχηις βρόδων
τῶν ἐκ Πιερίας, ἀλλ᾽ ἀφάνης κἀν Ἀίδα δόμωι
φοιτάσηις πεδ᾽ ἀμαύρων νεκύων ἐκπεποταμένα.

In these lines disparaging the unmusical lady, the second halves of the lines are marked both by the consistent word-end at the tenth and fourteenth position and by the sense. The content is repetitive, but, notwithstanding the enjambments, every line rises to a point of emphasis at the end. (There is reinforcement in the sound of the responding alphas of μναμοσύνα and κἀν Ἀίδα, picked up in the close of the six-syllable finale.) But the word-end pattern that is stressed is the normal one, with a cut between the choriambs. Before the tenth position

---

[18] In what follows I assume a rising scale of value for word-junctures, from clitic-junctures, which might fulfill the expectation of word-end but do not necessarily violate expected bridges, to elisions (including synizesis) to full word-divisions; the latter two can be reinforced by phrasing (punctuation). See Korzeniewski 1968:16–17.

there is more variety, with no or almost no word-ends repeated two lines in a row, save, as expected, between the first two choriambs.

Sappho 81:

σὺ δὲ στεφάνοις, ὦ Δίκα, πέρθεσθ' ἐράτοις φόβαισιν
ὄρπακας ἀνήτω συν<α>έρραισ' ἀπάλαισι χέρσιν·
εὐάνθεα † γὰρ - πέλεται† καὶ Χάριτες μάκαιρα<ι>
μᾶλλον †προτερην†, ἀστεφανώτοισι δ' ἀπυστρέφονται.

Here the cut between the choriambs is not so strongly marked, though it occurs at least once in the four lines at each position. What pattern of cuts there is, after the tenth syllable, is muted by elision (and a prepositive). These lines tend to have longer words (individual words of three or more syllables account for 50 of the 64 syllables in Sappho 81, 39 in Sappho 55), and the general effect is of variety and continuous flow, without any prominent interior structure. The sense, too, develops continuously across the two couplets.

Even if one deems such judgments excessively subjective, the patterning in these lines makes a clear contrast with what happens in the New Poem (West's text, without supplements):

	1	2	3	4	5	6	7	8	9	10	11	12	13	14	15	16
1	×	–	⏑	⏑	–	–	ǀ ⏑	⏑	–	– ǀ ⏑	⏑ ǀ –	⏑ ǀ –	–
2	×	–	⏑	⏑	–	– ǀ ⏑	⏑	–	– ǀ ⏑	⏑	– ǀ ⏑	–	–
3	×	–	⏑	⏑	–	–	⏑ ' ⏑	–	– ǀ ⏑	⏑ ǀ –	⏑ ǀ –	–
4	×	–	⏑	⏑	–	–	⏑	–	– ǀ ⏑	⏑ ǀ – ⦂ ⏑	–	–
5	⏑	– ⦂ ⏑ ǀ' ⏑ ⦂	–	– ǀ ⏑	⏑	–	– ǀ, ⏑	⏑ ǀ – ⦂ ⏑	–	–
6	⏑ ⦂ – ⦂ ⏑	⏑ ǀ –	– ' ⏑	⏑ ǀ –	– ' ⏑	⏑ ǀ –	⏑	–	–
7	⏑ ⦂ – ǀ ⏑	⏑	–	– ǀ ⏑	⏑	– ǀ. –	⏑ ǀ ⏑ ⦂ – ǀ ⏑	–	–
8	⏑	–	⏑	⏑ ǀ –	– ⏑ ǀ ⏑	– ' – ⦂ ⏑	– ǀ ⏑	–	–
9	– ⦂ – ⦂ ⏑	⏑ ǀ –	–	– ⏑ ǀ ⏑	–	– ǀ ⏑	⏑	–	– ⏑ ǀ –	–
10	⏑	– ǀ ⏑	⏑ ǀ† –	–	– ⏑	⏑ ' – ⦂ –	⏑	⏑ ǀ – ǀ ⏑	–	–
11	⏑	–	⏑ ǀ ⏑	– ǀ – ⦂ ⏑	⏑ ǀ, – ' –	⏑ ǀ ⏑	– ǀ ⏑	–	–
12	⏑	– ǀ ⏑	⏑	– ǀ –	⏑ ǀ ⏑	– ' –	⏑	⏑	– ǀ ⏑	–	–

× – ⏑ ⏑ – – ἰ]οκ[ό]λπων κάλα δῶρα, παῖδες,
× – ⏑ ⏑ – –]ν φιλάοιδον λιγύραν χελύνναν·
–]

× – ⏑ ⏑ – –] ποτ' [ἔ]οντα χρόα γῆρας ἤδη
× – ⏑ ⏑ – – ἐγ]ένοντο τρίχες ἐκ μελαίναν·
–]

βάρυς δὲ μ' ὀ [θ]ῦμος πεπόηται, γόνα δ' [ο]ὐ φέροισι,   5
τὰ δή ποτα λαίψηρ' ἔον ὄρχησθ' ἴσα νεβρίοισι.

τὰ <μὲν> στεναχίσδω θαμέως· ἀλλὰ τί κεν ποείην;
ἀγήραον ἄνθρωπον ἔοντ' οὐ δύνατον γένεσθαι.

—

καὶ γάρ π[ο]τα Τίθωνον ἔφαντο βροδόπαχυν Αὔων
ἔρωι ⏑ ⏑ – ανβάμεν' ἐς ἔσχατα γᾶς φέροισα[ν,   10

—

ἔοντα [κ]άλον καὶ νέον, ἀλλ' αὖτον ὔμως ἔμαρψε
χρόνωι πόλιον γῆρας, ἔχ[ο]ντ' ἀθανάταν ἄκοιτιν.

The expected cut between the second and third choriamb is entirely miss-ing in the second half of the verse for the first six lines, whereas a pyrrhic-shaped word—in every case an unelided, lexical word—is marked off in five of these lines. Such words are neither rare nor common. They occur on the average about once in every ten lines of the hendecasyllable of Book One, but never twice in a row. They were entirely absent from the eight lines I analyzed above.[19] The series of words here—κάλα, χρόα, τρίχες, γόνα, ἴσα—represents a notable rhythmic variation. This is combined with the persistent deviation from the normal line structure in the preceding four syllables of the first five lines, in which the preserved or highly probable word occupies a minor ionic shape that bridges the expected cut: ἰ]οκ[ό]λπων, φιλάοιδον, ποτ' [ἔ]ϱοντα, ἐγ]ένοντο, πεπόηται. Together these oddities must both unify the six lines that describe the singer's woes and contribute to a peculiar effect. There is an obvious parallel in the persistence of cuts after the fourth syllable and the absence of them after the fifth in the "pathography" of fr. 31. In this poem the deviations come to a sudden halt with punctuation between the choriambs in line 7, as the singer dismisses the complaints and turns to the consolation or recompense suggested by the myth. After that there are no more isolated pyrrhic words in the poem (only the word group καὶ νέον in line 11), and we find varied expressions of the normal structure for the last half of the verse. One the other hand, the trisyllabic final cadence—weakly (after a prepositive) and inconsistently marked in the first six lines—is enunciated with increasing clarity, so that only a god's name violates it in the last six lines.

The absence of the opening of the first four lines makes it impossible to know whether a similar rigidity characterized the beginnings of the verses, but the persistent absence of a cut between the choriambs from lines 5–10 and the word-end following the spondee in the fifth and sixth syllables in lines 5–7 suggest that it did. The supplements Μοίσαν and λεῦκον for lines 1 and 4, which seem certain for other reasons, would also fulfill the pattern, so it seems all the more likely. This could have consequences for how we supplement the rest of the text. Given the pattern, the article in line 2, καὶ τὰ]ν, printed by West (following Gronewald-Daniel's πάλιν τὰμ), which would be unexpected simply as an article, seems all the more improbable; I have suggested φώνα]ν or αὔδα]ν as the object of a verb (allowing the last two words of the line to be read as genitive plurals). If we are to keep ἄπαλον in line 3, then Gronewald's and Daniel's original suggestion of ἄπαλόν μοι would cause less variation than Di Benedetto's ἄπαλον πρὶν, printed by West.

---

[19] I suspect that those eight are somewhat unusual in having none at all; I count another eight instances in the scraps numbered 59–88 in Voigt's text (63.3, 7; 65.7, 9; 68.7, 8; 70.10; 71.5). Pyrrhic words may be slightly more common in lines with dactylic expansion; there are five in Sappho 44 V and one in almost every one of the remaining quotations from Book Two. The diminished opportunities to use words with internal spondees might have led to a different set of vocabulary choices (originally formulas) in the meter of Book Two. In discussing Book One I am including the third hendecasyllable.

In the last couplet of the poem, the expected cuts are expressed in all instances, softened only by elision. The return to the normative structure brings the myth and the emotional journey to a close (one can again compare Sappho 31 V, where, in the final hendecasyllable, the normative cut after the fifth syllable returns, and there is no cut after the fourth). This pattern is maintained by as much as can be recovered from the quotation by Athenaeus that would occupy lines 15 and 16, if these are part of the same poem.

The observation of these tendencies can have, at best, a suggestive value when it comes to answering the questions of what to print, and a cautionary value when we try to fill in verses with our own composition; more importantly, they can also aid us in appreciating the artistry of the texts that we do have or can reconstruct.

Bibliography

Campbell, D. A., ed. 1982. *Greek Lyric I.* Cambridge MA. Corrected second edition 1990.

Consbruch, M., ed. 1906. *Hephaestionis Enchiridion cum commentariis veteribus.* Leipzig. Reprinted Stuttgart 1971.

Gallavotti, C. 1957. *Saffo e Alceo: Testimonianze e frammenti.* Vol 1 *Saffo* rev. ed. 3. Naples.

Gronewald, M., and Daniel, R. W. 2004. "Ein neuer Sappho-Papyrus." *Zeitschrift für Papyrologie und Epigraphik* 147:1–8.

Hunt, A. S. 1922. "New Classical Fragments. 1787. Sappho, Book IV." *Oxyrhynchus Papyri Part XV* (ed. B. P. Grenfell and A. S. Hunt) 26–46. London.

Korzeniewski, D. 1968. *Griechische Metrik. Die Altertumswissenschaft.* Darmstadt.

Liberman, G., ed. 2002. *Alcée: Fragments.* Paris.

Liberman, G. 2007. "L'édition alexandrine de Sappho." *Atti del convegno internazionale di studi 'I papiri di Saffo e di Alceo': Firenze 8–9 giugno 2006* (ed. G. Bastianini and A. Casanova) 41–65. Studi e Testi di Papirologia n.s. 9. Florence.

Lidov, J. B. 1993. "The Second Stanza of Sappho 31: Another Look." *American Journal of Philology* 114:503–535.

Lobel, E., ed. 1925. ΣΑΠΦΟΥΣ ΜΕΛΗ: *The Fragments of the Lyrical Poems of Sappho.* Oxford.

Lobel, E., and Page, D. L., eds. 1963. *Poetarum Lesbiorum Fragmenta.* Oxford. First edition 1955. (= *L-P*)

L-P. See Lobel and Page 1963.

Nagy, G. 1996. "Metrical Convergences and Divergences in Early Greek Poetry and Song." *Struttura e storia dell'esametro greco* vol. 2 (ed. M. Fantuzzi and R. Pretagostini) 63–110. Studi di metrica classica 10. Rome. Revised version of Appendix to *Pindar's Homer* (Baltimore 1990).

Page, D. L. 1955. *Sappho and Alcaeus: An Introduction to the Study of Ancient Lesbian Poetry*. Oxford. Corrected reprint 1959.

Parker, L. P. E. 2001. "*Consilium et ratio?* Papyrus A of Bacchylides and Alexandrian Metrical Scholarship." *Classical Quarterly* 51:23–52.

Powell, J., trans. 1993. *Sappho, a Garland: The Poems and Fragments of Sappho*. New York.

V. See Voigt 1971.

van Ophuijsen, J. M. 1993. "On Poems: Two Hephaestionic Texts and One Chapter from Aristides Quintilianus on the Composition of Verse." *ANRW* II.34.1:796–869.

Voigt, E.-M., ed. 1971. *Sappho et Alcaeus: Fragmenta*. Amsterdam. (= V)

West, M. L. 1982. *Greek Metre*. Oxford.

Yatromanolakis, D. 1999. "Alexandrian Sappho Revisited." *Harvard Studies in Classical Philology* 99:179–195.

9

"Once" and "Now"
Temporal Markers and Sappho's Self-Representation

Eva Stehle

IT IS WELL KNOWN THAT MEMORY PLAYS AN IMPORTANT ROLE in Sappho's poetry. As scholars have emphasized, Sappho vividly evokes the past, even "blurs" past and present, through her poetic recall.[1] But the fragment and the apparently complete poem yielded by the new Cologne papyri call attention to a different dimension of Sappho's treatment of time, for temporal markers are surprisingly prominent in them.[2] Lines 1–8, the last lines of a poem that I call the Thalia poem, has *nun* twice, while the new version of 58 V (lines 9–20), which I call the Tithonos poem, has three instances of *pota*, and possibly one or more of *nun*, if suggested supplements are accepted.[3] *Nun* and *pota* as "now" and "once" are distinct in aspect as well as time. *Pota* is unaccented and indefinite, unlocated in calendric chronology, while *nun* is definite, emphatic, close at hand. They are common words, often found together, but Sappho uses them with unusual density in these two poems, and uses them in the context of her meditations on death and old age—two subjects intimately linked to time.[4]

---

[1] Hutchinson 2001 uses the word "blur." See also Greene 1994, Stehle 1997:297.

[2] See Gronewald and Daniel 2004a and 2004b for the new fragments.

[3] I accept the Cologne text as a complete poem. See Bernsdorff 2005a and 2005b and Edmunds, this volume, for the dispute over whether an "open ending" is plausible. Edmunds shows that it is rare in archaic monody, but Sappho is an innovative poet, and she draws the moral before adducing the myth. Moreover, lines 23–26 do not appear to pick up an earlier idea, whereas Sappho's return from myth, simile, etc, is sharp and elegant in 1, 2, 16, 31, and 96. It may be that the relevant idea was in 23–24, but the few extant words do not encourage that thought. See also Rawles 2006 for a nuanced view, di Benedetto 1985:153–63 for an older one. Gronewald and Daniel 2004a:3–4 suggest a reference to Phaon.

[4] Gronewald and Daniel 2004a:2–3 point out the thematic associations between the two poems. See also Clayman, this volume.

Indefinite past and emphatic present: how does Sappho see their relationship to her mortality? The new Sappho inspires me to reexamine the articulation of time in her poetry. What I find is that "once" is an imaginary time of mythic, erotic plenitude, and "now" is a time of performative speech that, among other things, looks forward to the heroization of the poet. In other words, Sappho as speaker presents herself as poised between two eras when she is close to divinity. My reading is inevitably subjective, and I include some fragments that consist of no more than a few suggestive words. But by teasing out the contrasts that these two words imply and taking them in the strongest sense they will bear, I think I can identify an underlying pattern that runs through Sappho's conception of her past, present, and future.

I begin with *pota* in the Tithonos poem. The three instances mark two different pasts: the first two refer to Sappho's own lost youth (lines 11 and 14), while the third in line 17 refers to the distant, heroic past, when Dawn carried off Tithonos.[5] The resonance among the adverbs suggests that Sappho's youth parallels Tithonos' youthful beauty when Dawn fell in love with him. Alerted by the multiple instances of *pota* here, we can look for similar double past times in other poems. The most striking case is Sappho's 16 V, even though it does not contain an explicit *pota*, for it also includes both a myth and Sappho's own past. It can help us understand the Tithonos poem, and the latter, in turn, can illuminate 16 by making us think about time.

In 16 V, as in the Tithonos poem, Sappho adduces a myth to illustrate a human truth that she states and applies to herself as well. In 16 V the truth is that the most beautiful is whatever one loves. The myth of Helen leaving home for Troy is introduced by *gar* in line 6 as an exemplum; there is no immediate indication that has deeper relevance for Sappho beyond its logical usefulness (hence perhaps no *pota*).[6] But the narrative quickly takes on a more complex form, for it contrasts conventional, male assessment (Helen as most beautiful of humans, 6–7; Menelaus as "best," 8) with the implied perception of the female lover (Paris as most beautiful).[7] Sappho then marks the transition to her own case with *nun* in line 15:

> . . . now reminded [me] of Anaktoria, who is not here, whose
> lovely walk I would rather see, and the bright sparkle of her

[5] For the story see *Homeric Hymn to Aphrodite* 218–38; Hellanikos FgrH 4 F 140, where the god changes him into a cicada; *LIMC* s.v. Eos.

[6] See Most 1981 on Sappho as exemplum.

[7] Stehle 1990; Worman 1997:167–70.

face, than the Lydian chariots and foot soldiers with their weapons.

Sappho does not simply name one who now seems most beautiful to her, but instead expresses longing to see her. Anaktoria's being beautiful is a memory, not a description of what Sappho actually sees when she looks.[8] Sappho and Anaktoria, now separated, were therefore together at some past time, and the poem's audience is invited to recall that army, fleet, and Menelaus forced Helen to return to her assigned place also. What is left implicit in Helen's story is her being violently separated from the one she loved, and what is left implicit in Sappho's story of loving Anaktoria is that they were once together. It is as though Sappho's story is the continuation and completion of Helen's story. Thus, in the deep structure of her poem, Sappho creates a temporal alignment that does not separate the mythic time of Helen from her own past but rather separates lovers together from lovers parted. In mythic time a female lover (Helen or Sappho) can choose her love and experience intimacy, whereas *nun* (for Helen and Sappho) is the time when the conventional social structure has intervened. This difference between mythic time and now is marked cognitively as well: Helen "did not remember" (*oude . . . emnasthē*, lines 10–11) her child or parents when [Aphrodite?] led her off to Troy, but her story "reminds" (*onemnais'*, lines 15–16) Sappho of Anaktoria. Helen, that is, could forget her assigned familial place, but Sappho can only remember her love.

We can read the Tithonos poem in light of *nun* in 16 V. It presents a similar temporal divide: "once" a goddess chose the young, beautiful Tithonos as her love. But in this case it is human feebleness, not the social structure, that intervenes: Tithonos grows old. What is left implicit this time is that Eos abandoned Tithonos and that Sappho was once the intimate of a goddess, Aphrodite surely. Sappho suggests as much when she laments (13–14), "my knees do not carry (me), which truly once were nimble to dance like fawns." *Orcheisthai* ("to dance") is not found in the rest of Sappho's extant work, but does occur in two fragments that Voigt lists as *incerti auctoris* but which many would consider Sapphic. The first is *inc. auct.* 16:

> Cretan women indeed once (*pot'*) thus gracefully with their
> tender feet danced around the lovely altar . . . treading the
> tender bloom of the grass . . .

---

[8] See Brown 1989 on the poetic associations of the "bright sparkle" of Anaktoria's face.

The time is "once," and this is an idealizing image. The other fragment is a scrap, *inc. auct.* 35:

> . . . Aphrodite . . . being freed . . . to you certainly . . . of women
> . . . blowing (?) . . . dance (OR: to dance), lovely Abanthis.

In both cases the adjective "lovely" (*eroeis*) occurs in the vicinity of "dance." Aphrodite appears in *inc. auct.* 35, and the altar in 16 could be hers.[9] In the Tithonos poem too, dancing may signify being in the presence of Aphrodite and/or being in a divinely-charged erotic space. If so, then "once" represents a time when Aphrodite was present for Sappho, whereas now that her knees are weak Aphrodite has abandoned her. Sappho would then finish Tithonos' story, his loss of the Dawn's love, just as she finishes Helen's story in 16 V. The Tithonos poem and 16 V, read together, suggest that for Sappho the time of myth extends up her own youth and past loves.

The mythic quality of Sappho's personal "once" is more explicit in 1 V, which shows Aphrodite coming in response to Sappho's prayer for help "once."[10] Poem 1 V contains both *pota* and *nun* within a prayer structure (as often). Sappho apostrophizes Aphrodite in the first stanza, then opens the second with a request (5–7): "But come here, if also once at another time (*ai pota k'aterota*), hearing my words from afar, you listened . . . ." With *pota* in line 5 Sappho opens the gates of memory, through which floods the picture of Aphrodite's past arrival(s) in her sparrow-chariot, and she again hears Aphrodite's voice. Aphrodite takes over Sappho's own voice to address Sappho, and, using it, promises Sappho fulfillment of her wish. In the final stanza (line 25) Sappho reclaims her voice and says, "Come to me *now* also . . . ." By using a standard prayer form to recount her experience of a god's undisguised presence and speech, Sappho again distinguishes two times, a "now" when she prays and a mythical time "once" when the goddess came in person, as if to a Homeric hero, in response to a call for help.[11] There is no myth except the one she creates by using epic imagery of a god's advent to recount her own past.[12] Rather than assimilate herself to a mythic figure as she does in 16 V to Helen, she

---

[9] An altar appears in 2.3 V in the enchanted landscape where Aphrodite is invited to pour nectar mixed with festivity (*thalia*) into golden cups.

[10] See esp. Greene 2002 on this poem.

[11] See Segal 1974.153 and *passim* on the incantatory quality of Sappho's poetry. With Sappho's mythicizing compare Ferrari 2002:17–19 and chs. 1–2 passim, who suggests that images of women together cannot be divided between mythic and genre scenes.

[12] Winkler 1990:167–70 discusses Sappho's self-identification with Diomedes and the parallels with Homer's description of Athena and Hera mounting and driving a chariot to go to the battle

here presents her own earlier self as the one whom Aphrodite favored. But Eos snatching Tithonos, Aphrodite leading Helen to Troy, and Aphrodite coming to Sappho to promise her erotic fulfillment all occupy the indefinite past time.

Sappho 1 V is not the only poem in which she places herself in a scene with Aphrodite in the indefinite past. Sappho encounters the goddess again in a more fragmentary poem, 22 V. After requesting (*kelomai*) another woman, possibly Abanthis, to sing and describing a third woman's desire for her (Abanthis), Sappho adds (14–19), "and I rejoice, for indeed Aphrodite herself once censured (me) because I pray . . . this . . . I want . . . ." One might think of Aphrodite blaming Helen in *Iliad* 3.414–17. Again, in the broken fragments at the end of 96 V appear the words (26–28), "Aphrodite . . . was pouring (OR: used to pour) nectar from a golden . . . ." This episode too must belong to "once" when she was visible to Sappho, and the nectar emphasizes the mythic, idyllic quality of the scene.[13] Thus in several poems Sappho portrays her past interaction with Aphrodite in the glow of myth, or, we could say, in a time continuous with the time of myth. To put it another way, Sappho "blurs" myth and memory but separates them from "now."

A subtler use of *pota* appears in 96 V.[14] Here an idyllic landscape is the setting for "once," the sort of place, perhaps, in which Sappho's knees were "nimble to dance like fawns." The first two preserved stanzas of 96 V are fragmentary, so we cannot tell whether *pota* was included, but the one legible clause (5) says "and she used to delight especially in your song." The imperfect gives the indefinite temporal sense of *pota*. The clause also shows that Sappho is addressing one woman about another and that those two were together in the past and are now separated. Other isolated words suggest a magical time; there are hints of divine beauty in *arignota* ("very eminent") and *theasikelan* ("like a goddess"), however they are to be emended and construed.[15]

Then in the third stanza we find *nun* (6) introducing the separation of the two women, for one of them is now in Lydia. Sappho does not use a first-person

---

at Troy in *Iliad* 5 lines 719–32, 767–72. For Diomedes' prayer see *Iliad* 5 lines 115–20. See also n. 25.

[13] See also 2 lines 13–16 V for the image of Aphrodite pouring nectar.

[14] On this poem see Snyder 1997:45–55, esp. 49–52 on *nun de* and the simile of the moon; Stehle 1997:300–302.

[15] Voigt obelizes *theasikelan arignota* but favors the interpretation *se theaic' ikelan Arignota*, taking Arignota as a proper name in vocative or nominative. Hutchinson 2001:179 also favors the proper name. Page 1955 ad loc. prefers to take *arignota<i>* as an adjective agreeing with singular *thea<i>*, citing *Od.* 6 line 108, where it is used of Artemis. Since, as he points out (89 ad 4–5), the name does not appear among those known later from her poems, I adopt his view. The word is used of Artemis in *Od.* 6 line 108.

verb of speaking here but describes the distant woman as if her gaze could reach that far (6–17):

> Now (*nun*) she is conspicuous among Lydian women as (was) once (*pot'*), the sun having set, the rose-fingered moon outshining all the stars; its light spreads over the salty sea and the flowery fields; the beautiful dew settles; roses bloom and tender chervil and flowerlike honey-lotus. Wandering often throughout, remembering gentle Atthis, she eats out . . . her delicate heart with longing.

In line 7 something odd occurs: within the account that begins with *nun* Sappho introduces the simile marked by *pot'*. The *pot'* is difficult, as Hutchinson remarks in his commentary on this poem; the verbs describing the moon's effect are all present (*epischei, kechutai, tethalaisi*), but taking *pot'* as "sometimes" is intolerably feeble.[16] However, in light of the earlier examples, I think that Sappho uses *pot'* to mark an unlocated mythic time, a past that is still visible when the moon fills the night with the same kind of erotic plenitude that Selene once did when she visited the sleeping Endymion and that Aphrodite does by her presence.[17] We know that Sappho told the story of the Moon's love for Endymion.[18] The flowers blooming under the stimulus of dew are those found in Sappho's imaginative erotic spaces belonging to sleep, death, and the gods.[19] The woman in Lydia becomes goddess-like by being identified with the moon and placed in this setting.[20] *Pot'* is the sign that she has been absorbed into myth.

In lines 15–17, Sappho returns to the woman with *zaphoitais'* ("wandering throughout"), an image ambiguously referring to her as permeating the space like the moon or wandering in lonely rootlessness. As the sentence continues, however, the latter meaning dominates: she is eating out her heart in longing. Time has shifted back to *nun*. Rhetorically it is as though the woman in Lydia is snatched away afresh from an embracing "once." Or we could say that, in a stunning poetic collage, Sappho shows us the woman as she lives

---

[16] Hutchinson 2001:180 ad 7–8. West emends to *os ot'* (Hutchinson ad loc and app. crit.) Contrast 34 V: "The stars around the beautiful moon hide their shining shape whenever (*hoppote*) it is full and lights most brightly the earth . . . ." The verb is subjunctive.

[17] Cf. the mixture of physical description and appeal to the goddess in *Homeric Hymn* 32 to Selene and in 154 V: "The moon appeared full and they (female) stood as around an altar . . . ." For association of altar with dancing, Aphrodite, and erotic landscapes, see below.

[18] Cf. 199 V and Stehle 1990, esp. 89 and n. 5 on Tithonos.

[19] See 2.6 V for roses, 95.12 V for lotus on the banks of Acheron; Boedeker 1979:47–50.

[20] See Williamson 1995:151–52 on this effect.

both in the seductive "once" of those who remember and fantasize about her (myth and memory blurred) and in her own painful "now."[21] This is a different poetic effect, created for speaking to one woman about another, from Sappho's self-description in the Tithonos poem, where she rigorously separates the two times, just as she does in speaking of herself in 1 V.

In both 96 V and 16 V Sappho uses a traditional trope—the moon/woman surpasses (*perrechoisa*) the stars as Helen is surpassing (*perschethoisa*, 6) in beauty among humans—but she uses it in unexpected ways, adding dimensions (Helen's choice as anti-conventional, the moon's erotic stimulus on flowering plants) and making them operate as implicit narratives rather than static comparisons. In the Tithonos poem she uses a less familiar image that combines innocent youth (the fawns) with erotic joy (dancing) to evoke a hint of the same landscape and potential for new love.

If *pota* signals the mythic time of female choice, erotic plenitude, and youth, what characterizes *nun*, time now? It is, first of all, a time of limitations recognized. In the Tithonos poem Sappho acknowledges (16) that "it is not possible for humans to be unaging" (note *ou dunaton genesthai*). In 16 V she says (21–22), in the first line of the stanza following the one quoted above, just as the papyrus gives out, ". . . it is not possible [for ?] to become (*ou dunaton genesthai*) . . . human(s) . . . to pray to share . . . ." Recognition of reality puts the time "now" beyond the boundary of myth. Her view is like Homer's at moments in the *Iliad* when he looks back from the perspective of his own time: "such as humans are *now*."[22] Of course, Tithonos' aging is as much a part of the myth as Dawn's carrying him off, but when Dawn closes the doors to lock him away from her, he disappears from myth and becomes part of "now," a cicada. By assimilating his old age to her own, Sappho draws a parallel between their experience.

Nun is also the time of remembering, as in 16.15–16 V. Recognition is the other face of memory; they provoke each other.[23] As the time of reality and recognition, separation and memory, *nun* is also the time of emphatic speech. In 16 V Sappho recalls, utters a wish, and asserts her perception (*egō de [phaimi]*, 3). In the Tithonos poem, Sappho says (15), "These things I groan over often,"

---

[21] Cf. 17 V, in which Sappho prays (?) to Hera. In the prayer (or memory; see Voigt ad loc), she refers to the Atreidai being unable to leave Troy, apparently to come to Lesbos. In line 11, with *nun*, she shifts from myth to her present concern, whatever that was. 62 V, a scrap with twelve line beginnings, contains *pot'* and *nun*. Fragment 166 V reads, "They say that Leda *once* found a hyacinthine . . . egg." Conversely, in 160 V we find "these delightful (?) things I *now* sing beautifully to my (female) companions."

[22] E.g., *Il.* 20 lines 285–87: Aeneas picks up a boulder "that even two men could not carry . . . ."

[23] For an interesting study from the perspective of rhetorical theory see Jarrett 2002.

or, with Richard Janko's metrical supplement, "These things I now groan over often" (*ta nun stenachizō thameōs*). As in 16 V, she articulates a truth based on the memory and a desire to return to the remembered time. In 1 V "now" is the time of her prayer (25): "come to me now also." In 22 V she commands and announces her gladness in light of her recollection. All of these are forms of expressive or performative speaking, a self-conscious measuring of the distance at which Sappho stands from the desired past.

In recalling mythic time Sappho is like a bard bringing the lost heroic past to light again through memory. But she is a bard for whom the memory and loss are personal as well as mythic, so she does not just recite. She groans, wishes, prays for the return of divine presence, or acknowledges its impossibility with a resigned rhetorical question. While, as bard, she tells us about that past, she presents herself as wishing to re-experience it herself. This combination of mythic grandeur and personal investment is one source of Sappho's poetic power.[24] But we cannot speak simply of Sappho's recapturing memory; she reshapes it into a different kind of past, emotionally absolute, supremely vivid, and now accessible only through poetry—like myth. In other words, the temporal divide gives Sappho's poetry its monumentality.[25]

This brings us to the Thalia poem, which can teach us more about *nun*. The word appears twice. In the first instance, *nun thalia* ("now festivity . . .," 3), she may have been making a declarative statement, or, as in other poems in which *nun* is the time of performative speech, she may be asserting that festivity should occur now. The first editors supply *ge[noito* or *ge[nesthō*, that is, "may there be (OR: let there be) festivity." In line 6 she refers to "now" when she is on earth rather than under it. In this poem (unlike the ones so far examined), she associates "now" with her singing.[26] *Thalia*, of course, involves music along with other kinds of festivity. More specifically (7–8), Sappho is now (apparently) *liguran* ("clear-voiced") "whenever taking hold of the lyre . . . I sing, Muse, beautiful things."

At the same time, in the extant lines, at least, these references to "now" do not contrast with the past; instead, they offer a model for the future. As artist, Sappho is concerned with her status in future time, so her performative speak-

---

[24] Cf. Stehle 1997:299–300 and 310–11.

[25] For Sappho's relationship to Homer see Winkler 1990:167–70, 175–77, Snyder 1997:63–78, Rosenmeyer 1997:133–47. For Hellenistic views of Sappho as a "female Homer" and bibliography on earlier studies, see Gosetti-Murrayjohn 2006:37–40.

[26] Di Benedetto 2005:11–12 notes the connections among *nun*, singing, and beauty.

ing in this context predicts the heroizing of the poet Sappho rather than recalling the mythic lover Sappho.[27] A tentative translation might read (4–8):

> [me being] . . . beneath the earth . . . having a prize-of-honor
> (*geras*) as is appropriate . . . may they [?marvel at] as now
> when I am on the earth . . . clear-voiced, whenever taking
> hold of the lyre . . . I sing, Muse, beautiful things.[28]

Sappho speaks of being remembered after death in other fragments: 147; Aristides, *Or.* 28.51 (= 55 V Test); and, implicitly, 55 and 150 V. She connects remembrance of her to her association with the Muses in all of these except 147, and speaks of the Muses as making her "honored" in 32 V.[29] Here, however, she takes the idea farther. She describes herself as "marveled at" now (if *[thauma]zoien* is the correct supplement) and hopes that she will still rouse wonder and have the *geras* she deserves after she is dead.[30] *Geras* is a concrete gift in honor of a human or a divinity.

With the Thalia poem we should compare 65.5–10 V. The remains are very fragmentary:

> Sappho, the queen (?) of Cyprus (= Aphrodite?) loves (?) you,
> although great(ly) . . . for as many people as shining [?the
> sun] . . . everywhere fame (*kleos*) . . . and you also in Acheron
> . . . .

This scrap adds *kleos* to Sappho's vocabulary of current renown and/or continued honor after death. [31] The Thalia poem together with 65 V thus gives us a list: *geras, kleos, thauma*. These suggest the honors paid to heroes. In the face of death, Sappho seems to claim for herself what Homer creates for his heroes:

---

[27] Cf. 147, and (by implication) 55 V and *test.* IV, including Aristides *Or.* 28.51 (=193 Lobel and Page), which refers to Sappho saying in a similar context that there will not be forgetfulness of her after death.

[28] Conceivably a lost noun is the subject of the feminine accusative participles and adjective in 5–7. The speaker's *aeidō* at the end of 8 would then belong to a short summary clause.

[29] Skinner 1991:80–90 identifies Aphrodite as Sappho's Muse; I would modify that conclusion to say that Aphrodite is the inspiration for Sappho's self-mythologizing, while she associates the Muses with her poetry as artistry. For a different view of Sappho's vision of the underworld and her continued existence, see di Benedetto 2005.

[30] See Hardie 2005:22–27 for the idea of immortality in the underworld here.

[31] Di Benedetto 2005:15 points out that *kleos* appears elsewhere in Sappho only in 44 V, a narrative in "epic" style of the wedding of Hector and Andromache. In 95 V Sappho recounts a past interchange with Hermes (?) about wishing to die and see the banks of Acheron dewy with lotus. Boedeker 1979:49 notes the similarity to Elysium.

fame and honors in response to lives lived at the extreme of intensity, lives in which the gods take an interest and that make more mundane humans wonder. So she desires to be heroized as the bard of her own "mythic" experience (and that of other women who choose their loves). In the future her "now" of song and the "once" of the mythic experience that it records will be united when future generations marvel at her vivid re-imagining of her interactions with Aphrodite and experience of female erotic subjectivity.

Her declaration, "now *thalia*," may therefore be a proclamation that festivity—the festivity with which she should be honored in the future—is to start now. Her performative words turn the present into that festivity for the audience of the poem. Since, within the poem, she is always still "now on earth," she must always inspire celebration of *thalia* "now." *Paides* are the next generation, who will pass on the message to celebrate by singing this song in her voice. (For readers, too, she is always still alive and marveled at, while hoping that the wonder will persist.)

I thus prefer the supplement to the first line of the Tithonos poem suggested by Gronewald and Daniel (*pherō tade Mousan io-*, which yields, "I bring these beautiful gifts of the violet-breasted Muses") to the one proposed by V. di Benedetto (*gerairete Moisan io-*, "Honor the beautiful gifts of the violet-breasted Muses").[32] The first makes Sappho claim the Muses' gifts. In light of the Thalia poem, where she views her poetic performance as a way of surviving death, she is surely more likely to emphasize her poetry and singing as the Muses' gift to her in old age.[33]

And that brings us back, finally, to Tithonos. I said earlier that what is left implicit in this poem is that Eos abandoned Tithonos and that Sappho was once the intimate of Aphrodite. But just as Sappho's story does not end with loss of Aphrodite's favor, neither does Tithonos'. In the version of the myth found in the *Homeric Hymn to Aphrodite* Tithonos becomes a singer in his old age (237–38). There has been debate over whether we should assume that Sappho is allud-

---

[32] Gronewald and Daniel 2004a:7, but see Luppe 2004:8; cf. Lidov, this volume, for another suggestion making Sappho the one with the gifts of the Muses; di Benedetto 1985:148–49. On 147 he adduces 21 V, where references to old age and a request to another to sing appear; we cannot assume that the situation there is parallel to that of the Thalia poem. West 2005:4–5 suggests *ummes peda Moisan io-* and *spoudasdete kai ta]n* for the first two lines, which yield, "you, together with the violet-breasted Muses, children, be eager for their beautiful gifts and for the song-loving, clear-voiced lyre."

[33] Unlike Homer, Sappho links the Muses with being remembered rather than remembering. Her "musicality" ensures her fame, another reason for her to claim the Muses' gift.

ing to that conclusion of the story.[34] I think that, just as she "finishes" Helen's story in 16 V with her wish to see her own love again, so it is open to us to construe this poem as Sappho completing Tithonos' story by singing in her old age. Tithonos becomes a singer when he loses the attention of Eos and drops out of the myth, and likewise Sappho presents herself as a singer who in old age can no longer experience the indefinite, mythic past of erotic plenitude. We should imagine Tithonos too, like the woman in Lydia in 96 V, as thrust out from "once" into "now," where he (still) sings beautifully about his lost youth, love, and life in loveliness with a goddess.

Together the poems seem to outline a temporal sequence: mythic plenitude in an indefinite past, song recreating or requesting renewal of that (imaginary) plenitude in the present, and immortality in hero-cult, figuratively or literally, in the future, based on the power of the singer's song and by analogy with Tithonos. *Thalia* now and Tithonos in the past and future (beloved beauty and eternal singer) comprise the trajectory Sappho envisions for herself and the place of her poetry in it.

Bibliography

Boedeker, D. 1979. "Sappho and Acheron." *Arktouros: Hellenic Studies Presented to Bernard M. W. Knox* (ed. G. W. Bowersock, W. Burkert, M. C. J. Putnam) 40–52. Berlin.

Brown, C. 1989. "Anactoria and the *Charitōn amarugmata*: Sappho fr. 16, 18 Voigt." *Quaderni Urbinati di Cultura Classica* 32:7–15.

Di Benedetto, V. 1985. "Il Tema della Vecchiaia e il fr. 58 di Saffo." *Quaderni Urbinati di Cultura Classica* 19:145–63.

Bernsdorff, H. 2005a. "Offene Gedichtschlüsse." *Zeitschrift für Papyrologie und Epigraphik* 153:1–6.

———. 2005b. "La Nuova Saffo e Dintorni." *Zeitschrift für Papyrologie und Epigraphik* 153:7–20.

duBois, P. 1995. *Sappho is Burning*. Chicago.

Ferrari, G. 2002. *Figures of Speech: Men and Maidens in Ancient Greece*. Chicago.

---

[34] Geissler 2005:107–8 argues that Sappho does not stress Tithonos' immortality, since she cannot achieve that, but that the open ending can imply the survival of his voice. Cf. also 101A V, a description of a cicada pouring out "clear-voiced song." It is not clear that Tithonos was identified with the cicada before the Hellenistic period, but the statement in the *Hymn to Aphrodite* (237) that "his voice flows ceaselessly," with its present tense, implies some such transformation. So, tentatively, Rawles 2006:5–7.

Geissler, C. 2005. "Der Tithonosmythos bei Sappho und Kallimachos: Zu Sappho fr. 58 V, 11–22 und Kallimachos, Aitia fr. 1 Pf." *Göttinger Forum für Altertumswissenschaft* 8:105–14.

Gosetti-Murrayjohn, A. 2006. "Sappho as the Tenth Muse in Hellenistic Epigram." *Arethusa* 39:21–45.

Greene, E. 1994. "Apostrophe and Women's Erotics in the Poetry of Sappho." *Transactions of the American Philological Association* 124:41–56. Repr. in Greene 1996:233–47.

———, ed. 1996. *Reading Sappho: Contemporary Approaches.* Berkeley.

———. 2002. "Subjects, Objects, and Erotic Symmetry in Sappho's Fragments." In Rabinowitz and Auanger 2002:82–105.

Hardie, A. 2005. "Sappho, the Muses, and Life after Death." *Zeitschrift für Papyrologie und Epigraphik* 154:13–32.

Hutchinson, G. O. 2001. *Greek Lyric Poetry: A Commentary on Selected Larger Pieces.* Oxford.

Jarrett, S. 2002. "Sappho's Memory." *Rhetoric Society Quarterly* 32:11–43.

Luppe, W. 2004. "Überlegungen zur Gedicht-Anordnung im neuen Sappho-Papyrus." *Zeitschrift für Papyrologie und Epigraphik* 149:7–9.

Most, G. 1981. "Sappho Fr. 16.6–7 L.-P." *Classical Quarterly* 31:11–17.

Page, D. 1955. *Sappho and Alcaeus: An Introduction to the Study of Ancient Lesbian Poetry.* Oxford.

Rabinowitz, N. S., and Auanger, L., eds. 2002. *Among Women: From the Homosocial to the Homoerotic in the Ancient World.* Austin.

Rawles, R. 2006. "Notes on the Interpretation of the 'New Sappho'." *Zeitschrift für Papyrologie und Epigraphik* 157:1–7.

Rosenmeyer, P. 1997. "Her Master's Voice: Sappho's Dialogue with Homer." *Materiali e Discussioni per l'Analisi dei Testi Classici* 39:123–49.

Segal, C. 1974. "Eros and Incantation: Sappho and Oral Poetry." *Arethusa* 7:139–60.

Skinner, M. 1991. "Aphrodite Garlanded: *Erôs* and Poetic Creativity in Sappho and Nossis." *Rose di Pieria* (ed. F. de Martino) 79–96. Bari.

Snyder, J. 1997. *Lesbian Desire in the Lyrics of Sappho.* New York.

Stehle, E. 1990. "Sappho's Gaze: Fantasies of a Goddess and Young Man." *differences* 2:88–125. Reprinted in Greene 1996:193–225.

———. 1997. *Performance and Gender in Ancient Greece: Nondramatic Poetry in its Setting.* Princeton.

West, M. L. 2005. "The New Sappho." *Zeitschrift für Papyrologie und Epigraphik* 151:1–9.

Williamson, M. 1995. *Sappho's Immortal Daughters.* Cambridge MA.

Winkler, J. J. 1990. *The Constraints of Desire: The Anthropology of Sex and Gender in Ancient Greece.* New York and London.

Worman, N. 1997. "The Body as Argument: Helen in Four Greek Texts." *Classical Antiquity* 16:151–203.

10

The New Sappho in a Hellenistic Poetry Book[1]

Dee Clayman

WHILE MOST OF THE INTEREST IN THE "NEW SAPPHO" (Köln. Inv. Nr. 21351 + 21376) has rightly centered on the "Tithonus" poem, fragments of another precede it on the Cologne papyrus and parts of a third follow.[2] I argue below that the ensemble of three appears to be part of an early Hellenistic[3] poetry book with editorial features familiar from the "new" Posidippus, Theocritus, Callimachus and Meleager, while evidence from the papyrus itself suggests that it is the anthologist's autograph.

The second poem, partly preserved on *P.Oxy.* 1787 (= 58 Voigt), is securely identified as the work of Sappho by a citation in Athenaeus 687b which also guarantees its meter.[4] Aeolic dialect forms and the same meter also characterize the first poem, which was previously unknown, but is very likely to be Sappho's as well. The third, however, is clearly the work of a different author from a later time. Its meter, though impossible to fully reconstruct, has too many contiguous brevi to be Aeolic, its dialect is mixed and some of the vocabulary is relatively "modern."[5]

---

[1] I would like to thank John Lundon for sharing with me a pre-publication version of his essential paper "Il nuovo testo lirico nel nuovo papiro di Saffo," now Lundon 2007, and for his careful reading of my own. I am also grateful to Nita Krevans and all the contributors to this volume for their helpful suggestions. I alone am responsible for the errors.

[2] On the constitution of the text and its divisions see Obbink and Hammerstaedt, Chapters 2 and 3 in this volume. I use Obbink's text below and substitute numbers for his titles as follows: "New Fragment" = poem 1; "The 'Tithonus poem'" = poem 2; and "Continuation 1" = poem 3. The numbers reflect the order of the poems on the papyrus.

[3] The papyrus is dated by its first editors to the early part of the third century BC on the basis of its handwriting which has partly "epigraphic" letter forms (Gronewald and Daniel 2004a:1).

[4] On the meter, see Lidov, Chapter 8 in this volume.

[5] On the non-Sapphic features of the third poem see Gronewald and Daniel 2005:7–8 and especially Lundon 2007:155–157.

It is clear from this that the Cologne papyrus is part of an anthology, but what kind?[6]

Unlike the components of some Hellenistic anthologies which seem to have no relationship to one another,[7] the three poems of *P.Köln.* were selected and arranged within the scope of a single theme: the mortal poet's immortal song. In the first poem, e.g., Sappho,[8] now on earth (ὡς νῦν ἐπὶ γᾶς ἔοισαν, 6), holds her clear-sounding lyre (λιγύραν [α]ἴ κεν ἔλοισα πᾶκτιν, 7) and sings (ἀείδω, 8) while referencing a place below the earth (νέρθε δὲ γᾶς, 4) where she will (or hopes to) receive honor due for the dead (γέρας, 5).[9]

Gronewald and Daniel demonstrate how closely this first poem is tied to the second. Not only are the meter and the Aeolic dialect the same, but striking verbal echoes lead the editors to suggest that the first poem is a Präludium and the second a Stichwort.[10] The verbal echoes highlight thematic ones, and the second poem also features the poet contemplating the end of life. Here she addresses a youthful chorus on "the lovely gifts of the violet-bosomed Muses" (1) and "the clear-sounding lyre" (2). From the pleasures of music, presumably here on earth, she turns to the physical indignities of old age: grey hair, heavy heart, and knees once as swift as fawns that no longer support her in the dance (3–6). But what can she do? (7). It is impossible for a human to avoid growing old (8). Her case in point is Tithonus, a mortal beloved by the goddess Dawn who carried him to the ends of the earth. Though he had an immortal wife, old age seized him (9–12).

Tithonus' story is told in more detail in the *Homeric Hymn to Aphrodite*, 218–38, in a version older than Sappho's. Dawn asked Zeus to make Tithonus immortal, but forgot to request eternal youth so he continued to age indefinitely until he became completely incapacitated, and his goddess-wife had to lock him away. Nevertheless his voice flows on eternally after all of his physical

---

[6] Gronewald and Daniel 2005:8 were the first to suggest that the papyrus did not represent any part of Sappho's collected works, but was instead an anthology. The argument is presented in greater detail in Lundon 2007:157–161.

[7] The poems of *P.Tebt.* I 1 & 2, for example, have no apparent connecting thread, see Lundon 2007:163–164.

[8] On the likelihood that Sappho is the speaker, see West 2005:2.

[9] This is essentially the interpretation of West 2005:2–3 who argues that it is consistent with fr. 65 Voigt and a notice in Aristides (*Or.* 28.51) that Sappho boasted that the Muses had made her blessed and envied and that she would not be forgotten in death. See also Hardie 2005:13–14 and Di Benedetto 1985. An example of Sappho's continued honor in death is Posidippus' "Doricha" poem (AB 122 = 17 GP), see Acosta-Hughes 2004:51–54, Yatromanolakis 2007:326–330 and Lidov 2002.

[10] Gronewald and Daniel 2004a:3.

strength has gone. Tithonus' fate seems like a depressing prospect for most mortals, but an aging poet, like Sappho, may well wish for an immortal voice. In fact, in later retellings of the tale, Tithonus turns into a cicada whose voice, in turn, becomes a paragon of stylistic purity for Hellenistic poets like Posidippus and Callimachus.[11] We do not know if Sappho herself was thinking in these terms, but a Hellenistic editor may well have been, and from this perspective the honor of an immortal voice like Tithonus' is the γέρας after death that Sappho anticipates in the first poem (5). She cannot expect physical immortality, but she can hope that her poetry will live on after her, and her voice will continue to sing as those on earth give her due rights by performing her compositions. The story of Tithonus, then, plays a key role in linking the first poem with the second. This is equally true whether Sappho ended her own poem with Tithonus, or the editor of the Cologne papyrus truncated a longer poem just at this point, as evidence from *P.Oxy.* 1787 seems to suggest.[12]

In any case, the conversation about poetry and death on the Cologne papyrus does not end with the second poem, but continues in the third. Like the first two poems, this one appears to be presented in the first person (ἀφέρπω, 3; ἀκούω, 8) by a female holding a lyre, ([εὔ]φθογγον λύραν.../[συ]νεργὸν ἔχοισα, 12–13), and it seems reasonable to assume, though it cannot be proven, that the narrator is meant to be "Sappho," who is here employing her lyric "I" as she seems to do in the two previous poems.[13] The presence of dicola in the text raises the possibility that she is in dialog with someone else, since dicola are sometimes used in dramatic texts and Platonic dialogs to indicate a change of speaker. The fragments, as they are, however, do not support this view, and it appears that there is only one, female speaker.[14] Dicola are often simply interpunctuations, and the placement in this text of two certain dicola after ἀφέρπω

---

[11] On Sappho and the cicada's immortal voice see Janko 2005; on the cicada in Callimachus, Acosta-Hughes and Stephens 2002:251–53 and Geissler 2005. On the likelihood that Sappho and her readers knew the *Hymn to Aphrodite*, see Rawles 2006:1–4.

[12] See Hammerstadt, pp. 22-24 in this volume.

[13] Gronewald and Daniel 2005:8 say cautiously that a reference to Sappho here is possible, but not certain. In the context of the first two poems, however, what other female would be holding a lyre?

[14] Nominatives probably describing a speaker are of uncertain gender (ἄπνους, 5) or feminine (ἔχοισα, 13). The only potential masculine is πᾶς (8), which, as the editors note, could also be read as πᾶσ', Gronewald and Daniel 2005:11. Lundon 2007:161 observes further that the initial string of vocatives addressed to a male figure are indecisive and that the fragments include no verbal forms in the 2nd person.

(3) and the metrically and grammatically equivalent ἀκούω (8), suggests that this is the case here.[15]

Though its meter and modern diction indicate that it is the work of another, later author, the third poem apparently presents itself as Sappho's own composition. It begins with an address to a deity who is called "slander-twister, crafty one" (ψιθυροπλόκε, δόλιε, 1), which rearranges and gives new direction to Sappho 1.2 Voigt, παῖ Δίος δολόπλοκε, where the epithet refers to Aphrodite. The vocatives continue in a similar vein: "inventor of stories" (μύθων αὐτουργ[έ, 1); "treacherous child" (ἐπίβουλε παῖ, 2); "companion" (ἑταῖρε, 3). These are all possible epithets for Aphrodite or her son Eros,[16] which recall Sappho 188 Voigt where Eros is a "weaver of stories" (μυθόπλοκος) and 1.28 Voigt where Sappho asks Aphrodite to be her "ally" (σύμμαχος). Both Aphrodite and Eros are central figures in Sappho's work, and a poet wishing to evoke it might well begin with an address to one or both of these deities. The clear reference to Sappho 1 Voigt[17] leaves no doubt that the author of the third poem knew her work and meant, at some level, to imitate it.

There is another possible addressee, however. Recently Rawles has called attention to four letters, βοτο, which were written in the second line and then crossed-off together with some others that followed. This he takes to be the first part of a compound adjective in the vocative case that points to an invocation of the cattle-thief Hermes, another deity familiar from Sappho for whom the epithets in verses 1–2 would be appropriate.[18] There is, however, no known Greek word that begins with βοτο-, though it might exist in theory, and further, an argument based on letters deliberately deleted and replaced by others is not an inherently strong one.[19]

After the invocation, the poem proceeds in the first person (ἀφέρπω, 3; ἀκούω, 8) as in the first and second poems. "Sappho" describes herself as "with-

---

[15] On the dicola in the text of poem 3, see Gronewald and Daniel 2005.8 and the detailed analysis of the dicola here and in parallel texts in Lundon 2007:161–163 and Esposito 2005:10–11.

[16] In addition to Sappho: ἐπίβουλος of Eros in Plato's *Symposium* 203d; Eros as the "son of crafty Aphrodite," παῖ δολομήδεος Ἀφροδίτας in Simonides 575 *PMG*. See Gronewald and Daniel 2005:10–11, Magnani 2005:42 n. 6, West 2005:1 and Lundon 2007:165 who adds that ἑταῖρε, 3 recalls Sappho's female ἕταιραι.

[17] It is thought that this poem opened the first book of the Alexandrian edition of Sappho, the work of Aristarchus which post-dates this papyrus. The importance of the poem here suggests that it also had a prominent position in an earlier edition. See Lundon 2007:164-165.

[18] Rawles 2006b:10. Hermes steals the cattle of Apollo in the *Homeric Hymn to Hermes* and uses trickery and deceit to exculpate himself.

[19] Lundon 2007:165-166 with n. 79.

out breath" (ἄπνους, 5), that is, near-dead,[20] and says "I go forth" (ἀφέρπω, 3), [leaving behind] the light of the stars and the fiery sun ([φ]άος ἀστέρων .../ [τ]ὸ πυριφεγγὲς ἀελ[ίου 6-7),[21] holding her "lovely... beautiful-sounding lyre ... her co-worker (τὰν ἐρατὰν... / [εὔ]φθογγον λύραν ... / [συ]νεργὸν ἔχοισα, 11-13). She who contemplates her death in the first poem (4-6) is now actively experiencing it as she leaves the world above for the world below, still holding the lyre she held there (7). Her descent to Hades, which dramatizes her musings in poems 1 and 2, brings them to a fitting conclusion.

Before her final departure, however, she makes reference to one more mythological exemplum, Orpheus the son of Oiagros (9), who charmed "every creeping thing" ([ἐρ]πετὰ πάντα,10). Orpheus' rapport with animals and nature, created by the power of his music, is well documented (A. *Ag.* 1629-30; E. *IA* 1211-14, *Ba.* 560-64) as are other aspects of his story.[22] In the absence of textual clues it is not possible to say which particular tale of Orpheus the author had in mind with this reference, but surely his descent to Hades fits the context perfectly. In poem three Sappho is on her way to Hades and can hope that her music will be as efficacious in triumphing over death as Orpheus'.[23]

Another aspect of his story that resonates with Sappho's concerns in the second poem is Orpheus' ultimate fate at the hands of furious maenads, who tear him from limb to limb while his head goes on singing. Most importantly, Orpheus' singing head had a special relationship with Sappho's island of Lesbos which is evident first in the early Hellenistic period though the tradition may be older.[24] Antigonus of Karystus tells us that "Myrsilus of Methymna, the chronicler of Lesbos, says that Orpheus' head is buried at Antissa, and its story is related by the local inhabitants. As a consequence, the nightingales there are more euphonious than others" (FGH XLV 477.2).[25] Singers are metaphori-

---

[20] Sometimes ἄπνους means "altogether dead" as in Leonidas *Epigrams* 15 GP and if the reading is correct, Callimachus *Epigrams* 14 GP, but "nearly dead" in Apolonius of Rhodes *Argonautica* 4.1403 where the tip of Ladon's tail is still twitching. The Περὶ τῆς ἄπνους of Plato's student Heracleides Ponticus featured a woman in a coma, brought back to life by Empedocles, Gottschalk 1980:11- 36. See also the discussion in Gronewald and Daniel 2005:11.

[21] Like the words of Praxilla's dying Adonis (*PMG* 747:1-2), Gronewald and Daniel 2005:11. This is a conventional way of saying farewell to life.

[22] Ziegler *RE* XXXV 1200-1316, West 1983, Segal 1989.

[23] There is evidence that Orpheus and his lyre were believed to have wider powers to protect the dead generally, see West 1983:24–25, Hardie 2004:28–29.

[24] For the impossibility of establishing the antiquity of the journey of Orpheus' head to Lesbos see Ziegler, *RE* XXXV 1293-1296 and Bömer 1980:237.

[25] On the date of Myrsilus also see Laqueur *RE* XXXI 1148–49 and Wilamowitz 1881:24. The citation of Myrsilus is said to be from the Ἱστοριῶν παραδόξων συναγωγή of Antigonus of Carystus who is dated by Wilamowitz 1881:16-26 to the early third century BC. More recently Dorandi

cally nightingales as early as Hesiod (*Erga* 203–208), and Myrsilus' contemporary Hermesianax calls Sappho a nightingale in an elegiac catalog of poets-in-love which begins with Orpheus' descent to Hades (47–50, fr. 7 Powell).[26] By the mid-third century "nightingales" are poems and Callimachus says that the "nightingales"of his friend Heraclitus of Halicarnassus "live untouched by the hand of Hades" though the poet himself is dead (Callimachus 34 G.-P. = AP 7.80). The fragments of Myrsilus do not suggest that he used much poetic language, but the especially sweet-sounding nightingales suggest that Orpheus' blessings had a literary expression which could, like their bestower, triumph over death.

Antissa is not the only location in Lesbos that claimed the honor of Orpheus' relics. In a detailed rendition of the head's journey, Phanokles, an elegiac poet also of early Hellenistic date[27], tells us that Maenads nailed the head to his lyre, and that it landed at Methymna after floating across the sea from Thrace:

> Τοῦ δ' ἀπὸ μὲν κεφαλὴν χαλκῶι τάμον, αὐτίκα δ' αὐτὴν   11
>   εἰς ἅλα Θρηϊκίην ῥῖψαν ὁμοῦ χέλυι
> ἥλωι καρτύνασαι, ἵν' ἐμφορέοιντο θαλάσσηι
>   ἄμφω ἅμα, γλαυκοῖς τεγγόμεναι ῥοθίοις.
> τὰς δ' ἱερῆι Λέσβωι πολιὴ ἐπέκελσε θάλασσα,   15
>   ἠχὴ δ' ὡς λιγυρῆς πόντον ἐπέσχε λύρης,
> νήσους τ' αἰγιαλούς θ' ἁλιμυρέας, ἔνθα λίγειαν
>   ἀνέρες Ὀρφείην ἐκτέρισαν κεφαλήν,
> ἐν δὲ χέλυν τύμβωι λιγυρὴν θέσαν, ἣ καὶ ἀναύδους
>   πέτρας καὶ Ὅρκου στυγνὸν ἔπειθεν ὕδωρ·   20
> ἐκ κείνου μολπαί τε καὶ ἱμερτὴ κιθαριστὺς
>   νῆσον ἔχει, πασέων δ' ἐστὶν ἀοιδοτάτη.

> They decapitated him with a bronze sword, and at once threw
> his head into the Thracian sea together with his lyre attached
> firmly by a nail, so that both could be carried in the water
> together, moistened by blue waves. And the grey sea brought
> them ashore at holy Lesbos, as the echo of the clear lyre com-

---

1999:XIV–XVII, following Musso, demonstrates that the Collection is a Byzantine compilation containing paradoxes extracted from a work by an Antigonus of unknown origin and date. If this is the case, as it seems to be, Myrsilus' association with Antignous says nothing about his date.

[26] Nightingales in Sappho herself are not obviously associated with human singers or song, e.g., "the sweet-voiced messenger of spring" (136 Voigt) and *P.Oxy.* 1787 6.7.

[27] On Phanokles' date see below, n. 32.

manded the waters, islands and shores flowing into the sea; and there men buried the clear-voiced head of Orpheus, and placed in the tomb his clear-sounding lyre, which once persuaded even mute rocks and the hateful water of Orcus. Since that time songs and the lovely art of the cithara hold that most musical of all the islands.

ap. Stobaeus 64.14 = 11–22, fr. 1,
Powell as emended by Lloyd-Jones[28]

Phanokles presents the tale as an aition which establishes a pedigree for lyric song on Lesbos through the death and suffering of Orpheus and the symbolic gift of his lyre. His telling of the tale unites the images and themes of all three poems of our anthology, which suggests, in turn, that the editor, or at least the author of poem 3, was aware of a connection between Orpheus and Lesbos, though neither Phanokles nor Myrsilus were necessarily the source of his information.[29] Like Tithonus, Orpheus became an immortal voice issuing from a compromised human frame, and through this image the second and third poems are joined in the same way as the first and second.

There is also another important aspect of Phanokles' treatment of Orpheus that resonates with Sappho. The verses above are from a 28 line segment of Phanokles' Ἔρωτες ἢ Καλοί, a catalog elegy with short segments describing the same-sex affairs of various figures of Greek myth. The section begins with a portrait of Orpheus singing and pining in vain for the love of Calais, one of the sons of Boreas and a fellow Argonaut (ap. Stobaeus 64.14 = 1–6 fr. 1, Powell).[30] The neat parallel of a homosexual Orpheus bringing his lyre and the gift of lyric to Sappho's Lesbos was surely the aim of Phanokles,[31] and if the Orpheus of our third poem was informed by this image, Sappho's own Orpheus-like descent to Hades is more richly evocative.[32]

Although it is not possible to establish a precise date for Phanokles, scholarly consensus places him towards the beginning of the third century, or roughly the

---

[28] The text of Phanokles follows Lloyd-Jones and Barns 1990:210, 214–15.

[29] Philostratus' report of an oracular shrine of Orpheus on the island (*VA* 4.14) suggests that the tradition was older than any of them.

[30] Lloyd-Jones and Barns 1990:210.

[31] Stern 1979:141.

[32] This seems to tell against the hypothesis that the third poem is Sappho's lament for her lost lover Phaon, see Gronewald and Daniel 2005:8, n. 5 and Lundon 2007:165-166 who rejects it on other grounds.

same period as the Cologne papyrus.[33] A reference to line 1 by Apollonius Rhodius (Ar. 4.905) suggests a very early Hellenistic date and this is confirmed by Lloyd-Jones's observation that the poem's diction includes very few words not found in Homer, the Homeric Hymns or early elegy.[34] Hopkinson notes Phanokles' penchant for repetition and rhyme, especially between words at the midpoint and end of the pentameter, and describes Phanokles' style as a "studied simplicity" quite different from the complexity of the high Hellenistic period.[35]

Poem 3 of the Sappho papyrus exhibits some of these same characteristics. The editors observe how ἀφέρπω (3) rhymes with ἀκούω (8), each followed by a dicolon in the same location in the verse.[36] And they demonstrate in their commentary that the poet uses virtually no vocabulary that cannot be found in early Greek lyric, tragedy and Plato. Indeed the only "new" word, ψιθυροπλόκε in line 1, is constructed on the model of Sappho's own δολόπλοκε (1.2 Voigt). Lastly, Phanokles' habit of repetition, illustrated above by λιγυρῆς ... λύρης (16), λίγειαν ... κεφαλήν (17–18), χέλυν ... λιγυρὴν (19), has a close parallel in words repeated across all three poems of the new Sappho papyrus: λιγύραν ... πᾶκτιν (7, poem 1), λιγύραν χελύνναν (2, poem 2) and [εὔ]φθογγον λύραν (12, poem 3).[37]

While none of these indications are decisive, the style and vocabulary of poem 3 seem to point to an early Hellenistic date—or approximately contemporary with Myrsilus, Phanokles and the Cologne papyrus itself which is, in effect, a terminus ante quem for its composition. Its monodic form and lyric litany of blame as well as its loose metrical scheme and some of its language has Hellenistic parallels in *P.Grenf.* I 1 (*P.Dryton* 50, "Des Mädchens Klage" = 117–80 Powell) and in Helen's song in *P.Tebt.* I 1,[38] though "Sappho" dispenses with her

---

[33] On Phanocles and his date see Lloyd-Jones and Barns 1990:209–214, Couat 1931.103–109 and von Leutsch 1857:66 who notes that Apollonius Rhodius (*Argonautica* 4.905) cites Phanokles 1.1, with its metrically unusual form θρηΐκιος. We do not have exact dates for Apollonius, but he is surely mid-third century BC. Clement of Alexandria, to whom we owe this text, says that Phanokles versified an idea of Demosthenes "that death is owed to us all." *Strom.* vi 750. If this is the case, Phanokles belongs to the end of the 4th or the early third century BC. His concern with aitiology, the poem's catalog structure in explicit imitation of Hesiod and his preference for recherché mythological variants all point to the Hellenistic period generally, Lloyd-Jones and Barns 1990:210.

[34] On Apollonius and Phanokles, Alexander 1988:17. On Phanokles' diction, Lloyd-Jones and Barns 1990:212–213.

[35] On Phanokles' style, Hopkinson 1988:178–179 and Alexander 1988 *passim*.

[36] Gronewald and Daniel 2005:8.

[37] It is not clear that λιγύραν on line 7 in poem 1 modifies πᾶκτιν, a kind of lyre, but in any case the words are in close proximity.

[38] Gronewald and Daniel 2005:8 and Lundon 2007:162–164. On *P.Dryton* 50, Esposito 1988 and Bing 2002, both with text and commentary.

complaints in just a few lines and focuses instead on the death scene which may be inspired by the tradition of Sappho's suicide.[39]

The poet's attempt to imitate Sappho's literary persona by couching the poem in the first person and addressing it to Sappho's signature deities, while using dialect forms that give an impression of being Aeolic,[40] all suggest that this is a tribute poem of a sort familiar in Hellenistic poetry. A well-known example is Callimachus' first *Iamb* which presents itself as a harangue by Hipponax, who lived and wrote some three centuries earlier. Though Callimachus uses Hipponax's unique meter, the choliamb, and his Ionic dialect, a reader is not expected to believe that this is really Hipponax's work. Rather it is a compliment to him and a statement about the aesthetics of Callimachus' own *Iambi*.[41] Poems like this are part of a larger cultural trend that Peter Bing has called the "memorializing impulse," which first appears in the late fourth century BCE and comes to full flower in the third.[42] That Sappho should be memorialized in this way is altogether consistent with her importance to Hellenistic poets generally.[43] Indeed, Theocritus' *Idylls* 28-31, which celebrate Sappho and Alcaeus by employing their meters, Aeolic dialect forms, and themes, offer an apposite example of this phenomenon.

Like *Iamb* 1, poem 3 has close connections with contiguous poems which raises the possibility that an editor placed them with care in a way that creates a complex composition with levels of meaning beyond its individual parts. This kind of careful construction of a new whole from smaller units is characteristic of Hellenistic poetry books, such as is the "new Posidippus," *P.Mil.Vogl.* VIII 309, dated by its hand to the end of the third century BC,[44] or not long after the Cologne papyrus. It contains some 112 epigrams of Posidippus of Pella (ca. 315–250 BCE) organized into divisions based on theme, each marked on the papyrus with a title.[45] Kathryn Gutzwiller has shown how poems within the divisions are linked by careful arrangement and verbal connections, while "a

---

[39] See Lundon 2007:165-166 who considers this hypothesis unproven.

[40] On the mixed dialect of poem 3, see Lundon 2007:155-156.

[41] On Callimachus' first *Iamb* see especially Clayman 1980:11–16, Acosta-Hughes 2002:21–59 and Kerkhecker 1999:11–48.

[42] See Bing 1993:620 for discussion of the memorializing impulse and its manifestations.

[43] On the reception of Sappho by Hellenistic poets see Skinner 1991, Bowman 1998, Gutzwiller 1998:85-87 and 260, Yatromanolakis 2007 *passim* and Acosta-Hughes, forthcoming.

[44] For the dating and a description of the handwriting see Bastianini and Gallazzi 2001:13–17 and Stephens and Obbink 2004:11 who suggest 230–200 BC.

[45] Krevans 2005:83–88.

sophisticated use of thematics" gives artistic shape to each section and provides links between them.[46]

Nita Krevans, who has examined some of the broader principles of arrangement in the Milan papyrus, finds that two predominate: "keep poems on similar topics adjacent to each other" and follow similar poems with variations and developments.[47] These same principles are at work in Callimachus' *Iambi* where the opening poems exhibit Hipponax's Ionic dialect and choliambic meter, but beginning with the fifth, the meters begin to change and with the sixth, the dialects, while the iambic spirit remains throughout. Likewise, in the Cologne papyrus two poems of Sappho in the same meter and dialect, and with similar content and theme, precede the third poem, which takes liberties with the first two criteria, but appears to be identical in the others.

Krevans also notes the close parallel between Posidippus' epigrams, particularly those in the sections on "Stones" and "Bird-signs," with Hellenistic wonder-books like Callimachus' *Collections of Marvels throughout the World by Location* and *On Birds* (frr. 407–11 Pf. and frr. 414–28 Pf).[48] These compilations, whether in Posidippus' poetry or Callimachus' prose, contain similar material on prodigies and unnatural phenomena meant to shock and amaze the reader. A similar interest in paradoxography is evident in the Cologne papyrus. Tithonus' wisp of a body pouring out perpetual chatter at the end of poem 2 surely belongs in this category, as well as Orpheus's singing head and his powers over the natural world. While Sappho herself might not have been interested in the bizarre aspects of her mythical exempla, they would not have been lost on a Hellenistic editor.

While the Cologne papyrus has these features in common with the "new Posidippus," it is not the work of a single author, as the Posippus is generally thought to be,[49] but is clearly part of an anthology containing poems of a well-known poet from the distant past set together with a new poem apparently composed for the context. One possible parallel for this arrangement may be an early collection of Theocritus' bucolica which included the spurious *Idylls* 8 and 9. We do not know precisely when it was produced, but it was certainly

---

[46] Gutzwiller 2005b on the thematic divisions, and on the intricate arrangement of poems within a single division, Gutzwiller 2004.

[47] Krevans 2005:93–95.

[48] Krevans 2005:88–92.

[49] On Posidippus as the sole author of the poems on *P.Mil.Vogl.* VIII 309 see the *editio princeps*, Bastianini and Gallazzi 2001:22–24 and Gutzwiller 2005a:1–3 with n. 3 containing references to contrary arguments.

before Virgil, who knew the spurious poems, and possibly as early as the late third or early second century BC.[50]

Idyll 9, which was apparently written as a conclusion to such a collection,[51] may be an analogue of poem 3. We do not know, of course, what, if anything, followed 3 on the papyrus, but Sappho's descent to Hades, which dramatizes her musings in poems 1 and 2, also brings them to a fitting conclusion.

Another important Hellenistic parallel, though later in time (c. 100 BC), is Meleager's *Garland*, a collection of epigrams containing the work of distinguished predecessors in that genre, arranged by Meleager and generously augmented with work of his own composition on the same themes. One of these served as an introduction to the collection (1 G-P = *AP* 4.1) and another, its conclusion (129 G-P = *AP* 12.257).[52] Although no manuscripts of the *Garland* itself have survived, extracts from it were preserved in the Byzantine anthology of Cephalus that forms the basis of what is now called the *Greek Anthology*.[53] Wifstrand's analyses of some of the extracts demonstrate that Meleager organized the poems thematically to create striking verbal repetitions, while Radinger's shows that Meleager characteristically placed his own variations after the original poems he wished to imitate.[54] Recent work by Kathryn Gutzwiller confirms these observations, and demonstrates how Meleager deploys his arrangements of his own and pre-existing compositions to create a work of art on a large scale, with its own aesthetics and a greater significance than any of its parts. Although Gutzwiller can identify no predecessors for Meleager in this editorial technique, she suggests that it probably predated him.[55] The Cologne Papyrus, with its two poems of Sappho followed by a later one on the same theme, appears to be a very early example of Meleager-like editing and composing.

To summarize, it appears that the Cologne papyrus contains part of an anthology consisting of two authentic poems of Sappho, closely connected by

---

[50] On early collections of Theocritus' *Idylls* and their possible dates see Gutzwiller 1996 who draws on the work of Wilamowitz, Gow, Van Sickle and others. *P.Oxy.* 2064 + 3548 of the late second century AD may be a copy of an early collection containing the spurious poems (Gutzwiller 1996:140). Unlike the author of poem 3, Pseudo-Theocritus composed in the same meter as Theocritus himself and probably intended that his poems would pass as Theocritus' own. By choosing another meter, the author of poem 3 is clearly aiming at a more creative tribute.

[51] For *Id.* 9 as the conclusion of a collection of *Idylls* see Gutzwiller 1996:125. An opposing view is in Gow 1952 vol. 2, 185 n. 1.

[52] For a description of how 1 and 129 G-P function as an introduction and conclusion see Gutzwiller 1997:170.

[53] On the history and nature of the text see Cameron 1993 and Gutzwiller 1998, 15-16.

[54] Radinger 1895:100–107, Wifstrand 1926. Both are reprinted in Tarán 1987.

[55] Gutzwiller 1998:46. Gutzwiller predicts that Meleager's techniques of arrangement could have come into use as early as the third century BC.

theme and verbal repetitions on the subject of old age, death and the immortality of song. These are followed by a Hellenistic poem, in the voice of Sappho, which repeats some of the same language, while it dramatizes the logical next step, Sappho's descent to Hades. The anthology is structured in a way that is familiar from Hellenistic poetry books, and an early Hellenistic date is consistent with the meter, dialect and language of the third poem, as well as the handwriting of the papyrus itself.

Following Gronewald and Daniel's description, the papyrus is written in a book hand, with epigraphic forms consistent with an early third-century date, until the ninth line of the second column where the third poem begins, after a short break, in a larger and rounder hand.[56] Lundon's exhaustive analysis shows that the two hands have more differences than similarities, but that they are more or less contemporary.[57] This suggests that the third poem was not simply added to a pre-existing collection of Sappho's work,[58] but rather, that some time in the first part of the third century someone copied the first two poems from another, presumably older manuscript of Sappho's, and perhaps arranged them with the anthology in mind, while another added the third poem within a short time frame. Alterations in the text of the third poem, where twice a series of letters has been crossed off and replaced with others, are typical of autographs[59] and this indicates, in turn, that the individual who inserted the third poem was also its composer. We do not know, of course, in what circumstances this took place, but *P.Köln.* seems to provide evidence that copyists and composers could collaborate in the creation of a complex work.[60]

Poems 1 and 2, removed from the context of their pre-Hellenistic source, do not provide us with any information about the transmission of Sappho's poetry before the work of the great Alexandrian editors, since we do not know whether they were extracted from the older manuscript separately or together.[61] Even if

---

[56] Gronewald and Daniel 2005:7.

[57] Lundon 2007:157-159. See also Hammerstadt's analysis of the hands in this volume, p. 20-22

[58] While Lundon 2007:158–160 does not rule out the possibility that the third poem was simply added to a pre-existing roll of Sappho's poetry, he raises important difficulties with this thesis. If 3 had been added to the end of a pre-existing collection we would expect its hand to be later than the other, and furthermore, we would expect a concluding title to occupy the blank space at the point where the hands change. He also provides examples of anthologies made by two collaborating copyists.

[59] Lundon 2007:159-160 with note 49.

[60] Lundon's (2007:159-160) suggestion that the text may in some way be connected to a symposium or similar occasion is certainly attractive. There is more work to be done on the relation between sympotic texts and early literary anthologies.

[61] On the pre-Alexandrian editions of Sappho see Lobel 1925:xiii–xxv, Edmonds 1922 and Yatromanolakis 1999. The canonical Hellenistic edition of Aristarchus was organized by meter with

their thematic unity reflects nothing more than Sappho's limited repertoire of images and themes, their arrangement in the anthology with the editor/author's own contribution, a tribute poem in honor of the same author carefully composed to enhance and develop the content and sequencing, exhibits an early Hellenistic interest in the principles of artistic arrangement, and looks forward to the complex Alexandrian literary creations that are still to come.

Bibliography

Acosta-Hughes, B. 2002. *Polyeideia: The Iambi of Callimachus and the Archaic Iambic Tradition*. Berkeley.

———. 2004. "Alexandrian Posidippus: On Rereading the GP Epigrams in Light of P.Mil.Vogl. VIII 309." In Acosta-Hughes et al. 2004:42–56.

———. Forthcoming. *Recalling Lyric in Alexandria. Five Readings*. Princeton.

Acosta-Hughes, B., and Stephens, S. A. 2002. "Rereading Callimachus' Aetia Fragment 1." *Classical Philology* 97:238–255.

Acosta-Hughes, B., et al., eds. 2004. *Labored in Papyrus Leaves: Perspectives on an Epigram Collection Attributed to Posidippus (P.Mil.Vogl. VIII 309)*. Hellenic Studies 2. Washington DC.

Alexander, K. 1988. *A Stylistic Commentary on Phanocles and Related Texts*. Classical and Byzantine Monographs 13. Amsterdam.

Bastianini, G., and Gallazzi, C., eds. 2001. *Epigrammi: P. Mil. Vogl. 8. 309*. With C. Austin. Papiri dell' Università degli studi di Milano 8. Milan.

Bernsdorff, H. 2005. "Offene Gedichtschlüsse." *Zeitschrift für Papyrologie und Epigraphik* 153:1–6.

Bing, P. 1993. "The Bios-Tradition and Poets' Lives in Hellenistic Poetry." *Nomodeiktes: Greek Studies in Honor of Martin Ostwald* (ed. R. M. Rosen and J. Farrell) 619–631. Ann Arbor.

———. 2002. "The 'Alexandrian Erotic Fragment' or 'Maedchens Klage'." *The Bilingual Family Archive of Dryton, his Wife Apollonia and their Daughter Senmouthis (P.Dryton)* (ed. K. Vandorpe) 381–390. Brussels.

Bömer, F. 1980. *P. Ovidius Naso Metamorphosen: Kommentar*. Heidelberg.

Bowman, L. 1998. "Nossis, Sappho and Hellenistic Poetry." *Ramus* 27:39–59.

---

the possible addition of a separate book of epithalamia. This papyrus containing two poems of Sappho and one by another author appears to confirm Yatromanolakis' conjecture that the canonical scholarly edition of her work was not the only context in which her poems were circulated in antiquity, Yatromanolakis 1999:180 with note 5 and Yatromanolakis 2007:278 nt. 438 and 360 nt. 341.

Cameron, A. 1993. *The Greek Anthology: From Meleager to Planudes.* Oxford.

Clayman, D. 1980. *Callimachus' Iambi.* Leiden.

Couat, A. 1931. *Alexandrian Poetry under the First Three Ptolemies.* Trans. J. Loeb. London.

Di Benedetto, V. 1985. "Il tema della vecchiaia e il fr. 58 di Saffo." *Quaderni urbinati di cultura classica* 48: 145-163.

Di Benedetto, V. 2004. "Osservazioni sul nuovo papiro di Saffo." *Zeitschrift für Papyrologie und Epigraphik* 149:5-6.

Dorandi, T., ed. 1999. *Antigone de Caryste: Fragments.* Paris.

Edmonds, J. M. 1922. "Sappho's Book as Depicted on an Attic Vase." *Classical Quarterly* 16.1-14.

Edmunds, L. 2006. "The New Sappho: ἔφαντο (9)." *Zeitschrift für Papyrologie und Epigraphik* 156:23-26.

Esposito, E. 2005. *Il Fragmentum Grenfellianum (P.Dryton 50): Introduzione, testo critico, traduzione e commento.* Eikasmos studi 12. Bologna.

Geissler, C. 2005. "Der Tithonosmythos bei Sappho und Kallimachos: Zu Sappho fr. 58 V., 11-22 und Kallimachos, Aitia fr. 1 Pf." *Göttinger Forum für Altertumswissenschaft* 8:105-114.

Gottschalk, H. B., ed. 1980. *Heraclides of Pontus.* Oxford.

Gow, A. S. F. 1952. *Theocritus.* 2nd ed. 2 vols. Cambridge.

Gow, A. S. F., and Page, D. L., eds. 1965. *The Greek Anthology: Hellenistic Epigrams.* 2 vols. Cambridge.

Gronewald, M., and Daniel, R. W. 2004a. "Ein neuer Sappho-Papyrus." *Zeitschrift für Papyrologie und Epigraphik* 147:1-8.

———. 2004b. "Nachtrag zum neuen Sappho-Papyrus." *Zeitschrift für Papyrologie und Epigraphik* 149:1-4.

———. 2005. "Lyrischer Text (Sappho-Papyrus)." *Zeitschrift für Papyrologie und Epigraphik* 154:7-12.

Gutzwiller, K. 1996. "The Evidence for Theocritean Poetry Books." *Theocritus* (eds. M. A. Harder, R. F. Regtuit, and G. C. Wakker) 119-148. Hellenistica Groningana 2. Groningen.

———. 1997. "The Poetics of Editing in Meleager's Garland." *Transactions of the American Philological Association* 127:169-200.

———. 1998. *Poetic Garlands: Hellenistic Epigrams in Context.* Berkeley.

———. 2003. "Posidippus on Statuary." *Il papiro di Posidippo un anno dopo. Atti del convegno internazionale di studi: Firenze 13-14 giugno 2002* (eds. G. Bastianini and A. Casanova) 41-60. Florence.

———. 2004. "A New Hellenistic Poetry Book: P. Mil. Vogl. VIII 309." In Acosta-Hughes et al. 2004:84-93.

———, ed. 2005a. *The New Posidippus: A Hellenistic Poetry Book.* Oxford.

———. 2005b. "The Literariness of the Milan Papyrus, or 'What Difference a Book?'" In Gutzwiller 2005a:287–319.

Hardie, A. 2004. "Muses and Mysteries." *Music and the Muses: The Culture of Mousike in the Classical Athenian City* (ed. P. Murray and P. Wilson) 11–37. Oxford.

———. 2005. "Sappho, the Muses and Life after Death." *Zeitschrift für Papyrologie und Epigraphik* 154:13–32.

Hopkinson, N. 1988. *A Hellenistic Anthology.* Cambridge.

Janko, R. 2005. "Sappho Revisited." *Times Literary Supplement* December 23.

Kerkhecker, A. 1999. *Callimachus' Book of Iambi.* Oxford.

Krevans, N. 2005. "The Editor's Toolbox: Strategies for Selections and Presentation in the Milan Epigram Papyrus." In Gutzwiller 2005a:81–96.

Leutsch, E. von. 1857. "Wann lebte Phanokles." *Philologus* 12:66.

Lidov, J. B. 2002. "Sappho, Herodotus, and the Hetaira." *Classical Philology* 97:203–237.

Lloyd-Jones, H., and Barns, J. B. W. 1990. "A New Papyrus Fragment of Hellenistic Elegy [= *SH* 970]." *Greek Comedy, Hellenistic Literature, Greek Religion, and Miscellanea: The Academic Papers of Sir Hugh Lloyd-Jones* 196–215. Oxford. Originally published 1963: *Studi italiani di filologia classica* n.s. 35:205–227.

Lobel, E., ed. 1925. ΣΑΠΦΟΥΣ ΜΕΛΗ: *The Fragments of the Lyrical Poems of Sappho.* Oxford.

Lundon, J. 2007. "Il nuovo testo lirico nel nuovo papiro di Saffo." *I Papiri di Saffo e Alceo: Atti del convengo internazionale di studi, Firenze, 8-9 Giugno 2006* (ed. G. Bastianini and A. Casanova) 149–166. Studi e Testi di Papirologia n.s. 9. Florence.

Luppe, W. 2004. "Überlegungen zur Gedicht-Anordnung im neuen Sappho-Papyrus." *Zeitschrift für Papyrologie und Epigraphik* 149:7–9.

Magnani, M. 2005. "Note alla nuova Saffo." *Eikasmos* 16:41–49.

Puelma, M., and Angiò. F. 2005. "Sappho und Poseidippos: Nachtrag zum Sonnenuhr-Epigramm 52 A.-B. des Mailänder Papyrus." *Zeitschrift für Papyrologie und Epigraphik* 152:13–15.

Rabinowitz, N. S., and Auanger, L., eds. 2002. *Among Women: From the Homosocial to the Homoerotic in the Ancient World.* Austin TX.

Radinger, C. 1895. *Meleagros von Gadara: Eine Litterargeschichtliche Skizze.* Innsbruck. Reprinted in Tarán 1987:1–115.

Rawles, R. 2006a. "Notes on the Interpretation of the 'New Sappho.'" *Zeitschrift für Papyrologie und Epigraphik* 157: 1-7.

Rawles, R. 2006b. "Musical Notes on the New Anonymous Lyric Poem from Köln." *Zeitschrift für Papyrologie und Epigraphik* 157:8–13.

Segal, C. 1989. *Orpheus: The Myth of the Poet.* Baltimore.

Skinner, M. B. 1991. "Aphrodite Garlanded: Erôs and Poetic Creativity in Sappho and Nossis." *Rose di Pieria* (ed. F. de Martino) 79–96. Bari. Revised and expanded version in Rabinowitz and Auanger 2002:60–81.

Stephens, S., and Obbink, D. 2004. "The Manuscript: Posidippus on Papyrus." In Acosta-Hughes et al. 2004:9–15.

Stern, J. 1979. "Phanocles Fragment 1." *Quaderni Urbinati di Cultura Classica* 32:135–143.

Tarán, S. L. 1987. *The Greek Anthology II.* New York.

Turner, E., and Parsons, P. 1987. *Greek Manuscripts of the Ancient World* ed. 2. Bulletin of the Institute of Classical Studies Supplement 46. London.

Voigt, E. M., ed. 1971. *Sappho et Alcaeus: Fragmenta.* Amsterdam.

West, M. L., ed. 1983. *The Orphic Poems.* Oxford.

———. 2005. "The New Sappho." *Zeitschrift für Papyrologie und Epigraphik* 151:1–9.

Wifstrand, A. 1926. *Studien zur Griechischen Anthologie.* Leipzig. Reprinted in Tarán 1987:1–39.

Wilamowitz-Moellendorff, U. von. 1881. *Antigonos von Karystos.* Berlin.

Yatromanolakis, D. 1999. "Alexandrian Sappho Revisited." *Harvard Studies in Classical Philology* 99:179–195.

———. 2007. *Sappho in the Making: The Early Reception.* Hellenic Studies 28. Washington DC.

11

Sappho 58
Philosophical Reflections on Death and Aging[1]

Ellen Greene

ALTHOUGH MOST CONTEMPORARY SCHOLARS are in agreement that Sappho's verse appropriates themes and poetic conventions employed by both Homer and male lyric poets, there is considerable disagreement about the extent to which Sappho's extant poetry ought to be considered 'woman-centered,' that is, poetry chiefly concerned with love, sexuality, and 'private' matters in general.[2] While Sappho's surviving poetry clearly depicts a female world apart from men, and is largely focused on issues connected with love and desire, there is, nonetheless, evidence that Sappho also had interests in politics and ethics, interests that show a more public dimension to her work.[3] Indeed, the ideas expressed in some of Sappho's poems are distinctly philosophical in character, and the content of the newly-recovered Poem 58 provides a further example of this.

There are at least two senses in which we may consider some of Sappho's work to be philosophical. Her poetry is clearly philosophical in the broad

---

[1] I wish to thank James Hawthorne, whose insights were extremely useful in writing this paper. I would also like to thank Marilyn Skinner, who first approached me about co-organizing a session on the new Sappho poem for the 2007 APA meeting. Finally, I want to express my deep appreciation of Gregory Nagy, whose enthusiasm and support for this project made this volume possible.

[2] Debates regarding the relationship between public and private discourses in Sappho have played a large role in Sappho scholarship over the last several decades. On these debates see especially; Hallett 1979, Stehle 1981, Winkler 1990, Calame 1996, Lardinois 1996, Snyder 1997, and Parker 2005. Discussions about whether Sappho's discourse may be considered peculiarly "feminine" have also occupied an importance place in recent Sappho scholarship. See, in particular; Stehle 1981, Skinner 1993, Greene 1994, Williamson 1995, Snyder 1997.

[3] See Parker 2005, in which he argues that Sappho's references and allusions to public and political life ought to be taken into account within the context of her body of work. While Parker acknowledges that Sappho's extant poetry is primarily focused on "feminine" concerns, he points out that ethical matters in general are also an important component of Sappho's poetry.

colloquial sense of reflecting on what has value in human life and exploring the nature of human existence more generally. But, arguably, her poetry is also philosophical in a narrower, more technical sense. While Sappho's poetry does not contain the kind of organized system of ideas one finds in Plato and Aristotle, her poetry treats some of the central metaphysical themes explored by such pre-Socratic thinkers as Thales, Heraclitus, and Anaximander—who are themselves explicitly recognized to be philosophers by Plato and Aristotle.[4] That is, although sixth-century (BCE) Greeks may not have had the concept of a 'philosopher,' Plato and Aristotle most certainly recognized the pre-Socratic thinkers as philosophical precursors. Aristotle himself explicitly refers to the pre-Socratics as "the first philosophers."[5] A major theme in the work of these pre-Socratic philosophers was the attempt to understand the nature of reality, and how the human experience of permanence and change is related to that reality. This theme of permanence and change was no doubt in the intellectual atmosphere of Sappho's culture. Thales of Miletus was probably her contemporary, so it is not altogether surprising that Sappho explores ideas about permanence and change in several of her poems. The newly-recovered Poem 58 is a particularly striking instance.

Considering that poem 58 is thought to be a complete poem, though its ending is subject to debate, it makes an especially important contribution to reinforcing the evidence for Sappho's concern with metaphysics and ethics, as well as erotics. My analysis of the poem will largely be based on Martin West's 12-line version of the text.[6] Some scholars, however, at least several in this volume for instance, offer persuasive arguments that there might have been two versions of Poem 58 based on two different performance traditions.[7] The Cologne version of the text ends with the myth of Tithonus, while the earlier Oxyrhynchus version continues for four more lines. The two versions of the poem's ending appear to emphasize very different responses, on the part of the speaker, to the problem of human mortality: a sense of resigned acceptance with her human lot, on the one hand, and the consolation arising from a confidence in her poetic immortality, on the other hand. I think it is worthwhile

---

[4] See Zellner 2007 for a discussion of how modern philosophical logic can be applied to Sappho 16. Although I do not agree with Zellner's main argument about the relativity of aesthetic evaluation in Sappho's poem, I do agree with his point that the significance of the intellectual background of the pre-Socratics in relation to Sappho "has not been sufficiently appreciated."

[5] See Aristotle *Metaphysics* A3:983b6.

[6] See West 2005 for an important and influential discussion of the recovery of Poem 58, with text and translation.

[7] See especially, in this volume, Hammerstaedt, Lardinois, Boedeker, and Nagy.

to consider how the alternative ending, that is, the continuation of the poem for four more lines from the Oxyrhynchus version, affects our interpretation of the poem—within the context of the poem's overall philosophical outlook. I shall argue that these last four lines reinforce the poem's demonstration of the speaker's ability to transcend the specificities of her mortal suffering, an ability evinced in several other poems of Sappho.[8]

***

I argue that Poem 58 constitutes a philosophical reflection on the human condition in light of the inevitability of aging and mortality. I see this as part of a philosophical thread that runs through at least several of Sappho's poems, which address what are now regarded as central philosophical issues: "what constitutes beauty" and "the nature of the good human life." [9] I will place Poem 58 in the context of other such didactic utterances in Sappho's work, arguing that the speaker's display of equanimity in the face of the body's decay and ultimate death in Poem 58 reflects Sappho's more general ruminations on the nature of human experience and existence. As West notes, the decay of the body described in Poem 58 mirrors the symptoms of love evoked in Poem 31.[10] Interestingly, both poems also show how the speaker "Sappho" achieves a kind of recovery from the debilitating effects of bodily dissolution and fragmentation.[11] This recovery is achieved through rational contemplation of the larger scheme of things, or to put it another way, through an ability to detach from the contingencies of self and see one's personal experience as part of a larger whole. We see this, most notably, in Fragments 1, 31, 94, 96, and 58, where the speaker is able to see her difficult, immediate situation—whether it be loss, separation, abandonment, helplessness, or aging—in a broader context and from a more objective perspective.

As in much of the archaic lyric poetry written by men , Sappho writes aphoristic lines about the nature of the virtuous life appropriate to a noble man. As Holt Parker points out, Fr. 148, cited below, "could have come from the mouth of Alcaeus."[12]

---

[8] See especially Poems 1, 31, and 94.
[9] These issues have been addressed by philosophers, at least since the time of Plato and Aristotle.
[10] For a discussion of parallels between Poems 31 and 58, in terms of the bodily effects of both love and old age, See West 2005.
[11] See in Greene 1999 an analysis of the speaker's collapse and recovery in Poem 31.
[12] Parker 2005:10.

ὁ πλοῦτος ἄνευ † ἀρέτας οὐκ ἀσίνη πάροικος
ἀ δ' ἀμφοτέρων κρᾶσις † εὐδαιμονίας ἔχει τὸ
   ἄκρον †

Wealth without virtue is not a harmless neighbor.
The mixing of them both is the height of good fortune.

Likewise, Fragments 3 and 50 show Sappho's concern for ethics and aristocratic social relations. More specifically, both fragments emphasize how, for Sappho, real beauty and goodness go hand in hand:

> ...to give...of the famous...of the beautiful and good...friends,
> and you grieve me...shame...having become swollen...you
>   might be
> disgusted by...for my mind not thus...is disposed...I understand...
> of baseness...others...minds...well-[...the blessed ones...[13]
>
>   (Fr. 3)

ὁ μὲν γὰρ κάλος ὄσσον ἴδην πέλεται (κάλος),
δὲ κἄγαθος αὔτικα καὶ κάλος ἔσσεται.

> For the beautiful man is beautiful as far as
> appearances go, while he that is good
> will consequently also become beautiful.
>
>   (Fr. 50)

The three fragments quoted above clearly demonstrate that Sappho is not merely interested in the private and domestic concerns typically associated with women in archaic Greek culture. They have, at the very least, a moral tone, in that they show Sappho's interest in declaring what she considers important, and in characterizing abstract notions of beauty and goodness. Sappho's association of love with beauty and moral excellence may also be said to anticipate Plato, for whom beauty and goodness are inextricably connected.[14]

We can see this connection most strikingly in one of Sappho's most famous poems, Fragment 16, in which Sappho uses the myth of Helen to explore the meaning of both beauty and desire.[15]

---

[13] I do not include the Greek here because the text is extremely fragmented.

[14] Socrates' speech in Plato's *Symposium* emphasizes a necessary connection between beauty and virtue.

[15] See, in Greene 2002, a discussion of Fragment 16 in more detail, with particular emphasis on the way the poem articulates a powerful connection between beauty and desire.

ο]ἰ μὲν ἰππήων στρότον οἰ δὲ πέσδων
οἰ δὲ νάων φαῖσ’ ἐπ[ὶ] γᾶν μέλαι[ν]αν
ἔ]μμεναι κάλλιστον, ἔγω δὲ κῆν’ ὄτ-
4   τω τις ἔραται·

πά]γχυ δ’ εὔμαρες σύνετον πόησαι
π]άντι τ[ο]ῦτ’, ἀ γὰρ πόλυ περσκέθοισα
κάλλος [ἀνθ]ρώπων Ἐλενα [τὸ]ν ἄνδρα
8   τὸν [πανάρ]ιστον

καλλ[ίποι]ς’ ἔβα ’ς Τροίαν πλέοι[σα
κωὐδ[ὲ πα]ῖδος οὐδὲ φίλων το[κ]ήων
πά[μπαν] ἐμνάσθη, ἀλλὰ παράγαγ’ αὔταν
12   ]σαν

               ]αμπτον γὰρ]
         ]... κούφως τ[   ]οησ[.]ν
   ..]με νῦν Ἀνακτορί[ας ὀ]νέμναι-
16   σ’ οὐ] παρεοίσας ·

τᾶ]ς κε βολλοίμαν ἔρατόν τε βᾶμα
κἀμάρυχμα λάμπρον ἴδην προσῶπω
ἢ τὰ Λύδων ἄρματα κἀν ὄπλοισι
20   πεσδομ]άχεντας.

(Fragments of a few lines follow that are largely unintelligible.)

Some say that a troop of horse-men,
some of foot-soldiers, some a fleet of ships,
but I say that it is whatever anyone loves
that is the most beautiful thing on the dark earth;

It is completely simple to make this
intelligible to all, for the woman
who far surpassed all mortals in beauty,

Helen, abandoning her most brave husband,
went sailing to Troy and took no thought
for child or dear parents, but
the [Cyprian goddess]
led her away...

> All of which] now reminds me
> of Anaktoria absent;
> Her lovely step and the bright sparkle
> of her face I would rather see than
> all the Lydian chariots
> and armed men fighting on foot...

Claude Calame has pointed out that the poem has a "Platonic flavor" in its close association of beauty and *eros*.[16] Although it may seem anachronistic to compare Sappho with Plato, a number of scholars have suggested that Sappho's poetry may be regarded as 'proto-philosophical' through its interest in abstractions, its search for absolutes, and its movement from mythical to rational thought.[17] Indeed, one of the hallmarks of early Greek philosophical thought, and perhaps most relevant to Poem 16, is the ability to organize perceptions 'from many into one' and to move from the particularities of human experience and existence to an abstract idea of what is common in those particularities.[18] As Page duBois has noted, Sappho's Poem 16 shows an ability to "move toward abstraction, toward definition, and the positing of one term that subsumes a variety of examples."[19] It is this move toward abstract thought and definition that leads duBois to assert that Sappho addresses questions and issues in her poetry that we might regard as philosophical in a contemporary sense.[20]

In Poem 16 the speaker considers an array of different examples of beauty from widely divergent realms. Beauty, the speaker tells us, is "whatever anyone loves." At first it may appear that she is offering *her* preference as a contrast to the preferences of those who find horsemen, infantry, and ships "the

---

[16] Calame 2005:62–6 discusses Sappho's use of beauty and memory in her treatment of eros, and suggests that the evocation of Anactoria's beauty in Poem 16 has a 'Platonic' flavor.

[17] See duBois 1995:114ff. for an insightful discussion of how Poem 16 constitutes a "protophilosophical" gesture in expressing and helping to define early Greek abstract thought. More generally, duBois 1995, Foley 1998, and Pender 2007 have argued that Sappho's depictions of *eros* as lack, her use of recollection as a way to transcend the specificities of loss and desire, may have had a direct influence on Plato's theory of recollection and his portrayals of eros in the *Phaedrus* and the *Symposium*. Pender's recent article, which examines Plato's praise of Sappho at Phaedrus 235c, offers a persuasive argument that Sappho's insights about love helped to shape Plato's treatment of *eros*.

[18] See Foley 1998:40–1, 58-9 for an analysis of how Sappho serves "in some critical respects as the 'mother' of Socrates' second argument about *eros* in *Phaedrus*." Foley uses evidence from Maximus of Tyre to show how the view that Sappho may have influenced Plato was already held in antiquity. Foley argues, therefore, that "Sappho's poetry—as Maximus hints—can be suggestively proto-philosophical (58)."

[19] DuBois 1995:110.

[20] DuBois 1995:110.

most beautiful." But the speaker's expression of what she finds beautiful, while emphatically an articulation of her particular identity, is presented as an instance of a *general* interconnectedness between beauty and *eros*.

In the first stanza of the poem the speaker, initially, presents beauty as subjective, but then asserts an objective, universal connection between beauty and love– one finds beauty in whatever one loves. In the stanzas that follow, the speaker subsumes the specific examples of Helen and her own object of desire, Anaktoria, to the more general connection between love and beauty put forth in the opening stanza. Sappho makes it clear from the beginning of the poem that she is attempting to find a unifying principle that will help to make sense of the diversity of human experience. In so doing, Sappho engages in the philosophical endeavor of searching for a defining idea or principle that helps to explain human identity and experience.

One of the most significant issues in discussions of Poem 16 has focused on whether Sappho presents a subjective view of beauty that prefigures cultural relativism. Fraenkel, Wills, and Race, for example, have all argued that Sappho's thesis in Poem 16, that beauty is "whatever anyone loves," undermines any concept of absolute value, and more specifically, points to all human evaluation of beauty as merely subjective.[21] DuBois takes a somewhat different view of Poem 16. While acknowledging that Sappho anticipates philosophical argument in the poem, duBois ultimately holds that Sappho's depiction of beauty has a 'specificity' and 'materiality' that presents a sharp contrast to Plato's association of beauty and abstract truth.[22] Foley, on the other hand, sees a closer relationship between Sapphic and Platonic erotics, arguing that "for both Plato and Sappho erotics involves far more than the body."[23] Although Foley maintains that Sappho's account of beauty does not "deliberately" look forward to "Platonic abstraction of the incorporeal from the corporeal," "it takes a step in that direction by moving the listener beyond beauty in the visual world to beauty in the world of the imagination and to potential poetic permanence."[24] My own view is closest to Foley's. For the power of Poem 16 derives from its ability to invoke beauty with incredibly vivid specificity while at the same time making us keenly aware of beauty in its paradigmatic form. Specificity and

---

[21] Fraenkel 1962, Wills 1967, Race 1989–90.

[22] DuBois 1995:87.

[23] Foley 1998:68. See also Snell 1960:50, who argues that Sappho's thesis in Poem 16 may sound like it is opening the door to "the arbitrary decision of personal taste." But, Snell asserts, Sappho is "evidently concerned to grasp a piece of genuine reality: to find Being instead of Appearance." This latter comment suggests that Sappho's poem has a Platonic ring to it.

[24] Foley 1998:62.

generality are held in a delicate balance in the poem, yet Sappho shows that the lover's encounter with beauty in the object of desire necessarily entails an encounter with the very nature of beauty itself since "the lover responds not just to the beloved but to beauty in the beloved."[25] As Foley points out, both Sappho and Plato insist upon *eros* as the motivating factor in the pursuits of both beauty and philosophy. Indeed, this implicit parallel between the lover and the philosopher can be inferred from Plato's description of the "madness" of the philosopher in the *Phaedrus*, who 'on seeing beauty here on earth' is reminded of 'true beauty.'[26] In Sappho 16, the lover's experience of visual beauty in the beloved leads to the contemplation of beauty in the abstract and, perhaps more importantly for Sappho, prompts the recollection of the beauty's beloved in the poet's imagination.

✱✱✱

It may be argued that, of all Sappho's surviving verse, the newly-recovered Poem 58 most touches on philosophical themes. As in Poem 16, we can see in 58 a concern with what is common or the same among things appearing to be diverse or different. Indeed, the poem reflects some of the central concerns addressed by early Greek philosophers, particularly the tension in Greek thought between the realm of the universal and unchanging, and the world of contingency and mortality. Based on their surviving texts, it appears that the pre-Socratic thinkers were looking for an underlying reality as an explanation of the nature of permanence and change. Sappho's near-contemporary, Thales, for example, sees the ever-changing world as composed of one underlying substance which he considers to be water. All change, for Thales, is modification or alteration of the qualities of that substance. Kirk and Raven, et. al. assert that the view of Thales as the first philosopher is justified, at the very least, on the grounds that Thales "evidently abandoned mythic formulations."[27] Anaximander, thought to have been slighter younger than Thales, is considered the first philosopher to have attempted a detailed and comprehensive explanation of all aspects of human experience.[28] Like Thales, Anaximander posits the existence of an underlying reality as an explanation of the nature of change and permanence. For him, the originative substance of the universe is what he

---

[25] Foley 1998:61.

[26] *Phaedrus* 249d5–e1.

[27] Kirk, Raven, and Schofield 1983:99. For commentary and the extant texts of the Ionian thinkers, including Thales, Anaximander, and Heraclitus, see Kirk, et al. 1983:76–213.

[28] For texts and commentary on Anaximander, see Kirk, et al. 1983:100–142.

calls the *Apeiron*, the indefinite or unlimited. He posits that all things come into being from the *Apeiron*.

Much more explicitly than Thales, Anaximander questions how things and qualities come to be and what their relationship is to the underlying and ever-lasting *Apeiron*, as the "first principle of things that are." Thus, as Wheelwright remarks, the *Apeiron* "has to account for all the innumerable changes that make up the incessant on-goingness of the world."[29] Like his predecessors, Heraclitus, nearly a century later, attempts to find one underlying principle of all reality. Among other things, he asserts that change is that underlying reality. Although things are always in flux for Heraclitus, the unchanging principle of flux itself, paradoxically, governs that flux eternally. Heraclitus attempts to explain all aspects of the world in relation to his central view, that "natural changes of all kinds are regular and balanced."[30]

Very briefly, I have tried to sketch the main ideas of some of the pre-Socratic thinkers in order to show that their concern with the nature of change and permanence was, most likely, part of the intellectual climate in which Sappho lived and wrote. I believe we can see in Sappho, particularly in Poems 16 and 58, some of the central themes in pre-Socratic philosophy: the relationship between the One and the Many and the relationship between permanence and change. I would argue that the latter theme can be seen most strikingly in Poem 58. The poem clearly presents change as fundamental to human nature. But it also suggests a kind of complementarity between what changes and what lasts. As the speaker of Poem 58 contemplates the ineluctable fact that human beings grow old and out of existence, she also alludes to an unchanging and immortal realm that, for her, may be encountered through art, or more generally, creative expression. That is, the poem seems to suggest that mortal humans may touch the immortal by engaging with the Muses. The centrality of this idea in the poem is at first only implicit, but is evoked more fully through reflection on the Tithonus myth.

I will explore these ideas in more detail after providing my own translation of West's text of the poem:

> You, children, pursue the violet-laden Muses' lovely gifts,
> and the clear-toned lyre so dear to song;

---

[29] See Wheelwright 1966 for commentary and texts, in translation, of all the extant pre–Socratic philosophers. See also Brumbaugh 1964 for a useful discussion of Greek philosophy, from Thales to Aristotle.

[30] Kirk, et al. 1983:212.

but for me–old age has now seized my once tender body,
and my hair has become white instead of black;

my heart has grown heavy, and knees do not support
that once were fleet for the dance like little fawns.

How often I lament these things. But what to do?
Being Human, one cannot escape old age.

For people used to say that rose-armed Dawn, overtaken by love,
took Tithonus, handsome and young then, and carried him off
to the world's end,

Yet in time grey age still seized him,
though husband of immortal wife.

In the first half of the poem the speaker draws on her own experience of growing old to impress upon her audience that their time for the dance is limited; she entreats them to engage fully with the "Muses' lovely gifts" while they can. In light of the hortatory nature of the poem's opening it can be argued that the speaker's personal experience of old age, at least implicitly, becomes an *exemplum* for her audience. The nature of the *exemplum*, however, becomes more complex in the second half of the poem, with the introduction of the Tithonus myth. As I will argue a bit later, the speaker may be identified with Tithonus who embodies the paradox of containing within himself both change and permanence. Further, the speaker's recognition that humans are by nature subject to the changing world of aging and death, in itself, touches on an ageless, unchanging *reality about* human nature.

In Poem 16 the speaker emphasizes the specificity of her desire for Anaktoria in the context of her more general ruminations on the interconnectedness of beauty and desire. She clearly sees individual experiences of beauty to be transitory and contingent, in that individuals differ in what they find beautiful. Yet she finds an immortal and necessary connection between beauty and desire. Indeed, it may be argued that the philosophical mood of these reflections is a way for her to come to terms with her sense of loss and separation from her beloved Anaktoria. Similarly, the speaker in Poem 58 puts the experience of loss– the loss of her youth, beauty, and bodily vigor– in perspective by adopting a philosophical attitude, which is to say that the speaker moves from an engagement with her immediate situation to a contemplation of the larger issues of mortality and eternality. That attitude is initially articulated in the speaker's urgent entreaty to her audience. Drawing on the wisdom of her experience, she exhorts her audience to engage in creative and joyous expression. This *carpe diem* message is reinforced by the reference to her addressees as *paides*. While it may be tempting to think of the poem's addressees, the *paides*, as referring to the girls whom many believe comprise a circle of affiliation in Sappho's poems, the poem itself does not support such a reading—as Richard Janko also argues.[31] The fact that the poem's addressees are ambiguously gendered gives the poem wider scope. Indeed, in the broader context of the poem, the speaker seems to be addressing not only the still youthful members of her time, but the *paides* of future generations, all of whom may benefit not only from the poem's *carpe diem* message, but also from the speaker's own ability to distance herself from the losses and sorrows associated with old age, as expressed in the remainder of the poem.

At line 7 the poem shifts from the temporality and specificity of the speaker's experiences to more general inquiries about the nature of the human condition. The central position of the word ἀλλά, introducing the speaker's question, "but what to do?", signals a move toward an introspective contemplation of human nature, life and death, mortality and eternity. At line 8 the speaker observes that being human necessarily entails growing old. The story of Tithonus is presented as an exemplum of that fact. But in the context of the whole poem, the Tithonus story suggests a more intricate understanding of the human condition and its relationship to the eternal.

The speaker contrasts her situation with that of the mythical figure Tithonus, whose beauty and youth so entrances the beautiful goddess Dawn that she takes him as her husband. At Dawn's request Zeus grants Tithonus immortality, but the goddess neglects to ask that Tithonus be given eternal youth as well. As a result, Tithonus continues to age, and ends up in a state of perpetual bodily decay, chattering endlessly while shut up in his room, repulsive to the once-enthralled Dawn.

There are two equally possible, though not mutually exclusive, readings of the myth. On the one hand, Sappho's image of Tithonus, condemned perpetually to endure the effects of old age, underlines the sense that death may provide a welcome relief from the indignities and suffering brought on by old age. On the other hand, the Tithonus exemplum may allude to Sappho's hope for her own poetic immortality. In the *Homeric Hymn to Aphrodite*, which Sappho was likely to have known, the story of Tithonus illustrates the horrors of old age. Though his body utterly fails him in the *Hymn*, Tithonus' voice "flows end-

---

[31] Janko 2005.

lessly." As Janko argues, the myth of Tithonus was also associated in Sappho's day with the cicada—who rejuvenates itself by shedding its skin and singing forever.[32] The myth of Tithonus may, thus, have appealed to Sappho not only because of its suggestions of poetic immortality—that her poems may sing on-but also because the story points to the dual nature of poetry itself—as both contingent and everlasting.

Like Tithonus, the speaker of Poem 58 was once young and beautiful, an object of desire herself, but also, like Dawn, consumed with love for others. Dawn is immortal, however, and the speaker clearly is not. Yet Sappho's description of Dawn carrying Tithonus to the ends of the earth may suggest the poet's own attempts to immortalize the beloved through verse. More than that, the image of Dawn mobilized by love to traverse the vast spaces of the world may be linked with Sappho's own poetic voice, in particular the confidence she often expresses in her eventual poetic immortality.[33] The four lines of the alternative ending would emphasize this point further:

>]ιμέναν νομίσδει
>]αις ὀπάσδοι·
> ἔγω δὲ φίλημμ' ἀβροσύναν,]τοῦτο κάμοι
> τὸ λάμπρον †ἔρος ἀελίω† καὶ τὸ κάλον λέλογχε.

> ....thinks ... might give ...
> I love refinement (delicacy).....
> Eros has granted to me (bestowed upon me) (obtained for me)
> the beauty and the brightness of the sun.

These additional lines signal a dramatic shift from the speaker's earlier expression of sadness, regret, and ultimately resigned acceptance of her mortal situation. Such a shift occurs in a number of Sappho's other extant poems, notably Frs. 1, 94, and 96, where the speaker is shown to overcome debilitating desire

---

[32] Janko 2005. In the legend of Tithonus, Janko points out, "the aged Tithonus turned into another winged creature, a cicada, that can continue to sing forever—an ideal image for the aged poetess herself (Sappho), with her well-attested wish to have her poetry win glory beyond the grave."

[33] See Fragment 147, perhaps the most famous of Sappho's fragments, which shows her confidence in her own poetic immortality:
μνάσεσθαί τινά φαιμι † καὶ ἕτερον † ἀμμέων.
Someone· I say, will remember us in the future.
See also Fragment 55, in which the speaker implies that, unlike the uneducated woman to whom she addresses her poem, the speaker will be remembered for "her share in the roses of Pieria."

and loss by means of her ability to invoke erotic fulfillment through memory and imagination.[34] We can see an analogous situation in Poem 58. While earlier in the poem the speaker's focus is on loss, in the last four lines she reflects on what she has gained through a life lived in passionate pursuit of the Muses, which is expressed by her declaration of love for refinement—a quality and way of life epitomized by the Muses.

While the speaker and Tithonus are closely identified with one another in that both are depicted as subject to the ravages of old age, the last four lines of the poem present a stark contrast between them. Tithonus, though immortal, is fated to become ever more decrepit, locked away alone in his dark room. By contrast, the speaker, aware of her own mortality, expresses in the last four lines a sense of exhilaration and fulfillment at having lived a life devoted to love, beauty, and the poetic imagination. These lines may also allude to her prospects of poetic immortality. The speaker's erotic experience as a mortal being and the poetry arising from it have brought her into communion with the incorruptible qualities of the immortal, represented by the beauty and brightness of the Sun. This associates her with Dawn, who by her nature also partakes of these immortal qualities. But whereas Dawn's desire fails to bestow everlasting beauty on its object, the speaker's passions and desires lead to the creation of the ageless and eternal images of beauty in her songs.

Clearly, the tone of Poem 58 is significantly altered if we include the last four lines from the earlier Cologne papyrus. It does seem to be the case that this alternative ending accords with the energy and enthusiasm expressed by the speaker at the beginning of the poem. The potential benefits that will accrue to those who pursue the Muses are fully realized by the speaker herself at the end of the poem, when she asserts so confidently that, because of *Eros*, she has obtained the sun's brightness and beauty.[35] The implication of this assertion is that her creative endeavors (i.e. erotic poetry) have illuminated not only her life but her "afterlife" as well. Although it may be said that Sappho's artistic progeny, her poems, live in the realm of eternal ideas (the realm of the ageless and immortal muses), Sappho's songs also possess a contingent nature, in that

---

[34] For further discussions of the role of memory and imagination in Sappho, see Burnett 1979, Greene 2002, and Rayor 2005.

[35] Here, we can see evidence of Foley's point (1998) that Sappho moves beyond physical beauty to beauty in the imagination and to "potential poetic permanence (62)." Moreover, as Pender 2007:31–2 suggests, the image of the sun, used here in the context of poetic creativity and inspiration, anticipates Plato's presentation of the Form of Beauty as 'shining.' Pender argues that Plato draws on motifs of the "radiance of love," "familiar in lyric poetry," including Sappho, to describe the Form of Beauty.

they only have vitality so long as dynamic, mortal beings perform them. This contingent nature of poetic immortality brings us back to the poem's beginning. Thus, the speaker's urgent entreaty of the *paides* in the first line of the poem may be read not only as a powerful call to embrace song and dance while one can, but also as an invocation to future generations to keep her songs alive in the only way they *can* live, through performance.

Bibliography

Brumbaugh, R. 1966. *The Philosophers of Greece.* London.

Burnett, A. 1979. "Desire and Memory (Sappho Frag. 94)." *Classical Philology* 74:16–27.

Calame, C. 1996. "Sappho's Group: An Initiation into Womanhood." *Reading Sappho: Contemporary Approaches* (ed. E. Greene) 113–24. Berkeley.

———. 1999. *The Poetics of Eros in Ancient Greece.* Princeton.

duBois, P. 1995. *Sappho is Burning.* Chicago and London.

Foley, H. 1998. "The Mother of the Argument: *Eros* and the Body in Sappho and Plato's *Phaedrus*." *Parchments of Gender: Deciphering the Bodies of Antiquity* (ed. M. Wyke) 39–70. Oxford.

Fraenkel, H. 1962. *Early Greek Poetry and Philosophy.* Oxford.

Greene, E. 1994. "Apostrophe and Women's Erotics in the Poetry of Sappho." *Transactions of the American Philological Association* 124:41–56.

———. 1999. "Refiguring the Feminine Voice: Catullus Translating Sappho." *Arethusa* 32:1–18.

———. 2002. "Subjects, Objects, and Erotic Symmetry in Sappho's Fragments." *Among Women: From the Homosocial to the Homoerotic in the Ancient World* (ed. N. S. Rabinowitz and L. Auanger) 82–105. Austin.

Hallett, J. 1979. "Sappho and Her Social Context: Sense and Sensuality." *Signs* 4:447–64.

Kirk, G.S., Raven, J.E., Schofield, M. 1983. *The Presocratic Philosophers* ed 2. Cambridge. First edition 1957.

Janko, R. 2005. "Sappho Revisited." *Times Literary Supplement* December 23.

Lardinois, A. 1996. "Who Sang Sappho's Songs?" *Reading Sappho: Contemporary Approaches* (ed. E. Greene) 50–74. Berkeley.

Parker, H. 2005. "Sappho's Public World." *Women Poets in Ancient Greece and Rome,* (ed. E. Greene) 3–24. Norman.

Pender, E. E. 2007. "Sappho and Anacreon in Plato's Phaedrus." *Leeds International Classical Studies* 6.4:1–57.

Race, W. H. 1989–90. "Sappho, fr. 16 L-P and Alkaios, fr. 42 L-P: Romantic and Classical Strains in Lesbian Lyric." *Classical Journal* 85:16–33.

Rayor, D. 2005. "The Power of Memory in Erinna and Sappho." *Women Poets in Ancient Greece and Rome* (ed. E. Greene) 59–71. Norman.

Skinner, M. 1993. "Woman and Language in Archaic Greece, or, Why is Sappho a Woman?" *Feminist Theory and the Classics* (ed. N. S. Rabinowitz and A. Richlin) 125–44. New York.

Snell, B. 1960. *The Discovery of the Mind: The Greek Origins of European Thought.* Trans. T.G. Rosenmeyer. New York.

Snyder, J. M. 1997. *Lesbian Desire in the Lyrics of Sappho.* New York.

Stehle, E. 1981. "Sappho's Private World." *Reflections of Women in Antiquity* (ed. H. Foley) 45–61. New York.

West, M. L. 2005. "The New Sappho." *Zeitschrift für Papyrologie und Epigraphik* 151:1–9.

Wheelwright, P., ed. 1966. *The Presocratics.* New York.

Williamson, M. 1995. *Sappho's Immortal Daughters.* Cambridge MA.

Wills, G. 1967. "The Sapphic Umwertung aller Werte." *American Journal of Philology* 88:434–42.

Winkler, J. J. 1990. "Double Consciousness in Sappho's Lyrics." *Constraints of Desire: The Anthropology of Sex and Gender in Ancient Greece.* New York.

Zellner, H. 2007. "Sappho's Alleged Proof of Aesthetic Relativity." *Greek, Roman, and Byzantine Studies* 47:257–70.

12

A Reading of Sappho Poem 58, Fragment 31 and Mimnermus[1]

Marguerite Johnson

UCH HAS BEEN WRITTEN ON THE SAPPHIC GAZE, primarily in relation to the representation of the various personae in her poems and fragments.[2] I would like to address this subject as it relates to the poet's depiction of herself, or her artistic construct, with a focus on poem 58 and fragment 31, to illustrate what Eva Stehle defines as "poetry in and through which the gaze opens the self to disintegration, shifting position, identification with the other, or mirroring of the viewer's desiring self" (Stehle 1996:221). In addition to this feature of Sapphic poetic technique, I wish to consider further viable connections between the two pieces—specifically a similarity of theme (*eros*, *geras* and death) and one of artistic allusion (the poetry of Mimnermus). The results of this comparative study will hopefully shed some light on poem 58 in relation to an established fragment, fragment 31, as well as extend discussion of the latter piece—not only in terms of the themes of age and aging per se—but also in terms of the possibilities of the influence of Mimnermus, whose voice I suggest is not only audible in fragment 31 but in poem 58 as well.

In poem 58 Sappho laments the bodily effects of old age (58.3–6) while in fragment 31, writing on the physiological urgency of intense desire, she describes her body in crisis (31.5–16). In both pieces the same poetic devices are employed to evoke the Sapphic self-gaze: hyperbole, vivid imagery and the theme of transformation. The approach to the representation of the Sapphic body is also the same: viewing her body as if from above, the singer watches

[1] For the opportunity to present my views on poem 58, I am grateful to Ellen Greene and Marilyn Skinner for the invitation to present at the APA Special Panel, "The New Sappho on Old Age," in San Diego (January 2007). Translations of Sappho are my own, and those of Mimnermus by Terry Ryan (The University of Newcastle). Terry Ryan also provided insightful commentary on this paper.
[2] On the Sapphic gaze, cf. Stehle 1996, Snyder 1997, Keeling 1998 and Greene 2002.

physical transformations caused by external factors, namely old age in poem 58 and, in part, the forces of *eros* in fragment 31. In keeping with an almost homogenous Greek belief, nothing is directly ascribed as coming from within. Additionally, from a conceptual perspective, Sappho connects *eros* with *geras* and death.[3] In poem 58 she sings of Eos and Tithonos (58.9ff.), specifying the goddess as "mad with" *eros* because of his youthful beauty. Desperate to prolong his life for eternity—to conquer death—she achieves perpetuity for him but forgets to preserve his adolescent body. As Tithonos unendingly approaches death, engulfed by *geras* (58.12) like the poet herself, there is the metaphorical implication that *eros* dies with Eos' repulsion at the aging youth. These themes, *eros* and death, also feature in fragment 31. Like Eos, Sappho is in the grip of erotic madness and her body acts involuntarily, with each symptom drawing her closer to a dramatic fatality. But this threat of fatality may well be, I suggest, as much the result of *geras* as it is *eros*—thus the tripartite theme of *eros-geras*-death may be regarded as featuring in fragment 31 also, thereby establishing further connections between the two Sapphic pieces in question.

A comparison of poem 58 and fragment 31 reveals three stylistic features of Sappho's artistic composition. Sappho chooses hyperbole to convey emotional as well as physical states. The intensity of the hyperbole in poem 58 is heralded in the opening stanza with the use of the (conjectural) simple present, σπουδάσδω (line 2), which taken as an imperative, urges the chorus of *paides* (addressed in the vocative in 58.1) to zealously pursue the gifts of the Muses. Such dramatic urgency is continued with the use of the emphatically placed aorist, ἐπέλλαβε (58.4), the subject of which, γῆρας (58.3), governs ἔμοι δ᾽ ἄπαλον πρίν] ποτ᾽ [ἔ]οντα χρόα (58.3). Thereafter are bodily transformations: whitening hair (58.4) and unstable knees (58.5). To emphasise these changes, Sappho juxtaposes them to earlier physical states: her hair was once dark (58.4) and her knees once as capable of dancing as fawns (58.6). The same poetic devices of hyperbole, vivid imagery and the theme of transformation are employed in fragment 31. As this piece has been the subject of extensive academic analysis, it is sufficient to summarise the techniques as follows: hyperbole governs the fragment from the very beginning with the simile comparing the unnamed

---

3 While it may be argued that 58.7–8 is more about agelessness than death—and a case can be made for Tithonos as the *exemplum*—I am suggesting that Tithonos represents more than immortality; he becomes a symbol of the inevitable and unrelenting journey towards death, never reaching it, but nevertheless perpetually awaiting it. On the theme of *geras* and immortality in Mimnermus' *fragment 4*, Janko is in keeping with the first interpretation of the Tithonos topos offered above, writing: "it is Tithonus' miserable fate *not* to perish, but to have an 'imperishable' old age" (1999:155).

man—designated by the demonstrative pronoun κῆνος ('that man there' or 'whatever man')—to the gods. This Homeric echo[4] is continued in the dramatic self-representation of the Sapphic ἐγώ characterised by more Homeric flavouring via the subversion of Iliadic and Odyssean passages to evoke the narrator's erotic crisis. Bodily transformations that lead the singer to "the very point of death" (31.16) are described in economically vivid language.

In fragment 31 it has traditionally been argued that it is the presence of the woman that causes Sappho's crisis. Yet the theme of *geras* may well be present in the fragment also—an external force equally as powerful as the object of desire. It is Mimnermus, composing a generation before Sappho, whose poetry strengthens this hypothesis. Before analysing Mimnermus *fragment 2*, however, it is necessary to briefly consider whether or not he is a viable source of influence for the songs of Sappho. In relation to this hypothesis, it is pertinent to note that during the Archaic age there was no fixed or privileged version of poetry or individual poems but rather a formulaic yet nonetheless fluid tradition of oral composition and re-composition (by 'fluid,' in contrast to 'formulaic,' the distinction between *adopting* and *adapting* canonical composition is meant). R. Rawles (2006:1–7), in an analysis of poem 58 and the links it presents to the *Homeric Hymn to Aphrodite*, for example, demonstrates how, in an artistic environment based on oral composition, Sappho constructs imitative songs by establishing "an allusive relationship" with her predecessors and contemporaries (Rawles 2006:2). Such a relationship may not always be predicated on "close lexical parallels" (Rawles 2006:2), but can just as legitimately—in terms of allusion—turn to other circumstantial points of poetic reference. Motifs in this sense are a pan-Hellenic[5] corpus of "quotable quotes" originating from a discernibly oral tradition. In this environment of composition there is naturally occurring parallel subject matter "handled with parallel sequences of thematic development, which in turn will be expressed with remarkably parallel formulaic patterns" (Nagy 1985:48).

On the basis of such a system of analysis, then, we may argue for a similarity of approaches to the specific theme of ageing by both Mimnermus and

---

[4] There are several significant Homeric echoes in fragment 31; cf. Page 1955:21ff., Wills 1967:174ff., Marcovich 1972:22ff., Rissman 1983:66–118, Edwards 1989:593ff, Winkler 1996:92ff. These echoes can be divided into two categories: [i] allusions to Homeric accounts of emotions, particularly those associated with fear and astonishment; [ii] goddess imagery, particularly the accounts of mortal responses to god-like women. On the Homeric ἴσος θέοισιν (fr. 31.1), cf. Winkler 1996:98–101 and Furley 2000:10ff. For further discussion of the imagery, particularly as medical, cf. Lanata 1966, Di Benedetto 1985 and Bonanno 1990.

[5] Cf. Nagy 1979, and especially Nagy 1985.

Sappho that is a natural product of this particular environment of composition. The problem with this analysis is, however, the obvious question: given the generic approaches to given themes, in this instance *geras*, is Sappho necessarily invoking Mimnermus? In reply I would suggest that as Mimnermus comes at an earlier stage in the history of Greek oral lyric his material—in all its glorious oral variations—was in the likely position of pre-eminence in regards to sources for allusion. Secondly, his treatment of *geras* matches Sappho's not only in terms of general thematic approaches, but, more significantly, in a series of echoes of more precise motifs. The first of these two areas of compatibility is perhaps best seen in *fragment 2*, in which Mimnermus sings of old age:

ἡμεῖς δ', οἷά τε φύλλα φύει πολυάνθεμος ὥρη
    ἔαρος, ὅτ' αἶψ' αὐγῆς αὔξεται ἠελίου,
τοῖς ἴκελοι πήχυιον ἐπὶ χρόνον ἄνθεσιν ἥβης
    τερπόμεθα, πρὸς θεῶν εἰδότες οὔτε κακὸν
οὔτ' ἀγαθόν· Κῆρες δὲ παρεστήκασι μέλαιναι,
    ἡ μὲν ἔχουσα τέλος γήραος ἀργαλέου,
ἡ δ' ἑτέρη θανάτοιο· μίνυνθα δὲ γίνεται ἥβης
    καρπός, ὅσον τ' ἐπὶ γῆν κίδναται ἠέλιος.
αὐτὰρ ἐπὴν δὴ τοῦτο τέλος παραμείψεται ὥρης,
    αὐτίκα δὴ τεθνάναι βέλτιον ἢ βίοτος·
πολλὰ γὰρ ἐν θυμῷ κακὰ γίνεται· ἄλλοτε οἶκος
    τρυχοῦται, πενίης δ' ἔργ' ὀδυνηρὰ πέλει·
ἄλλος δ' αὖ παίδων ἐπιδεύεται, ὧν τε μάλιστα
    ἱμείρων κατὰ γῆς ἔρχεται εἰς Ἀΐδην·
ἄλλος νοῦσον ἔχει θυμοφθόρον· οὐδέ τίς ἐστιν
    ἀνθρώπων ᾧ Ζεὺς μὴ κακὰ πολλὰ διδοῖ.

We, indeed, are just like leaves that the season of flowers
    produces, springing up swiftly beneath the warm rays of the
        sun:
for us, like them, brief is the span of time when we take delight
    in the blooming of youth; the good or bad to come the
gods keep a secret, while alongside us stand the two dark Spirits of
        Death,
    one offering us the harshness of old age,
the other one bringing death. The fruitful time of youth
    is all too brief, as brief as the day's sunlight upon the earth:
and once the full ripeness of this season has passed,

from that moment it is preferable to be dead than to go on
living.
A multiplicity of evils afflict one's heart. One man's property
wastes away, and painful poverty ensues;
another man is bereft of sons and feels this lack the keenest
as he makes his way down to Hades;
another endures illness that saps the spirit. There is no mortal
to whom
Zeus does not allot a multiplicity of evils.

In this fragment, Mimnermus, in keeping with Greek cultural and literary tradition, regards *geras* as an external force that attacks the human body, mentioning "the two dark Spirits of Death, / one offering us the harshness of old age, / the other one bringing death" (*fr.2.5–7*). Mimnermus' external forces are the Keres, the Spirits of Death, agents of the Moirai. While Sappho does not refer to specific deities—personifications of *geras*—that assail her, *geras* per se is certainly represented as an active, external force. Additionally, Sappho's treatment of old age as it relates to youth is also found in Mimnermus. Sappho views age as a desperate condition and one to be mourned. Thus she reminds—or even warns—the *paides* to be aware of what they have (as in Mimnermus' *fr.2.7–8*). Likewise, Mimnermus looks ahead to old age and reminds himself that it is inevitably close.

It is possible that Sappho was drawing from the works of Mimnermus in poem 58 as well as additional pieces by him in her other lyrics, most notably, fragment 31. As previously signposted, it has long been read as her response to the woman in fragment 31 that causes her seizure. It is noteworthy however, that in terms of the theme of old age in poem 58, fragment 31, when read in conjunction with another piece—Mimnermus *fragment 5*—is perhaps even closer to poem 58 than ascertained at first glance.[6] In *fragment 5*, the poet mourns fleeting youth and the onset of *geras*:

αὐτίκα μοι κατὰ μὲν χροιὴν ῥέει ἄσπετος ἱδρώς,
πτοιῶμαι δ' ἐσορῶν ἄνθος ὁμηλικίης
τερπνὸν ὁμῶς καὶ καλόν· ἐπὶ πλέον ὤφελεν εἶναι·
ἀλλ' ὀλιγοχρόνιον γίνεται ὥσπερ ὄναρ
ἥβη τιμήεσσα· τὸ δ' ἀργαλέον καὶ ἄμορφον

---

[6] There is a series of persuasive arguments in favour of the attribution to Mimnermus; cf. West 1989:221, Adkins 1985:101-106, and Nagy 1985:48. Cf. also Young 1964. Contra Gerber 1999:84–85.

γῆρας ὑπὲρ κεφαλῆς αὐτίχ' ὑπερκρέμεται,
ἐχθρὸν ὁμῶς καὶ ἄτιμον, ὅ τ' ἄγνωστον τιθεῖ ἄνδρα,
βλάπτει δ' ὀφθαλμοὺς καὶ νόον ἀμφιχυθέν.

The sweat pours down me, and my heart is filled with trembling
  when I gaze upon my generation in full flower of
pleasure and what is beautiful. If only it would last much longer!
  But as transient as a mere dream is
precious youth; soon ugly, dire, loathsome
  old age looms above us,
disgusting and without honour, that renders a man
  unrecognisable, and overwhelms both his eyes and his mind.

Once again, as in both pieces by Sappho, the physical response or condition of the mortal is a result of external forces: *geras* "looms above us" (*fr.*5.6) and "overwhelms" our "eyes and mind." Closer comparison of all three pieces suggests that Sappho had more than a passing familiarity with the poetry of Mimnermus and has not only imitated it in poem 58 but utilised it in fragment 31. Of significance here is the two-line reference to Tithonos and the *kakon* of *geras* in *fragment 4*, which is combined with *fragment 5* (with a lacuna between) in the Gentili-Prato edition:

Τιθωνῷ μὲν ἔδωκεν ἔχειν κακὸν ἄφθιτον< >
  γῆρας, ὅ καὶ θανάτου ῥίγιον ἀργαλέου.

To Tithonos, he [Zeus] granted possession of an
      immortal evil <...>,
  old age, something even more horrible than painful death.

In poem 58, *geras* "seizes" Sappho (58.4)[7] as it "overwhelms" Mimnermus; Sappho urges the *paides* to make the most of their time—a sentiment urgently expressed, and symbolised by reference to the "beautiful gifts of the fragrant-breasted Muses" (58.1) and "for the clear, sweet-singing lyre" (58.2) just as Mimnermus, significantly, "gaze[s] upon" his "generation in full flower of / pleasure and what is beautiful" (*fr.*5.2-3), then, as does Sappho (58.7-8), laments its brevity. As she sings of bodily transformations, he sings of old age that renders a man "unrecognisable" (*fr.*5.8). If we adopt the combined reading offered

---

[7] Cf. Annis 2005:1 on ἐπι-λαμβάνω as "used to describe affliction by a disease." Verbs for "snatching up" are often associated with death in the Greek lyric and epic tradition, cf. Nagy 1996b:52.

by Gentili and Prato, the similarities between poem 58 and the piece(s) by Mimnermus are substantially reinforced. *eros-geras*-death thereby become a tripartite poetic concept in the compositions of both.

In fragment 31, Sappho sings of her bodily reactions—transformations—externally instigated. The woman's "sweet replies" (31.4), "desire-inducing laugh" (31.5) and the mere sight of her are dramatised by the exclamation:

ὡς γὰρ ἔς σ' ἴδω βρόχε' ὥς με φώναι-
σ' οὐδ' ἒν ἔτ' εἴκει,

For just gazing at you for a second, it is impossible
for me even to talk (31:7–8)[8]

This lends itself to an erotic interpretation. The forces of *eros* have assaulted Sappho. Yet the recollection of Mimnermus' *fragment 5* in fragment 31 adds layers of additional meaning to Sappho's external assailants. He opens his poem with a powerful statement of a body in crisis, a device Stehle credits to Sappho in poetry "in and through which the gaze opens the self to disintegration" (Stehle 1996:221): "sweat pours down" him, and his "heart is filled with trembling" (*fr.*5.1) when he "gaze[s] upon" his designated object of wonder (*fr.*5.2–3). Additionally, the external force—*geras*—assails his eyes and mind. Sappho's heart, as we know, pounds in her "breast" (31.6), her mind is not mentioned but its ally, the "tongue," "is broken" (31.9) and she cannot talk; like Mimnermus, her mind is overwhelmed. As "a soft / flame" steals "beneath" her "flesh" (31.9–10), "sweat pours down" her (31.13) and, perspiring thus, like him she too is blinded (31.11). As old age brings Mimnermus closer to (inevitable) death, so Sappho reaches the point of no return in fragment 31. Both confront their own limited mortality.

As extensively documented by scholars, Sappho's use of Homeric imagery, inverted from military or battlefield death scenes to an erotic context, has been at the forefront of analyses of fragment 31.[9] In support of her use of Mimnermus *fragment 5* in the same piece, we may likewise argue in favour of clever inversion of the language of ageing to effect erotic verse. Her crisis, however, may be more complex than straightforward desire. It may well be the yearning of one who is old gazing at one who is young. This reading is strengthened by a reappraisal of Sappho's opening line, the famous φαίνεταί μοι. Academic interpretations have focussed on the man's equation with the gods in terms of

---

[8] Cf. Lidov 1993.
[9] Cf. n3.

his ability to calmly endure the presence of the woman or because he occupies the woman's attention.[10] These are more than appropriate interpretations of the simile, yet it may be suggested that, if read in the context of the theme of ageing, the male in question may be regarded as fortunate because he is young, while Sappho is old. In a less poetic context, it may be useful to recall M. I. Finley's seminal paper, "The Elderly in Classical Antiquity," in which he states the basic facts of what the ancient doctors knew and wrote of ageing: "They knew that pulse rates changed with age, for example, that the elderly tended to ... failing sight, and deafness" (Finley 1981:157–58).[11] Such symptoms of ageing, specifically blindness, are mentioned by Mimnermus when he sings of *geras* overwhelming "both his eyes and his mind" (*fragment 5*:8). The assault on the mind may well be a reference to the onset of dementia and while this may seem a somewhat farfetched interpretation of Mimnermus' line, dementia was a symptom of ageing discerned by the ancients at least by the time of Pythagoras.[12] Perhaps this is also what besets Sappho in fragment 31—a symptom of ageing combined with an established symptom of erotic crisis to create a superb metaphor. As for the ancient view on youth, Finley continues: "Youth meant a healthy physique, beauty, and sexual attraction" (Finley 1981:162). Mimnermus and Sappho were clearly—and painfully—aware of both conditions.

Returning to the topic of the Sapphic gaze, notably the self-gaze, we detect further echoes of Mimnermus' poetry. His tendency to self-observe, however, is not as consistent a poetic device in the extant fragments as it is in her work. While the use of the self-gaze as descriptive signifier appears in Mimnermus *fragment 5*, it is not there in *fragment 2*. It appears, however, in both pieces by Sappho as expressing personal and physical trauma. To better identify the Sapphic self-gaze, I acknowledge the definition by Bret L. Keeling, who, while writing on her erotic gaze, offers clear interpretive parameters: "a steadily intense way of looking at ... a way of looking after (following with the eye), looking into (inquiring with the mind) ... looking upon (considering and beholding), looking ahead ..., and looking back (reviewing and returning)" (Keeling 1998:178).

When read in connection with poem 58 and fragment 31, these ways of looking at oneself exemplify what Keeling refers to as "specifically multiple ways of seeing" (Keeling 1998:178). In picturing her body through the multiplicity that is the Sapphic self-gaze, the poet better communicates, and simul-

---

[10] For a survey of the academic interpretations, cf. Furley 2000.

[11] Much has been written on ageing in antiquity since Finley; cf. for example, Falkner and De Luce 1989, Falkner 1995, Pratt 2000. Prior to Finley is Kirk 1971 and Bertman 1976.

[12] Cf. Román 2002:200.

taneously evokes, the themes of *eros* and death. In poem 58, for example, she employs "a steadily intense way of looking" at herself, establishing through the aforementioned poetic devices a dual picture of herself as once youthful and active *and* old and decrepit. So too does she "look" "into" a more holistic image of both herself as an ageing person and old age per se, Keeling's "inquiring with the mind." This is best illustrated by the simple aphorism of lines 7–8, effectively amplified by the Tithonos exemplum immediately following, which typifies the themes of *eros* and death. As she looks upon herself, "considering and beholding," the audience knows—as does Sappho—that the erotic gaze of others dies with the onset of *geras*. Herein is Keeling's final component of the Sapphic gaze, as something that looks "ahead" and "back (reviewing and returning)," a feature of Mimnermus *fragment 5*. Once young, lithe and, by implication, desirable, she is now old, slow and, by implication, unattractive, and the future entails death. As Mimnermus expresses in *fragment 1.1-5*

> τίς δὲ βίος, τί δὲ τερπνὸν ἄτερ χρυσέης Ἀφροδίτης;
>   τεθναίην, ὅτε μοι μηκέτι ταῦτα μέλοι,
> κρυπταδίη φιλότης καὶ μείλιχα δῶρα καὶ εὐνή,
>   οἷ' ἥβης ἄνθεα γίνεται ἁρπαλέα
> ἀνδράσιν ἠδὲ γυναιξίν·

> What is it to be alive, what is pleasure without golden Aphrodite?
>   I trust that I will die by the time I no longer care for
> secret love affairs and tender gifts and for bed,
>   the delightful flowers that adorn the prime of youth
> for men and for women.

Admittedly, in comparison to Sappho, Mimnermus is more overt in his lamentation of *geras* and its repercussions vis-à-vis *philotes* (fr.1.3). More so than Sappho, his stated fear is that he will live into old age, and the desires of the body will still remain, sentiments of lines 2–4 that alter the opening line with depressing irony. Sappho's approach is subtler, with poem 58 suggestive of the sentiments of Mimnermus' theme of *philotes* at lines 7–8, coming as they do after her imperative to the *paides* and the description of her ageing body, and followed by the Tithonos reference.

In fragment 31, Sappho is sick with a desire that brings her close to death. As she "watches" her own body waste away in poem 58, so too does she "watch" (and feel)—what I posit to be her ageing body—sickened as she listens to and gazes at the object of desire in fragment 31. Sappho, by turning her gaze on herself in both instances, recasts a preoccupation demonstrated elsewhere in her work, namely the gazing at others. One of the poetic accomplishments of this self-externalization, whereby the singer casts herself as protagonist and victim, is the evocation of the inevitable human condition—utter defenceless-ness against the forces of old age, death and *eros*, all of which coalesce, I sug-gest, in both pieces.

There is, it could be argued, an impasse to this new interpretation of frag-ment 31, which is, of course, Catullus' *poem 51*. The latter clearly reveals that Catullus has interpreted the Sapphic piece in terms of erotic verse without any discernable cogency of ageing imagery in the original. Nevertheless, it is important to remember that Catullus was practising *imitatio* and his rendition is demonstrably his own, particularly with (i) the inclusion of his own name and that of Lesbia and (ii) the *otium* stanza.[13] It could be argued that the latter, if accepted as part of the new version and not, as has been argued, a section of another poem or a self-contained piece in its own right, inadvertently mis-placed in the manuscript tradition, is a deliberate move away from the themes of ageing and death contained in the original. Despite scholars who argue that the *otium* stanza is misplaced owing, in part, to the sudden change of direction that is, allegedly, not a feature of Catullan poetry, the movement towards this stanza is signposted by the changes made to fragment 31 in *poem 51* prior to lines 13–16, most notably the removal of the reference to the closeness of death at 31.15–16. This change—an acceptable if not expected feature of the best of the poetry of *imitatio*—centres *poem 51* more completely within the realm of eroticism per se. Additionally, if we accept the traditional reading of the Lesbia Cycle being the outpourings of a younger man to an older woman, we witness a necessary poetic reversal of the traditional reading of the Sapphic corpus as poems written by an older woman to younger companions. Ageing, therefore, is a more probable theme of interpretive detection in Sappho's oeuvre than it is in the works of Catullus.

The *otium* stanza, taken by most scholars as part of *poem 51*, is perhaps an example of Catullan *imitatio* in more ways than one; expressly, it may not only be a rendering of a specific poem by Sappho but also a rendering of Sapphic *imitatio* per se. What we have detected in this analysis of Sappho's use of Mim-nermus—in the true spirit of intertextual allusion—is detectable comparison

---

13 In support of original inclusion of the *otium* stanza, cf. Lattimore 1944, Elder 1951, Kidd 1963, Commager 1965, Fredricksmeyer 1965, Woodman 1966, Wills 1967, Frank 1968, Lejnieks 1968, Segal 1970, Kinsey 1974, Shipton 1980, Adler 1981, Baker 1981, Itzkowitz 1983, Knox 1984, Finamore 1984, Vine 1992; contra, cf. Bowra 1961.223, Wormell 1966, Jensen 1967, Fordyce 1978:219, Richmond 1970, Copley 1974, Wilkinson 1974.

as well as diversion. The diversions from Mimnermus have been discussed in relation to her use of *fragment 1*, and the same techniques of Sapphic *imitatio* can be detected in her use of *fragment 5*. In regard to the latter fragment by Mimnermus, we note his emphasis on the physical aspects of beauty, which is the focus that sets Sappho's approach apart; she sings of non-erotic beauty in poem 58 whereas he gazes at the young in a different light. Catullus, too, practises the same techniques. While we detect similarities between *poem 51* and fragment 31, there is individualism (as discussed above). The *otium* stanza, while arguably the most distinctive departure from the original, is also very much a "gaze" piece, and one that is self-referential in the extreme—"looking into" and "looking upon." Both Sappho and Catullus transform not translate.

Bibliography

Adkins, A. H. W. 1985. *Poetic Craft in the Early Greek Elegists*. Chicago.

Adler, E. 1981. *Catullan Self-Revelation*. New York.

Allen, A. 1993. *The Fragments of Mimnermus: Text and Commentary*. Stuttgart.

Annis, W. S. 2005. "Sappho: Fragment 58." ΑΟΙΔΟΙ: Poetic Texts. http://www.aoidoi.org/poets/sappho/sappho-58.pdf

Baker, R. J. 1981. "Propertius' Monobiblos and Catullus 51." *Rheinisches Museum* 124:312–24.

Bertman, S., ed. 1976. *The Conflict of Generations in Ancient Greece and Rome*. Amsterdam.

Bonanno, M. G. 1990. "Patemi d'amore (Apollonio, Teocrito e Saffo)." *L'allusione necessaria. Eicerche intertestuali sulla poesia greca e latina* , 147–81. Rome.

Bowra, C. M. 1961. *Greek Lyric Poetry: From Alcman to Simonides* ed. 3. Oxford.

Commager, S. 1965. "Notes on Some Poems of Catullus." *Harvard Studies in Classical Philology* 70:83–110.

Copley, F. O. 1974. "The Structure of Catullus C.51 and the Problem of the Otium-Strophe." *Grazer Beiträge* 2:25–37.

Di Benedetto, V. 1985. "Il tema della vecchiaia e il fr. 58 di Saffo." *Quaderni Urbinati di Cultura Classica* n.s. 19:145–63.

Edmunds, L. 2006. "The New Sappho: ἔφαντο." *Zeitschrift für Papyrologie und Epigraphik* 156:23–25.

Edwards, M. J. 1989. "Greek into Latin: A Note on Catullus and Sappho." *Latomus* 48:590–600.

Elder, J. P. 1951. "Notes on Some Conscious and Subconscious Elements in Catullus' Poetry." *Harvard Studies in Classical Philology* 60:101–36.

Falkner, T. M. 1995. *The Poetics of Old Age in Greek Epic, Lyric and Tragedy*. Oklahoma.

Falkner, T. M., and De Luce, J., eds. 1989. *Old Age in Greek and Latin Literature*. New York.

Finamore, J. 1984. "Catullus 50 and 51: Friendship, Love, and Otium." *Classical World* 78:11–19.

Finley, M. I. 1981. "The Elderly in Classical Antiquity." *Greece & Rome* 28:156–71.

Fordyce, C. J. 1978. *Catullus: A Commentary*. Oxford.

Frank, R. I. 1968. "Catullus 51: Otium Versus Virtus." *Transactions of the American Philological Association* 99:233–39.

Fredricksmeyer, E. A. 1965. "On the Unity of Catullus 51." *Transactions of the American Philological Association* 96:153–63.

Furley, W. D. 2000. "'Fearless, Bloodless ... like the Gods': Sappho 31 and the Rhetoric of 'Godlike.'" *Classical Quarterly* 50:7–15.

Gentili, B., and Prato, C., eds. 1988. *Poetae Elegiaci. Testimonia et Fragmenta*. Leipzig.

Gerber, D. E. 1991. "Early Greek Elegy and Iambus 1921–1989." *Lustrum* 33:7–225.

———. 1999. *Greek Elegiac Poetry from the Seventh to the Fifth Centuries BC*. Cambridge MA.

Greene, E., ed. 1996. *Reading Sappho: Contemporary Approaches*. Berkeley.

———. 2002. "Subjects, Objects, and Erotic Symmetry in Sappho's Fragments." *Among Women: From the Homosocial to the Homoerotic in the Ancient World* (eds. N. S. Rabinowitz and L. Auanger) , 82–105. Austin.

Gronewald, M., and Daniel, R. W. 2004a. "Ein neuer Sappho-Papyrus." *Zeitschrift für Papyrologie und Epigraphik* 147:1–8.

———."Nachtrag zum neuen Sappho-Papyrus." *Zeitschrift für Papyrologie und Epigraphik* 149:1–4.

———. 2006. "Lyrischer Text (Sappho-Papyrus)." *Zeitschrift für Papyrologie und Epigraphik* 154:7–12.

Hardie, A. 2006. "Sappho, the Muses, and Life after Death." *Zeitschrift für Papyrologie und Epigraphik* 154:13–32.

Itzkowitz, J. B. 1983. "On the Last Stanza of Catullus 51." *Latomus* 42:129–34.

Janko, R. 1990. "Mimnermus, Fragment 4 West: A Conjecture." *American Journal of Philology* 111:154–55.

———. 2005. "Sappho Revisited." *Times Literary Supplement* December 23.

Jensen, R. C. 1967. "Otium, Catulle, tibi molestum est." *Classical Journal* 62:363–65.

Keeling, B. L. 1998. "H.D. and 'The Contest': Archaeology of a Sapphic Gaze." *Twentieth Century Literature* 44:176–203.

Kidd, D. A. 1963. "The Unity of Catullus 51." *Journal of the Australasian Universities Language and Literature Association* 20:298–308.

Kinsey, T. E. 1974. "Catullus 51." *Latomus* 33:373–78.

Kirk, G. S. 1971. "Old Age and Maturity in Ancient Greece." *Eranos* 40:123–58.

Knox, P. E. 1984. "Sappho, fr.31 LP and Catullus 51: A Suggestion." *Quaderni Urbinati di Cultura Classica* n.s. 17:97–102.

Lanata, G. 1966. "Sul linguaggio amoroso di Saffo." *Quaderni Urbinati di Cultura Classica* n.s. 2:63–79.

Lattimore, R. 1944. "Sappho 2 and Catullus 51." *Classical Philology* 39:184–87.

Lejnieks, V. 1968. "Otium Catullianum Reconsidered." *Classical Journal* 63:262–64.

Lidov, J. B. 1993. "The Second Stanza of Sappho 31: Another Look." *American Journal of Philology* 114:503–35.

Marcovich, M. 1972. "Sappho Fr.31: Anxiety Attack or Love Declaration?" *Classical Quarterly* 22:19–32.

Nagy, G. 1979. *The Best of the Achaeans: Concepts of the Hero in Archaic Greek Poetry*. Baltimore. Revised second edition 1999.

———. 1985. "Theognis and Megara: A Poet's Vision of His City." *Theognis of Megara: Poetry and the Polis* (eds. T. J. Figueira and G. Nagy) 22--81. Baltimore.

———. 1996a. *Poetry as Performance: Homer and Beyond*. Oxford.

———. 1996b. "Phaethon, Sappho's Phaon, and the White Rock of Leukas: 'Reading' the Symbols of Greek Lyric." In Greene 1996:, 35--57.

Page, D. L. 1955. *Sappho and Alcaeus*. Oxford. Corrected reprint 1959.

Pratt, L. 2000. "The Old Women of Ancient Greece and the Homeric Hymn to Demeter." *Transactions of the American Philological Association* 130:41–65.

Rawles, R. 2006. "Notes on the Interpretation of the 'New Sappho'." *Zeitschrift für Papyrologie und Epigraphik* 157:1–7.

Richmond, A. J. 1970. "Horace's Mottoes and Catullus 51." *Rheinisches Museum* 113:197–204.

Rissman, L. 1983. *Love as War: Homeric Allusion in the Poetry of Sappho*. Konigstein.

Román, G. C. 2002. "Historical Evolution of the Concept of Dementia: A Systematic Review from 2000 BC to AD 2000." *Evidence-Based Dementia Practice*, (eds. N. Qizilbash et al.), 199–227. London.

Segal, C. 1970. "Catullan Otiosi: The Lover and the Poet." *Greece & Rome* 17:25–31.

Shipton, K. M. W. 1980. "Catullus 51: Just Another Love Poem?" *Liverpool Classical Monthly* 5:73–76.

Snyder, J. M. 1997. *Lesbian Desire in the Lyrics of Sappho*. New York.

Stehle, E. 1996. "Sappho's Gaze: Fantasies of a Goddess and Young Man." In Greene 1996:, 193–25.

Vine, B. 1992. "On the 'Missing' Fourth Stanza of Catullus 51." *Harvard Studies in Classical Philology* 94:251–58.

West, M. L. 1974. *Studies in Greek Elegy and Iambus*. Berlin.

———, ed. 1989. *Iambi et elegi Graeci ante Alexandrum cantati* ed. 2. Oxford.

———. 2005a. "A New Sappho Poem." *Times Literary Supplement* June 24.

———. 2005b. "The New Sappho." *Zeitschrift für Papyrologie und Epigraphik* 151:1–9.

Wilkinson, L. P. 1974. "Ancient and Modern: Catullus 51 Again." *Greece & Rome* 21:82–85.

Wills, G. 1967. "Sappho 31 and Catullus 51." *Greek, Roman and Byzantine Studies* 8:167–97.

Winkler, J. J. 1996. "Gardens of Nymphs: Public and Private in Sappho's Lyrics." In Greene 1996:, 89–109.

Woodman, A. J. 1966. "Some Implications of Otium in Catullus 51.13–16." *Latomus* 25:217–26.

Wormell, D. E. W. 1966. "Catullus as Translator." *The Classical Tradition: Literary and Historical Studies in Honor of Harry Caplan* (L. Wallach) , 187–201. Ithaca.

Young, D. 1964. "Borrowings and Self-Adaptions in Theognis." *Miscellanea Critica Teubner* (I. J. Irmscher, et al.), 307–390. Leipzig.

13

The "New Sappho" Reconsidered in the Light of the Athenian Reception of Sappho

Gregory Nagy

THE TEXT OF THE "NEW SAPPHO," FOUND IN A COLOGNE PAPYRUS dated to the third century BCE (P.Köln inv. 21351 + 21376), is different from a later text of Sappho, found in an Oxyrhynchus papyrus dated to the second or third century CE (*P.Oxy.* 1787). In the two papyri, the songs of Sappho are evidently arranged in a different order. Both papyri contain fragments of three songs, but only the second of the three songs in each papyrus is the same. The other two songs in each papyrus are different from each other. The sameness of the second song in each papyrus is evident from an overlap between the wording of lines 9–20 in the earlier papyrus (Π^1 in the working edition of Obbink) and of lines 11–22 in the later papyrus (Π^2). But even this same song, which is about Tithonos, is not really the same in the two papyri. The text of Sappho's "song of Tithonos" in the later papyrus is longer: after line 22, which corresponds to line 20 of the earlier papyrus, the song seems to keep going for another four lines, all the way through line 26, before a third song starts at line 27. By contrast, the text of Sappho's "song of Tithonos" in the earlier papyrus is shorter: after line 20, there are no further lines for this song, and a third song starts at line 21. This difference between the two texts of Sappho's "song of Tithonos" leads to a question: which of the texts is definitive—the shorter one or the longer one? In what follows, I will formulate an answer based on what we know about the reception of Sappho in Athens in the fifth century BCE.

This reception, as I argue, was an aspect of the actual transmission of Sappho's songs, starting from their foundational context in Lesbos around 600 BCE. In other words, the Athenian reception of Sappho was not some revival of an Aeolian lyric tradition that had been discontinued. This is not a story of Sappho interrupted and then revived. Instead, it is a story of Sappho continued—and thereby transformed. As an analogy for the reception of Sappho in Athens during the fifth century I think of the reception of Homer in the same city during the same period. This Athenian Homer was not some revival of an Ionian epic tradition that had been discontinued: rather, the Homeric tradition in Athens was an organic continuation of earlier epic traditions stemming from Ionia.[1]

An essential aspect of Sappho's reception in Athens, I argue, was the tradition of performing her songs in a sympotic context, which differentiated these songs from what they once had been in their primarily choral context.[2] Before proceeding further, I pause for a moment to review what I mean by <u>sympotic</u> and <u>choral</u> contexts.

When I speak of a <u>choral</u> context, I have in mind the general idea of performances by a *khoros*, conventionally translated as 'chorus'. I offer a working definition of the *khoros*: <u>it is a group of male or female performers who sing and dance a given song within a space (real or notional) that is sacred to a divinity or to a constellation of divinities.</u>[3] In the case of songs attributed to Sappho, they were once performed by women singing and dancing within such a sacred space.[4] And the divinity most closely identified with most of her songs is Aphrodite.[5]

When I speak of a <u>sympotic</u> context, I have in mind more specifically the idea of <u>comastic</u> performances, that is, performances by a *kōmos*, which is a group linked with an occasion conventionally termed a 'revel'. Pragmatically speaking, we can say that the *kōmos* is both the occasion of a 'revel' and the group engaged in that 'revel'. I offer a working definition of the *kōmos*: <u>it is a group of male performers who sing and dance a given song on a festive occasion that calls for the drinking of wine.</u>[6]

Here I review the implications of this definition. The combination of wine and song expresses the ritual communion of those participating in the *kōmos*. This communion creates a bonding of the participants with one another and with the divinity who makes the communion sacred, that is, Dionysus.[7] To the extent that the *kōmos* is a group of male performers who sing and dance in a

---

[1] Nagy 2007b.

[2] Nagy 2007a and c. Hereafter I refer to Nagy 2007c as "SA." My views on the transmission of Sappho's songs converge with those of Deborah Boedeker, who has kindly shared with me a copy of a forthcoming work of hers (see the Bibliography) about the transmission of Sappho's songs in sympotic as well as choral contexts.

[3] SA 211. Also PP 53–54, with extensive references to Calame 1977/2001; Bierl 2003:98–101.

[4] Nagy 2007a:24–43; PH 371 [12§62]; PP 87; cf. Lardinois 1994 and 1996.

[5] Nagy 2007a:26–35; PP 96–103; cf. Gentili 1988:216–222.

[6] SA 212. For the *kōmos*, see in general Bierl 2001:ch. 2 pp. 300–361; also Pütz 2003 and the review by Bierl 2005.

[7] SA 212. Frontisi-Ducroux and Lissarrague 1990:230.

space (real or notional) that is sacred to Dionysus, it can be considered a sub-category of the *khoros*.[8]

The concept of the *kōmos* is linked with the more general concept of the symposium.[9] That is why I have found it convenient to use the more general term <u>sympotic</u> as well as the more specific term <u>comastic</u> in referring to the context of the *kōmos*. I should note, however, that the ancient symposium, in all its attested varieties, could accommodate other kinds of singing and dancing besides the kinds we find attested for the *kōmos*. And, for the moment, I concentrate on the specific concept of the *kōmos*.

Back when Sappho is thought to have flourished in Lesbos, around 600 BCE, we expect that her songs would be performed by women in the context of the *khoros*. Around the same time in Lesbos, the songs of Alcaeus would be performed by men in the context of the *kōmos*. This context is signaled by the use of the verb *kōmazein* 'sing and dance in the *kōmos*', which is actually attested in one of his songs (Alcaeus F 374.1).

There is an overlap, however, in performing the songs attributed to Sappho. I argue that such songs could be performed not only by women in a *khoros* but also by men in a *kōmos*.[10] To avoid any misunderstanding here, I should note that the *kōmos* involves forms of "high art" as well as "low art." A prominent example of the higher forms is the epinician poetry of Pindar and Bacchylides, which is stylized as comastic performance. And, within the mythological framework of the stylized *kōmoi* of Pindar and Bacchylides, the male singers and dancers could be imagined at special moments as female singers and dancers who are performing in a chorus. A case in point is Song 13 of Bacchylides, which features a mythically performing *khoros* 'chorus' of nymphs embedded within a ritually performing *kōmos* of men.[11]

I trace this kind of embedded choral performance from Lesbos to Samos, where it became part of the court poetry of Anacreon:[12]

> Anacreon was court poet to Polycrates of Samos, the powerful ruler of an expansive maritime empire in the Aegean world of the late sixth century. The lyric role of Sappho was appropriated by the imperial court poetry of Anacreon.

---

[8] SA 212.

[9] SA 212; PP 85; Nagy 2004:31n17.

[10] SA 212.

[11] Power 2000; cf. Stehle 1997:106 and Fearn 2003:359n48.

[12] SA 226–227.

This appropriation can be viewed only retrospectively, however, through the lens of poetic traditions in Athens. That is because the center of imperial power over the Aegean shifted from Samos to Athens when Polycrates the tyrant of Samos was captured and executed by agents of the Persian empire. Parallel to this transfer of imperial power was a transfer of musical prestige, politically engineered by Hipparkhos the son of Peisistratos and tyrant of Athens. Hipparkhos made the powerful symbolic gesture of sending a warship to Samos to fetch Anacreon and bring him to Athens ("Plato" *Hipparkhos* 228c). This way, the Ionian lyric tradition as represented by Anacreon was relocated from its older imperial venue in Samos to a newer imperial venue in Athens. Likewise relocated was the Aeolian lyric tradition as represented by Sappho—and also by Alcaeus.

The new Aegean empire that was taking shape under the hegemony of Athens became the setting for a new era in lyric poetry, starting in the late sixth century and extending through most of the fifth. In this era, Athens became a new stage, as it were, for the performing of Aeolian and Ionian lyric poetry as mediated by the likes of Anacreon. The most public context for such performance was the prestigious Athenian festival of the Panathenaia, where professional monodic singers performed competitively in spectacular restagings of lyric poetry. The Aeolian and Ionian lyric traditions exemplified by Anacreon figured prominently at this festival.

This kind of poetry, despite the publicity it got from the Panathenaia as the greatest of the public festivals of Athens, could also be performed privately, that is, in sympotic contexts. Most telling are the references in Athenian Old Comedy to the sympotic singing of Aeolian and Ionian lyric. I cite an example from Aristophanes (F 235 ed. Kassel/Austin), where singing a song of Anacreon at a symposium is viewed as parallel to singing a song of Alcaeus: ᾆσον δή μοι σκόλιόν τι λαβὼν Ἀλκαίου κ'Ἀνακρέοντος 'sing me some *skolion*, taking it from Alcaeus or Anacreon'.[13]

---

[13] The word *skolion*, as used in the time of Aristophanes, is a distinctly sympotic term. Details in Nagy 2004:37n31.

Elsewhere, in the *Sympotic Questions* of Plutarch (711d), singing a song of Anacreon at a symposium is viewed as parallel to singing a song of Sappho herself: ὅτε καὶ Σαπφοῦς ἂν ᾀδομένης καὶ τῶν Ἀνακρέοντος ἐγώ μοι δοκῶ καταθέσθαι τὸ ποτήριον αἰδούμενος 'whenever Sappho is being sung, and Anacreon, I think of putting down the drinking cup in awe'.

In general, the Dionysiac medium of the symposium was most receptive to the Aeolian and Ionian lyric traditions exemplified by the likes of Anacreon, Alcaeus, and Sappho. There is an anecdote that bears witness to this reception: it is said that Solon of Athens became enraptured by a song of Sappho as sung by his own nephew at a symposium (Aelian via Stobaeus 3.29.58).[14]

The correlation of Aeolian lyric with the Ionian lyric of Anacreon in these contexts is relevant to an explicit identification of Anacreon with the Dionysiac medium of the symposium. In a pointed reference, Anacreon is pictured in the lavish setting of a grand symposium hosted by his patron, the tyrant Polycrates, in the heyday of the Ionian maritime empire of Samos. The reference comes from Herodotus (3.121), who pictures Polycrates in the orientalizing pose of reclining on a sympotic couch in the company of his court poet Anacreon: καὶ τὸν Πολυκράτεα τυχεῖν κατακείμενον ἐν ἀνδρεῶνι, παρεῖναι δέ οἱ καὶ Ἀνακρέοντα τὸν Τήιον 'and he [= a Persian agent] found Polycrates reclining in the men's quarters, and with him was Anacreon of Teos'.[15]

In a future project, I will have more to say about the convergence of private and public in media controlled by tyrants. I will focus on such media as the poetry of Anacreon in Samos, which incorporated the earlier poetry of Sappho and Alcaeus in Lesbos. The performance traditions of Anacreontic poetry, which explicitly combined the private with the public, lived on in Athens, where the performance traditions of this poetry were further shaped and reshaped by

---

[14] PP 219.

[15] Commentary by Urios-Aparisi 1993:54 on the explicitly sympotic features of the description given by Herodotus.

both the private conventions of the symposium and the public conventions of the Panathenaia.

A symbol of the convergence of sympotic and Panathenaic traditions of performing the songs of Anacreon—and of Sappho and Alcaeus—was an exotic string instrument of Lydian origin known as the *barbiton* (a byform is *barbitos*), as we see from references in the visual as well as the verbal arts.[16] The morphology of this instrument made it ideal for a combination of song, instrumental accompaniment, and dance. With its elongated neck, the *barbiton* produced a low range of tone that best matched the register of the human voice, and its shape was "ideally suited to walking musicians, since it could be held against the left hip and strummed without interfering with a normal walking stride."[17] What is described here as "a normal walking stride" could modulate into a dancing pose, as we see in pictures representing Anacreon himself in the act of singing and dancing while accompanying himself on the *barbiton*.[18]

The figure of Anacreon as a performer at the Panathenaia is parodied in the verbal as well as the visual arts:

> A case in point is *Women at the Thesmophoria*, a comedy by Aris-
> tophanes. Here the tragic poet Agathon is depicted as wear-
> ing a turban and a woman's *khitōn*—costuming that matches
> the costume of the lyric poet Anacreon as depicted by the
> Kleophrades Painter (Copenhagen MN 13365).[19] In the com-
> edy of Aristophanes, the stage Agathon even says explicitly
> that his self-staging is meant to replicate the monodic stag-
> ings of Ibycus, Anacreon, and Alcaeus (verses 159–163). This
> reference indicates that Agathon as a master of tragic poetry
> was strongly influenced by the tradition of performing lyric
> poetry monodically at the Panathenaia.[20]

Another source of influence was the tradition of performing lyric poetry in an ensemble like the *kōmos*. There is a potential for choral as well as monodic parody in Old Comedy:[21]

---

[16] SA 233, 237–238–246.

[17] Price 1990:143n30.

[18] SA 238.

[19] Price 1990:169, with further bibliography.

[20] For more on Anacreon in Aristophanes' *Women at the Thesmophoria*, see Bierl 2001:160–163; on Agathon as a stage Anacreon, see Bierl p. 158 n137, 165; on Agathon as parody of Dionysus see Bierl pp. 164–168, 173, 321n60.

[21] SA 246.

The case in point is again the *Women at the Thesmophoria*. In this comedy of Aristophanes, the Panathenaic persona of the tragic poet Agathon extends into a Dionysiac persona when the acting of the actor who plays Agathon shifts from dialogue to chorus. Once the shift takes place, there can be a choral as well as monodic self-staging of the stage Agathon.[22] And such choral stagings would most likely be comastic in inspiration.

Returning to the symbolic value of the *barbiton*, I next consider two conflicting myths about the invention of this string instrument. According to one myth, the inventor was Anacreon (Athenaeus 4.175e); according to the other, the inventor was an archetypal poet from Lesbos known as Terpander (Athenaeus 14.635d). I interpret the symbolic value of these myths as follows:[23]

Just as the figure of Anacreon was associated with the *kithara* as well as the *barbiton*, so too was the older figure of Terpander. In fact, Terpander of Lesbos was thought to be the prototype of *kitharōidoi* 'kithara-singers' (Aristotle F 545 Rose and Hesychius s.v. μετὰ Λέσβιον ᾠδόν; Plutarch *Laconic sayings* 238c). Pictured as an itinerant professional singer, he was reportedly the first of all winners at the Spartan festival of the Karneia (Hellanicus *FGH* 4 F 85 by way of Athenaeus 14.635e).[24] Tradition has it that the Feast of the Karneia was founded in the twenty-sixth Olympiad, that is, between 676 and 672 BCE (Athenaeus 14.635e–f).

Not only was Terpander of Lesbos thought to be the prototypical *kitharōidos* or 'kithara-singer' ("Plutarch" *On Music* 1132d, 1133b–d). He was also overtly identified as the originator of *kitharōidia* or 'kithara-singing' as a performance tradition perpetuated by a historical figure named Phrynis of Lesbos; just like Terpander, Phrynis was known as a *kitharōidos* ("Plutarch" *On Music* 1133b). And the historicity of this Phrynis is independently verified: at the Panathenaia of 456 (or possi-

---

[22] Price 1990:169–170.
[23] SA 244.
[24] PH 86–87 [3§§6–9], with further discussion.

bly 446), he won first prize in the competition of *kitharōidoi*
(scholia to Aristophanes *Clouds* 969).[25]

Given the interchangeability of *barbiton* and *kithara* in traditions about Ter-
pander as the prototypical *kitharōidos* 'kithara-singer', I return to the traditions
about Anacreon as shown in Anacreontic vase paintings: here too we find an
interchangeability of *barbiton* and *kithara*.

In both cases of interchangeability, it is implied that the *kithara* is the more
traditional of these two kinds of instrument, since the *barbiton* is figured as
something invented by the Asiatic Ionian Anacreon according to one version
(Athenaeus 4.175e) or by the Asiatic Aeolian Terpander according to another
(Athenaeus 14.635d).

Pursuing further the idea of a Panathenaic context for the performance of
songs attributed to Anacreon—and, by extension, of songs attributed to Sappho
and Alcaeus—I turn to the evidence of a picture painted on a red-figure vase
of Athenian provenance. This vase, a krater shaped like a *kalathos* and made in
Athens sometime in the decade of 480–470 BCE (Munich, Antikensammlungen
no. 2416; *ARV2* 385 [228]), shows on its two sides two paintings attributed to the
so-called Brygos Painter. I analyze these two paintings with reference to two
line drawings I have provided, Image 1 and Image 2:[26]

> In Image 1 we see two figures in a pointedly musical scene.
> The figure on the left is Alcaeus playing the specialized string
> instrument known as the *barbiton*, while the figure on the
> right is Sappho playing her own *barbiton*. [...] The two figures
> in the painting are described as follows by a team of art his-
> torians:
>
> [They are] side by side in nearly identical dress. But under
> the transparent clothing of one—a bearded man—the sex is
> clearly drawn. The other is a woman—her breasts are indicat-
> ed—but a cloak hides the region of her genitals, apparently
> distancing her from any erotic context. She wears a diadem,
> while the hair of her companion is held in a ribbon (*tainia*).
> Each holds a *barbiton* and seems to be playing. The parallel-
> isms of the two figures, male and female, is unambiguous
> here. A string of vowels (O O O O O) leaving the man's mouth

[25] PH 98 [3§32]. On the date 446 see Davison 1968 [1958] 61–64.
[26] SA 233–234, 237.

Image 1

indicates song. An inscription, finally, gives his name, <u>Alcaeus</u> [ΑΛΚΑΙΟΣ], and indicates the identity of his companion, <u>Sappho</u> [ΣΑΦΟ—*sic*]. [...] The long garment and the playing of the *barbiton* are [...] connected with Ionian lyric.[27]

Next we turn to Image 2 as painted on the Munich vase. Here we see two figures in a pointedly sympotic scene. The figure on the left is Dionysus, while the figure on the right is a female devotee, that is, a Maenad. Sympotic themes predominate. Dionysus, god of the symposium, is directly facing the Maenad, who appears to be coming under the god's possession, transfixed by his direct gaze. The symmetry of Dionysus and the Maenad is reinforced by the symmetrical picturing of two overtly sympotic vessels, one held by the god and the other, by his newly possessed female devotee: he is holding a *kantharos* while she is holding an *oinokhoē*. The pairing creates a sort of sympotic symmetry.

---

[27] Frontisi-Ducroux and Lissarrague 1990:219.

Image 2

Matching the sympotic symmetry of Dionysus and the Maenad in Image 2 is the musical symmetry of Alcaeus and Sappho in Image 1. Both Alcaeus and Sappho are shown in the musical moment of striking all seven strings of the *barbiton* in a sweep of the *plēktron* held in the right hand. Each of the two figures has just executed this masterful instrumental sweep, and now the singing may begin. Alcaeus has already begun to sing, but Sappho has yet to begin. She appears to be waiting for her own turn to sing.

The idea of taking turns in performing a song, as I have just expressed it, is essential for the rest of my essay. What I have just described as a musical scene in Image 1 of the Munich vase is more specifically a Panathenaic scene, which is symmetrical with the sympotic scene in Image 2. I say Panathenaic scene because Sappho and Alcaeus are being pictured here as if they were citharodes competing with each other at the festival of the Panathenaia in Athens.[28] And

---

[28] SA 234–254.

the idea of <u>taking turns in performing a song</u> is a defining feature of <u>singing in competition</u>.

This idea of <u>taking turns in performing a song</u> brings me back full circle to the question I asked at the beginning of this essay, with reference to the two different texts of Sappho's "song of Tithonos" as written in two different papyri. The question was: which text of the song is definitive—the shorter one as written in the earlier Cologne papyrus (Π¹) or the longer one as written in the later Oxyrhynchus papyrus (Π²)?

My answer is this: I think that the shorter and the longer texts of Sappho's "song of Tithonos" are actually two versions of the same song, and that both the shorter and the longer versions can be considered definitive. This definitiveness, however, has to be viewed in terms of performing the song, not in terms of writing the text of the song.

Viewed in this light, the longer version of Sappho's "song of Tithonos" as written in the later Oxyrhynchus papyrus did not result from a textual addition. Conversely, the shorter version as written in the earlier Cologne papyrus did not result from a textual subtraction. Rather, both the addition and the subtraction were a matter of alternative performances. And the differences in addition or subtraction correspond to differences in the contexts of alternative performances.

I think that the longer version of Sappho's "song of Tithonos," where the additional four lines express a hope for an afterlife, would have been most appropriate for performance in the context of choral singing and dancing at public events like the festivals of Lesbos. As for the shorter version, which is without those four lines and without an expression of hope for an afterlife, I think it would have been more appropriate for performance in the context of monodic singing at (1) public events like the competition of citharodes at the festival of the Panathenaia in Athens or at (2) private events like the competitions of symposiasts at symposia. Such Panathenaic and sympotic events are analogous to (1) the <u>Panathenaic scene</u> and (2) the <u>sympotic scene</u> as depicted in Images 1 and 2 of the Munich vase.

I do not mean to say, however, that the longer version of Sappho's "song of Tithonos" would have been inappropriate for Panathenaic or sympotic performances at Athens. That version too could have been appropriate. I am only saying that there was something special about the shorter version that made it particularly appropriate for Panathenaic or sympotic performances. That special something is what I call the mentality of <u>relay performance</u>. In terms of this mentality, it is not that the speaker has given up hope for an afterlife. Rather, the hope for an afterlife is being expressed indirectly, by way of a relay from one performance to the next.

In the the epigrams of Posidippus, we find a learned reference to such a mentality of <u>relay performance</u> in the poetics of Sappho. This reference has to do with the noun *oaros*, which I propose to translate as 'song of courtship'. In the dictionary of Liddell and Scott, I should note for background, this noun *oaros* is said to be the synonym of the noun *oaristus*, which is glossed as 'familiar converse, fond discourse'. But there is more to it: from a survey of attestations, we find that these nouns *oaros* and *oaristus* refer specifically to <u>love songs</u>.[29] Viewed in this light, the combined use of the terms 'familiar' and 'fond' in the definition of Liddell and Scott is apt. And it goes without saying that the 'familiar converse' or 'fond discourse' indicated by the words *oaros* and *oaristus* may be seen as songs of homoerotic as well as heterosexual courtship.

With this background in place, let us consider a reference in the epigrams of Posidippus to the medium of Sappho as *oaros*: Σα<π>φώιους ἐξ ὀά<ρ>ων ὀάρους 'oaroi of Sappho, one continuing after the next' (Posidippus 55.2 ed. BA).
In the poetics of Sappho, as we see from this learned reference, one *oaros* comes from another, over and over again. Each *oaros* is a coming full circle from the previous *oaros*. Each song extends from the previous song into the next song. The singing of the songs of Sappho is envisioned as an unbroken cycle of song, a singing by relay. Such <u>relay performance</u>, I argue, is analogous to what we see in the competitions of citharodes—and of rhapsodes—at the festival of the Panathenaia in Athens.

Just as Sappho's medium comes full circle from one *oaros* or 'amorous converse' to the next, so also Sappho herself comes full circle, for eternity. She is a girl who becomes a woman who becomes a girl again, coming full circle. That is the perennial poetic theme of Sappho.

In order to come to terms with this theme, I begin by returning to the poetry of Posidippus. In one of his epigrams (52 ed. BA), the closing words of the sixth and last verse focus on the image of the beautiful sun (52.6: τὸν καλὸν ἥέλιον), and the beauty of the sun is linked with the accumulation of years (52.6: σωρὸν ἐτέων), which is being measured by a *skiotheron* 'sundial' set up to commemorate a dead man named Timon (52.1). Observing the sundial is a *pais* 'girl' named *Astē* (52.3), whom the dead man has left behind just as he has left behind the sundial. On the surface, the girl seems to be the dead man's surviving daughter. But there is more to it, as we may glimpse from the conclusion of the epigram, where this girl *Astē* is addressed as a *korē* 'girl' (52.5). The adjective *astos*, including the feminine *astē*, is conventionally used to indicate a native of a given city, and so it seems perfectly appropriate to a local girl who is native

---

[29] GM 200n123, with reference to *Iliad* XXII 126–127; also GM 253.

to the city where the sundial is located. But there is still more to it, as we see from the fact that the feminine substantive byform of this adjective, *Astos*, is attested as the epithet of the local *Korē* in Paros (*IG* 12[5] 225, 5th century BCE). In such a sacral context, *korē* refers to the goddess nymph par excellence. In such a context, *korē* refers to the primary local nymph worshipped by the local population.

In the epigram of Posidippus (52), the name *Astē*—whether or not we read it as an epithet—may evoke the idea of a local *Korē* or nymph goddess in the making. It seems as if this local nymph is pictured as part of the object of art that functions as a sundial. The dead man who notionally commissioned the sundial expects the *parthenos* 'maiden' to keep time, 'to watch the time go by' or *hōrologeîn*—even as the sundial watches the time go by (52.4: ἐνδέχετ' ἐλπίδ' ἔχειν παρθένον ὡρολογεῖν). There she is, this *parthenos* or 'maiden' who is ever watching time go by. It happens on her ancient watch, as it were, which is a sundial ever watching the movement of time, ever observing the solar radiance that is ever loved by this lamenting *pais* or 'girl'. The sundial 'measures one *hōra* after the next *hōra*'—let us translate *hōra* here as 'hour' (52.1–2: ἵνα μετρῇ | ὥρας). That is its purpose. That is why the sundial is there, marking time to compensate for the death of the dead man. The sundial measures time, which is the passage of one seasonal phase or *hōra* to the next. The sundial measures one *hōra* at a time, counting the hours from one *hōra* to the next one. The plural of *hōra*, *hōrai*, is a metonymic expression of this eternal passage of time. As we hear in a song of Sappho, παρὰ δ' ἔρχετ' ὥρα 'and time [*hōra*] goes by' (PMG 58.3).

The maiden in this epigram of Posidippus (52) is herself measuring time just as the sundial measures time, and, as she is measuring, she is addressed as *korē* 'girl': ἀλλὰ σὺ γῆρας ἱκοῦ κούρη· παρὰ σήματι τούτῳ | σωρὸν ἐτέων μέτρει τὸν καλὸν ἠέλιον 'So now, come to the point of old age [*gēras*], you *korē*: at this marker [*sēma*] of yours, keep on measuring [*metreîn*] the accumulation of years, the beautiful sun' (52.5–6). If we apply terminology that suits the poetics of the Hellenistic era, we may say that there is an *adunaton* or 'impossibility' at work here at the close of this epigram. The fact is, this closure cannot really be a closure because the wording leaves everything openended. The *korē* cannot ever reach *gēras* 'old age' because the sundial cannot ever finish counting one *hōra* after the next—just as the lamenting girl cannot ever finish measuring the radiance of the sun that shines its light for the sundial to measure time. So the *korē* cannot be simply a 'girl' interrupted.[30] The girl cannot be interrupted by

---

[30] The expression "girl interrupted" comes from the title of the 1993 book of Susanna Kaysen.

gēras 'old age'. She cannot grow old with the passage of time, despite the abrupt command for her to reach *gēras* 'old age' finally. That is because she measures the passage of time by observing the sun just as the sundial observes the radiance of the sun. She can be a 'girl' for eternity because the passage of time can never come to an end, just as the sun can never lose its radiant light.

Such a sense of *pais* as 'girl' is evident in the invocation addressed to the ensemble of singers and dancers at the beginning of Sappho's "song of Tithonos" as written down in the Cologne papyrus of the "New Sappho" (Π¹). The song begins at line 9 of the papyrus. The invocation is being made to *paides* 'girls' (Π¹ 9). The speaker in the song speaks to them as she laments the passage of time and the coming of *gēras* 'old age' (Π¹ 13). The theme of old age persists till the end of the song as we see it written on this papyrus: in the last line, we hear of the *gēras* 'old age' that afflicts Tithonos, mortal lover of Eos the goddess of dawn (Π¹ 20). In the later papyrus (Π²), however, the song keeps going for four more lines, culminating in an affirmation of hope for the afterlife. In the last line, the speaker affirms her 'love of the sun'—her ἔρως ἀελίω (Π² 26).[31] This love is what makes it possible for the speaker to possess everything that is bright and beautiful in life – and to prevail over old age and death.

Here is my translation of the last line of the longer and later version of Sappho's "song of Tithonos" (Π² 26): 'Love [*erōs*] of the Sun has won for me its radiance and beauty'.[32] In terms of an alternative interpretation, the translation would be this: 'Love [*erōs*] has won for me the radiance and beauty of the Sun'.[33] I prefer the first of these two translations, which makes the Sun the objective genitive of *erōs* 'love'. Such a genitive construction would be parallel to the phrase ὄττω τις ἔραται 'whatever one loves' in another song of Sappho (F 16), where this 'whatever' (16.3–4) is described as κάλλιστον 'the most beautiful thing' in the whole wide world (16.3).[34]

There are three things to compare with 'the most beautiful thing' in this song of Sappho (F 16), but each one of them pales in comparison to 'whatever' that thing is that 'one' loves. These three things to be compared are three radiant visions of beauty. The first of these visions is the dazzling sight of magnificent chariot-fighters in their luminous war-chariots massing for frontal assault against their terrified enemy; the second vision is of footsoldiers on

---

[31] The noun ἔρως in the phrase ἔρως ἀελίω (F 58.26) is a byform of ἔρος in the diction of Sappho (as also at F 23.1).

[32] GM 261–262; PH 285 [10§18]; PP 90, 102–103. For more on this interpretation, see Boedeker in this volume.

[33] Again, see Boedeker in this volume.

[34] For more on this song, see Bierl 2003.

the battlefield; and the third vision is of battleships at sea (16.1–2). But none of these three radiant visions of beauty can match that ultimate brightness radiating from the speaker's love-object, Anaktoria (16.15–16). When Anaktoria sings and dances in the chorus, the loveliness of her steps and the brilliant light you see radiating from her looks (16.17–8: ἔρατόν τε βᾶμα | κἀμάρυχμα λάμπρον ἴδην προσώπω) cannot be surpassed by anything in the whole wide world. That radiance of Anaktoria is now directly compared with the radiance of the luminous chariots and the other two luminous foils (16.19–20).

According to the logic of Sappho's poetic cosmos, nothing can surpass the radiance of the sun. So the all-surpassing radiance of 'whatever' it is that the speaker says she loves more than anything else in the whole wide world must be the same thing as the sun—or at least it must be a metonymic extension of the sun, such as the radiance of Anaktoria herself as she sings and dances in the chorus.

Similarly in the song of Sappho about the terrors and sorrows of dark old age, the speaker's declared love for the sun is what turns her life into a world of radiance and beauty. As we read in the text of the later papyrus, she loves *habrosunē* 'luxuriance' (Π^2 25: ἔγω δὲ φίλημμι' ἀβροσύναν), which is associated with the sun. In the poetics of Sappho, this association extends to the beautiful heroes Adonis and Phaon, lovers of Aphrodite and projected lovers of Sappho: they are *habroi* 'luxuriant' and they shine like the sun in their radiant attractiveness.[35]

In this song of Sappho, then, the sun is the promise of recycling for the girl who fears the interruption of her youth by old age, for the woman who fears the termination of her life. The love or eros (ἔρως) for the sun as experienced by Sappho in the longer and later text of this song (Π^2 26) is the converse of the love or eros (ἔρος) for Tithonos as experienced by the goddess of dawn, Eos, in the shorter and earlier text that we now call the "New Sappho" (Π^1 18). As we see from the wording that survives in the earlier papyrus, the beauty of Tithonos, who was *kalos* 'beautiful' as a *neos* 'young man' (Π^1 19), will be ruined by what is described as a *polion gēras* 'gray old age' (Π^1 20), just as the speaker's beauty has been ruined (Π^1 11) by the graying of her hair (Π^1 12) because of *gēras* 'old age' (Π^1 11)—after all, no human can remain *agēraos* 'ageless' forever (Π^1 16). For a human to remain *agēraos* 'ageless' is *ou dunaton* 'impossible' (Π^1 16). This impossibility, this *adunaton*, is keenly felt by the speaker as she laments her inability to dance any more—now that her knees are no longer nimble for dancing – no longer nimble like the limbs of playful fawns (Π^1 13–14).

---

[35] PH 285 [10§18], 298 [10§29] n113; GM 235, 255, 257, and especially 261–262; PP 90, 102–103.

Such a poetic *adunaton* is a specifically choral poetic *adunaton*, as we see from a comparable expression in a choral song of Alcman (Song 26) where the speaker declares that he is too old and weak to dance with the chorus of women who sing and dance his song: by implication, he continues to sing as the lead singer—even if he cannot dance any more.[36]

The promise of the girl who comes back full circle, as expressed in the longer and later version of the text of Sappho's song when the speaker declares her love (ἔρως) for the sun (Π² 26), is withheld in the shorter and earlier version of the song. As Lowell Edmunds has shown, the shorter version fails to return to the present poetic situation that had started the song—and had introduced the myth of Tithonos.[37] There is no return to the start, which is the present. Such failure to return to the present suspends the coming full circle that is being promised by the present. And this suspension creates a sense of suspense. It is not so much a truncation of something that is thereafter left out of mind as it is a withholding of something that is thereafter kept in mind. I find this effect comparable to the suspense created by the narrative device of ending one performance with a *men*-clause ('on the one hand') and then beginning the next performance with a *de*-clause ('on the other hand').[38] Such a device is typical of transitions in the relay-performances of rhapsodes competing at the Panathenaia, as we see for example in the transition from Rhapsody ii of the *Odyssey* (ending with a *men*-clause at verse 434) to the subsequent Rhapsody iii (starting with a *de*-clause at verse 1).[39]

Such transitions are to be expected in the relay-performances of citharodes as well as rhapsodes. If it is true that the songs of Sappho were included in the repertoires of citharodes competing at the Panathenaia, then the shorter and earlier version of Sappho's song featuring the myth of Tithonos and Eos may be viewed as a variant stemming from the performances of citharodes competing at the Panathenaia.

I should add that both the shorter and the longer versions of Sappho's song may also be viewed as variants stemming from the performances of participants in private symposia. Variations in the singing of Sappho's songs by men and boys at Athenian symposia help explain differences in the textual

---

[36] PH 352 [12§32]; Nagy 2007a:22.

[37] Edmunds 2006.

[38] PP 161–162, with reference to Plutarch *Quaestiones convivales* 736e.

[39] PP 161–162n30. Further examples in PR 61–69. Relay-performances in rhapsodic contests at the Panathenaia require collaboration as well as competition: see PR 22. For a comparative perspective on the concept of competition-in-collaboration, see PP 18.

Image 3

transmission of Sappho—including differences that have come to light with the discovery of the "New Sappho."

In the case of Song 2 of Sappho, for example, we find two attested versions of the closure of this song. In the version inscribed on the so-called Florentine ostrakon dated to the third century BCE, at lines 13–16, the last word is οἰνοχόεισα 'pouring wine', referring to Aphrodite herself in the act of pouring not wine but nectar. In the "Attic" version of these lines as quoted by Athenaeus (11.463e), on the other hand, the wording after οἰνοχοοῦσα 'pouring wine' continues with τούτοις τοῖς ἑταίροις ἐμοῖς γε καὶ σοῖς '(pouring wine) for these my (male) companions [*hetairoi*], such as they are, as well as for your (male divine) companions [= Aphrodite's]'.[40] Both kinds of sympotic closure, I argue, are compatible with the singing of Sappho's songs by men and boys at Athenian symposia.

---

[40] On the relevance of this wording to questions of genre, see Yatromanolakis 2004 [2003]:65. On the "Attic" transmission of the sympotic songs of Alcaeus, see Nagy 2004:37–41. The term *Attic* here is used not only to indicate the Attic dialect but also the Athenian cultural context of transmission.

Image 4

On the basis of such sympotic contexts, I infer that the shorter version of Sappho's song, attested in the earlier papyrus containing the "New Sappho" (Π²), is not necessarily an earlier version than the longer version as attested in the later papyrus (Π¹)—or the other way around. Without making judgments about the relative lateness or earliness of the version containing the "New Sappho," I conclude this essay by comparing a parallel from the visual arts, dated to the fifth century BCE.

In the case of the "New Sappho" as transmitted in the older papyrus, the failure of the song to return to its own present time, back from the timeless myth of Tithonos and Eos, means that the speaker's contact with the *paides* 'girls' whom she addresses (Π¹ 9) has been for the moment suspended. There is a comparable sense of suspension between Sappho and her *paides* 'girls' in the visual arts of Athens in the fifth century. I have in mind an image of Sappho that is painted on a red-figure kalyx-krater dated to the first third of the fifth century BCE and attributed to the Tithonos Painter (Bochum, Ruhr-Universität Kunstsammlungen, inv. S 508). On the obverse side of this vase (Image 3) we see the image of a woman in a dancing pose that resembles the "walking stride" of Anacreon.[41] She is wearing a cloak or *himation* over her *khitōn*, and a snood (net-cap) or *sakkos* is holding up her hair. As she "walks," she carries a *barbiton* in her left hand, while her gracefully extended right hand is holding a *plēktron*. The inscribed lettering placed not far from her mouth indicates that she is Sappho (ΣΑΦΟ).

This picture of Sappho on the obverse side of this vase painted by the Tithonos painter must be contrasted with the picture on the reverse side (Image 4), as Dimitrios Yatromanolakis has shown.[42] Applying an anthropological approach to the images painted on both sides of this vase, he argues that the obverse and the reverse must be viewed together. He sees a symmetry in the depiction of Sappho on the obverse and the depiction of another female figure dressed similarly on the reverse: she too, like Sappho, is wearing a cloak or *himation* over her *khitōn*, and a snood or *sakkos* is holding up her hair. This symmetry as analyzed further by Yatromanolakis:

> The symmetry is clarified as soon as we realize that there is a second, hitherto unknown, inscription on the reverse of this vase. Near the *sakkos* holding up the hair of this female figure paired with Sappho is lettering that reads HE ΠΑΙΣ (= *hē pais*), meaning 'the girl'. If the viewer's eye keeps rotating the vase, the two female figures eternally follow each other, but because their position is symmetrically pictured, they can never gaze at each other. Nor can a viewer ever gaze at both figures at the same time—at least, without a mirror.[43]

So the *pais* 'girl' is eternally pursued by the singing and dancing Sappho as painted by the Tithonos painter. But Sappho is in turn eternally pursued by the girl. The girl of the present time will become the woman of a future time who will pursue a girl of that future time just as she herself had once been pursued in time past. As we hear from Sappho's own wording in another song, καὶ γὰρ αἰ φεύγει, ταχέως διώξει 'for if she fleeing now, soon she will be pursuing' (Song 1 line 21).

---

[41] I have more to say in SA about the stylized dance implied by such a "walking style" in fifth-century Athenian paintings.

[42] Yatromanolakis 2001, 2005; also 2007: 88–110, 248, 262–279.

[43] SA 239, following Yatromanolakis 2001 and 2005, who was the first to read and publish this inscription. Yatromanolakis 2001 features photographs of the obverse and the reverse sides. See also Yatromanolakis, Forthcoming-1 and 2008.

So the moment of catching up is eternally deferred. The woman cannot catch up with the girl she once had been, and the girl cannot catch up with the woman she will become. This is not just *amor versus*, it is *amor conversus*. It is a yearning for a merger of identities as woman pursues girl pursues woman. Such a merger could conceivably happen, but only in the mentality of myth fused with ritual. I have studied this mentality elsewhere, comparing it to the concept of the "Changing Woman" in the female initiation rituals and songs of the Navajo and Apache peoples:[44] as we learn from interviews with women who experience such rituals, Changing Woman defies old age even as she grows old, since "she is always able to recapture her youth."[45]

I come to the end of this essay without being able to come to the full stop. I end with a glimpse of Sappho as she heads off to Hades, holding in her hand a lyre of one kind or another. All three of the songs contained in the new Cologne papyrus offer variations on the theme of Sappho the citharode holding on to her exotic lyre, holding on to her exotic life for just an hour longer.

But Sappho is not a woman whose life is about to be terminated. She is a woman to be continued. More than that, she is the girl who comes back full circle. This girl will not be interrupted.

Bibliography

Basso, K. H. 1966. "The Gift of Changing Woman." *Smithsonian Institution, Bureau of American Ethnology Bulletin* 196:113–173. Anthropological Papers no. 76. Washington DC.

Bierl, A. 1991. *Dionysos und die griechische Tragödie. Politische und 'metatheatralische' Aspekte im Text*. Tübingen.

———. 2001. *Ritual und Performativität (unter besonderer Berücksichtigung von Aristophanes' Thesmophoriazusen und der Phalloslieder fr. 851 PMG)*. München and Leipzig.

———. 2003. "'Ich aber (sage): das Schönste ist, was einer liebt!': Eine pragmatische Deutung von Sappho Fr. 16 LP / V." *Quaderni Urbinati di Cultura Classica* 74:91–124.

———. 2005. Review of Pütz 2003. *Classical Review* 55:422–424.

---

[44] PP 101–103.
[45] Basso 1966:151.

———. 2006. "Tragödie als Spiel und das Satyrspiel. Die Geburt des griechischen Theaters aus dem Geiste des Chortanzes und seines Gottes Dionysos." *Kind und Spiel* (ed. J. Sánchez de Murillo and M. Thurner) 111–138. Aufgang: Jahrbuch für Denken, Dichten, Music 3. Stuttgart.

———. 2007a. *Ritual and Performativity: The Chorus in Old Comedy.* Trans. A. Hollmann. Hellenic Studies 20. Washington DC.

———. 2007b. "L'uso intertestuale di Alcmane nel finale della Lisistrata di Aristofane. Coro e rito nel contesto performativo." *Dalla lirica corale alla poesia drammatica. Forme e funzioni del canto corale nella tragedia e nella commedia greca* (ed. F. Perusino) 259–290. Pisa.

Boedeker, D. Forthcoming. "Sappho Old and New (P.Köln 21351 and 21376, and P.Oxy. 1787): An Overview of Texts and Contexts." *Symposium Lesbium: Poetry, Wisdom and Politics in Archaic Lesbos: Alcaeus, Sappho, Pittacus* (ed. A. Pierris). Oxford.

Calame, C. 1974. "Réflexions sur les genres littéraires en Grèce archaïque." *Quaderni Urbinati di Cultura Classica* 17:113–123.

———. 1977. *Les choeurs de jeunes filles en Grèce archaïque.* Rome.

———. 1989. "Apprendre à boire, apprendre à chanter: L'inférence énonciative dans une image grecque." *La part de l'oeil* 5:45–53.

———. 1994-5. "From Choral Poetry to Tragic Stasimon: The Enactment of Women's Song." *Arion* 3.2:136–154.

———. 2001. *Choruses of Young Women in Ancient Greece: Their Morphology, Religious Role, and Social Function* ed. 2. Trans. D. Collins and J. Orion. Lanham MD.

Davison, J. A. 1958. "Notes on the Panathenaea." *Journal of Hellenic Studies* 78:23–41. Reprinted in Davison 1968:28–69.

———. 1968. *From Archilochus to Pindar: Papers on Greek Literature of the Archaic Period.* London.

Edmunds, L. 2006. "The New Sappho: ἔφαντο (9)." *Zeitschrift für Papyrologie und Epigraphik* 156:23–26.

Fearn, D. 2003. "Mapping Phleious: Politics and Myth-Making in Bacchylides 9." *Classical Quarterly* 3:347–367.

Figueira, T. J., and Nagy, G., eds. 1985. *Theognis of Megara: Poetry and the Polis.* Baltimore.

Frontisi-Ducroux, F. 1995. *Du masque au visage: Aspects de l'identité en Grèce ancienne.* Paris.

Frontisi-Ducroux, F. and Lissarrague, F. 1983. "De l'ambiguïté à l'ambivalence: un parcours Dionysiaque." *Annali del Seminario di studi del mondo classico: Sezione di archeologia e storia antica* 5:11–32.

———. 1990. "From Ambiguity to Ambivalence: A Dionysiac Excursion Through the 'Anakreontic' Vases." Before Sexuality: The Construction of Erotic Experience in the Ancient Greek World (ed. D. M. Halperin, J. J. Winkler, and F. Zeitlin) 211–256. Princeton.

Gentili, B. 1985. *Poesia e pubblico nella Grecia antica. Da Omero al V secolo.* Rome and Bari.

———. 1986. "Il coro della tragedia greca nella teoria degli antichi." *Teatro e pubblico nell'antichità: Atti del Convegno Nazionale Trento 25-27 April 1986* (ed. L. De Finis) 27–44. Trento.

———. 1988. *Poetry and its Public in Ancient Greece: From Homer to the Fifth Century.* Trans. A. T. Cole. Baltimore MD.

GM. *See* Nagy 1990b.

Greene, E., ed. 1996a. *Reading Sappho: Contemporary Approaches.* Berkeley.

———, ed. 1996b. *Re-Reading Sappho: Reception and Transmission.* Berkeley.

Kaysen, S. 1993. *Girl Interrupted.* New York.

Lardinois, A. 1994. "Subject and Circumstance in Sappho's Poetry." *Transactions of the American Philological Association* 124:57–84.

———. 1996. "Who Sang Sappho's Songs?" In Greene 1996a:150–172.

Murray, O. 1983. "The Greek Symposion in History." *Tria Corda: Scritti in onore di Arnaldo Momigliano* (ed. E. Gabba) 257–272. Como.

———. 1990a. "The Affair of the Mysteries: Democracy and the Drinking Group." In Murray 1990b:149–161. Oxford.

———., ed. 1990b. *Sympotica: A Symposium on the Symposium.* Oxford. Note especially the introduction by Murray, "Sympotic History," pp. 3–13.

Nagy, G. 1979. *The Best of the Achaeans: Concepts of the Hero in Archaic Greek Poetry.* Baltimore. Second edition, with new introduction, 1999.

———. 1985. "Theognis and Megara: A Poet's Vision of His City." In Figueira and Nagy 1985:22–81.

———. 1989. "The 'Professional Muse' and Models of Prestige in Ancient Greece." *Cultural Critique* 12:133–143. Rewritten as part of Ch. 6 in Nagy 1990a.

———. 1990a. *Pindar's Homer: The Lyric Possession of an Epic Past.* Baltimore. Paperback edition, with corrections, 1994. (= PH)

———. 1990b. *Greek Mythology and Poetics.* Ithaca NY. Paperback edition, with corrections, 1992. (= GM)

———. 1993. "Alcaeus in Sacred Space." *Tradizione e innovazione nella cultura greca da Omero all' età ellenistica: Scritti in onore di Bruno Gentili* (ed. R. Pretagostini) 221–225. Rome.

———. 1994-1995a. "Transformations of Choral Lyric Traditions in the Context of Athenian State Theater." *Arion* 3.2:41–55.

———. 1994–1995b. "Genre and Occasion." *Métis* 9–10:11–25.

———. 1996a. *Poetry as Performance: Homer and Beyond.* Cambridge. (=PP)

———. 1996b. *Homeric Questions.* Austin.

———. 2004. "Transmission of Archaic Greek Sympotic Songs: From Lesbos to Alexandria." *Critical Inquiry* 31:26–48.

———. 2007a. "Lyric and Greek Myth." *The Cambridge Encyclopedia of Classical Mythology* (ed. R. D. Woodard) 19–51. Cambridge.

———. 2007b. "Homer and Greek Myth." *The Cambridge Encyclopedia of Classical Mythology* (ed. R. D. Woodard) 52–82. Cambridge.

———. 2007c. "Did Sappho and Alcaeus ever meet?" *Literatur und Religion. Wege zu einer mythisch-rituellen Poetik bei den Griechen* (ed. A. Bierl, R. Lämmle, K. Wesselmann) 211–269. MythosEikonPoiesis 1.1. Berlin and New York. (= SA)

———. Forthcoming-1. *Homer the Classic.* Cambridge MA and Washington DC.

———. Forthcoming-2. *Homer the Preclassic.* Berkeley and Los Angeles.

Page, D. L. 1955. *Sappho and Alcaeus: An Introduction to the Study of Ancient Lesbian Poetry.* Oxford.

PH. *See* Nagy 1990a.

Power, T. 2000. "The Parthenoi of Bacchylides 13." *Harvard Studies in Classical Philology* 100:67–81.

PP. *See* Nagy 1996a.

Price, S. D. 1990. "Anacreontic Vases Reconsidered." *Greek, Roman, and Byzantine Studies* 31:133–75.

Pütz, B. 2003. *The Symposium and Komos in Aristophanes.* Drama: Beiträge zum antiken Drama und seiner Rezeption 22. Stuttgart and Weimar.

SA. *See* Nagy 2007c.

Schmitt-Pantel, P. 1990. "Sacrificial Meal and Symposion." In Murray 1990b:14–33.

Stehle, E. 1997. *Performance and Gender in Ancient Greece: Nondramatic Poetry in Its Setting.* Princeton.

Urios-Aparisi, E. 1993. "Anacreon: Love and Poetry (On 358 PMG, 13 Gentili)." *Quaderni Urbinati di Cultura Classica* 44:51–70.

Yatromanolakis, D. 2001. "Visualizing Poetry: An Early Representation of Sappho." *Classical Philology* 96: 159–168. On visual performability of song and the Bochum vase.

———. 2003. "Ritual Poetics in Archaic Lesbos: Contextualizing Genre in Sappho." *Towards a Ritual Poetics* (D.Yatromanolakis and P. Roilos) 43–59. Athens. Also in Yatromanolakis and Roilos 2004:56–70. In referring to this work, I will use the pagination of the 2004 version.

———. 2005. "Contrapuntal Inscriptions." *Zeitschrift für Papyrologie und Epigraphik* 152:16–30. On an inscription newly discovered by D.Y. on the Bochum vase (examined here in the context of numerous other vase-inscriptions).

———. 2007. *Sappho in the Making: An Anthropology of Reception.* Hellenic Studies 28. Washington DC.

———. 2008. "P.Colon. inv. 21351+21376 and *P.Oxy.* 1787 fr.1: Music, Cultural Politics, and Hellenistic Anthologies." *Hellenika* 58.2:1–19.

———. Forthcoming-1. "Alcaeus and Sappho." *The Cambridge Companion to Ancient Greek Lyric* (ed. F. Budelmann). Cambridge.

———. Forthcoming-2. *Fragments of Sappho: A Commentary.* Hellenic Studies series. Washington DC.

Yatromanolakis D., and Roilos, P. eds. 2004. *Greek Ritual Poetics.* Hellenic Studies 3. Washington DC.

About the Contributors

DEBORAH BOEDEKER, Professor of Classics at Brown University, works mainly on archaic and classical Greek poetry, historiography, and religion. Her publications include *Aphrodite's Entry into Greek Epic*; *Descent from Heaven: Images of Dew in Greek Poetry and Religion*; and essays on Herodotus, lyric poetry, Athenian religion, Simonides, tragedy, and traditions about the Persian Wars. She has edited and co-edited a number of volumes, including *Herodotus and the Invention of History*; *Democracy, Empire, and the Arts in Fifth-Century Athens*; and *The New Simonides: Contexts of Praise and Desire*. Currently she is working on poetic and prosaic commemorations of the past, and the textualization of early Greek poetry.

DEE L. CLAYMAN is Professor of Classics and Executive Officer of the PhD Program in Classics at the Graduate Center of the City University of New York. She is the Editor-in-Chief of Oxford Bibliographies Online: Classics and the Director of the Database of Classical Bibliography. She has published widely on Greek poetry, especially the work of Callimachus and his contemporaries in the Hellenistic age.

LOWELL EDMUNDS is Professor of Classics Emeritus at Rutgers University. His recent publications include *Oedipus* (Routledge, 2006) and "Helen's Divine Origins," *Electronic Antiquity* 10.2 (2007) 1-45. His "Deixis in Ancient Greek and Latin Literature: Historical Introduction and State of the Question" is forthcoming in the first number of *Philologia Antiqua*.

ELLEN GREENE is the Joseph Paxton Presidential Professor of Classics at the University of Oklahoma. She received her Ph.D. from UC Berkeley in 1992. Her research specialization is Greek and Roman lyric poetry, with an emphasis on issues in gender and sexuality. Her published books include: *The Erotics of Domination: Male Desire and the Mistress in Latin Poetry* (1999), *Reading Sappho: Contemporary Approaches* (1997), *Re-Reading Sappho: Reception and Transmission* (1997), *Women Poets in Ancient Greece and Rome* (2005), and *Gendered Dynamics in Latin Love Poetry* (with Ronnie Ancona) (2005). Greene has also published numerous articles on Greek and Latin love lyric. She is currently working on a book-length study of Sappho for Blackwell.

JÜRGEN HAMMERSTAEDT has held the Chair of Classics and Papyrology at Cologne University since 2004 and there directs the research unit for papyrology, epigraphy and numismatics of the Northrhine-Westfalian Academy. Previously he worked for several years at Naples on the Herculaneum Papyri, at Bonn University at the Reallexikon für Antike und Christentum, and at Jena University, where he held the Chair of Greek. His main interests are ancient philosophical literature of the Hellenistic and Imperial periods and ancient literary and Christian papyri. He also takes part in the epigraphic and archaeological survey at Oinoanda, Turkey, which explores the largest inscription of antiquity, containing Epicurean texts.

MARGUERITE JOHNSON is Lecturer in Classics at the University of Newcastle, Australia. She is the author of several articles on Latin poetry, co-author of *Sexuality in Greek and Roman Society and Literature* (Routledge); and author of *Sappho* for the Duckworth *Ancients in Action* series.

ANDRÉ P.M.H. LARDINOIS (Ph.D. Princeton 1995) is professor of Greek Language and Culture at the Radboud University Nijmegen in the Netherlands. His main interests center on Greek lyric poetry and Greek drama. He has written various articles on Sappho and other Greek poetry. He is the author, together with T.C. Oudemans, of *Tragic Ambiguity: Anthropology, Philosophy and Sophocles' Antigone* (Leiden 1987), and the co-editor of *Making Silence Speak: Women's Voices in Greek Literature and Society* (Princeton 2001) and *Solon of Athens: New Historical and Philological Approaches* (Leiden 2005).

JOEL LIDOV (Ph.D Columbia University) is a professor of Classics at Queens College and the Graduate School of the City University of New York. He has written articles and reviews on Greek meter, Pindar, and Sappho, and is completing a book on metrical theory and form in Greek lyric.

GREGORY NAGY is the author of *The Best of the Achaeans: Concepts of the Hero in Archaic Greek Poetry* (The Johns Hopkins University Press, 1979; 2nd ed., with new Introduction, 1999). Other publications include *Plato's Rhapsody and Homer's Music: The Poetics of the Panathenaic Festival in Classical Athens* (Cambridge: Harvard University Press 2002). He co-edited with Stephen A. Mitchell the second 40th anniversary edition of Albert Lord, *The Singer of Tales* (Harvard Studies in Comparative Literature vol. 24; Harvard University

Press, 2000), co-authoring with Mitchell the new Introduction, pp. vii-xxix. Since 2000, he has been the Director of the Harvard Center for Hellenic Studies in Washington DC, while continuing to teach at the Harvard campus in Cambridge as the Francis Jones Professor of Classical Greek Literature and Professor of Comparative Literature.

DIRK OBBINK is Lecturer and Fellow of Christ Church College, Oxford University. He is the Editor of the Oxyrhynchus Papyri and is the recipient of a MacArthur Fellowship. He specializes in Greek literature and papyrology. His publications include *Philodemus on Piety Part I: Critical Text with Commentary* (Oxford 1996), "Anoubion, Elegiacs" in *The Oxyrhynchus Papyri*, Vol. 66 (ed. N. Gonis et al., nos. 4503-7), Egypt Exploration Society (London 1999), and *Matrices of Genre: Authors, Canons and Society* [with M. Depew] (Cambridge, MA 2000).

MARILYN B. SKINNER is Professor of Classics at the University of Arizona in Tucson. She received her Ph.D. from Stanford University in 1977. Before taking up her present post in 1991, she held faculty positions at Reed College, the University of California at Los Angeles, and Northern Illinois University and visiting appointments at the University of Texas in Austin and Colgate University. Her primary research specialization is Roman literature of the Republican and Augustan eras. She has authored two monographs, *Catullus' Passer: The Arrangement of the Book of Polymetric Poems* (1981) and *Catullus in Verona* (2003), and has co-edited two collections of scholarly essays, *Vergil, Philodemus, and the Augustans* (2004) and the Blackwell *Companion to Catullus* (2007). Skinner is well known for her work on sexuality and gender in antiquity, as both co-editor of *Roman Sexualities* (1997) and author of *Sexuality in Greek and Roman Culture* (2005). Lastly, she has also published numerous articles on the Greek female poetic tradition, dealing with Sappho and her successors Korinna, Erinna, Anyte, Moero, and Nossis.

EVA STEHLE teaches at the University of Maryland. Her major interests are Greek poetry and performance, ancient women, and Greek religion, and especially the intersections among these. Her 1997 book *Performance and Gender in Ancient Greece* is on gender images in poetry as a form of self-positioning for performers. She is finishing a book on women's religious ritual in classical Greece.

Index

A

A-B-A structure. *See* ring-composition

abrosuna (refinement): as consolation, 72, 80; Muses, associated with, 158–59; and sun, 190

abstract concept: of beauty, in Fr. 16: 152–54

acephalous Hipponacteans: as aeolic form, 104. *See also* meter

adunaton (impossibility): divine aid, overcome by, 77, 78–79; in Fr. 58.11–26, 80; in other Sappho poems, 76–79; prayer, juxtaposed to, 77; of remaining ageless, 191; in Tithonus poem, 76

adversative statement: as closural device, as, 4

Aelian: *ap.* Stobaeus *Florilegium* 3.29.58, 75n12, 180

Aelius Aristides: *Orat.* 28.51, 92–93, 126

aeolic forms: ancient authorities, as described by, 105; expansion of, 104–5; in Lesbian poetry, 105; modern description of, 105

Aeschylus: *Agamemnon* 72–75, 104–9, 98–99; *Agamemnon* 1629–30, 135; *Eumenides* 788, 97

Agathon: influence of lyric poetry on tragedies of, 181

aiolikon: as term for meter of New Sappho, 103

aition (cause): death of Orpheus as, 137

Alcaeus: Fr. 38a V, 60; Fr. 38a.10 V, 64; Fr. 42 V, 60, 64; Fr. 44 V, 61; Fr. 48 V, 105; Fr. 50 V, 79–80; Fr. 61 V, 105; Fr. 129.9–12 V, 96; Fr. 283.3–6 V, 96; Fr. 298 V, 61; Fr. 308b.1–2 V, 95–96; Fr. 374.1 V, 178; open conclusions in, 60–61

Alcman: Fr. 1.16–20, 79; Fr. 26, 51–52, 85, 191; and Tithonus poem, 51–52

Alexandrian edition of Sappho: arranged by meter, 86, 106–11; content of book 2, 89; content of book 4, 18; content of book 5, 89; song exchanges collected in, 100

allusion: in oral culture, 164–65; in Pindaric and tragic exempla, 59

allusion or riddle: absence of, in lyric exempla, 65, 67

alternative endings: of Sappho Fr. 2, 192–93

ambiguity: in Fr. 58.26, 43–44, 72, 189

Anacreon: appropriates lyric role of Sappho, 178–80; on Athenian vase, 181; Fr. 50/395, 79–80; Fr.